WARRIORS AND WORRIERS

WARRIORS
AND
WORRIERS

The Survival of the Sexes

JOYCE. F. BENENSON

WITH

HENRY MARKOVITS

OXFORD
UNIVERSITY PRESS

OXFORD
UNIVERSITY PRESS

Oxford University Press is a department of the University of Oxford.
It furthers the University's objective of excellence in research, scholarship,
and education by publishing worldwide.

Oxford   New York

Auckland   Cape Town   Dar es Salaam   Hong Kong   Karachi
Kuala Lumpur   Madrid   Melbourne   Mexico City   Nairobi
New Delhi   Shanghai   Taipei   Toronto

With offices in

Argentina   Austria   Brazil   Chile   Czech Republic   France   Greece
Guatemala   Hungary   Italy   Japan   Poland   Portugal   Singapore
South Korea   Switzerland   Thailand   Turkey   Ukraine   Vietnam

Oxford is a registered trademark of Oxford University Press
in the UK and certain other countries.

Published in the United States of America by
Oxford University Press
198 Madison Avenue, New York, NY 10016

Library of Congress Cataloging-in-Publication Data
Benenson, Joyce F.
Warriors and worriers : the survival of the sexes / Joyce F. Benenson with Henry Markovits.
p. cm.
ISBN 978-0-19-997223-4 (hardback)
1. Sex differences (Psychology)   2. Sex differences.   I. Title.
BF692.2.B456 2014
155.3'3—dc23
2013034100

1 3 5 7 9 8 6 4 2
Printed in the United States of America
on acid-free paper

CONTENTS

◆

PREFACE

—◆—

I wrote this book to provide a developmental psychologist's perspective on sex differences. Observing the same behaviors over and over again in boys, and other behaviors over and over again in girls, I became interested in designing experiments to see whether these behaviors occur without the props and people that natural environments provide. When they did, I wanted to know whether others had seen these behaviors across diverse cultures. The more cross-cultural similarities I found, the more I became intrigued.

Over the past 30 years, I have come to believe that boys and girls differ in some of their basic interests and accordingly behave in different ways. What are these sex-specific interests? I find in my own studies, and in research reports from diverse cultures, that boys enjoy physical fighting, find enemies captivating, and cannot beat competition for pure entertainment. Most important of all, boys want to engage in these behaviors with other boys.

What kind of enterprise would allow boys to practice all of their interests at once? The obvious answer is intergroup competition, such as warfare, politics, or business, where several entities compete against one another. Here I focus on warfare. I suggest that because the ingredients that contribute to warfare appear so early in development and across so many diverse cultures, there is likely an innate basis for males' interest.

This led me to the work of Harvard primatologist Richard Wrangham, who was studying warlike behaviors in chimpanzees, *Pan troglodytes*. Since then, I have adopted many of the models that he and other primatologists use for studying behavior and applied them to my studies with children.

Primatologists record the behaviors that most individuals in a species exhibit. They then ask what benefit a specific behavior provides by suggesting a problem it solves. For example, if individuals in a species generally come to a watering hole only in the dark, this is probably because they will be more likely to be eaten if they drink during the day.

I consider myself a human primatologist, or ethologist. When I see a behavior exhibited by virtually all members of one sex, but rarely by members of the other sex, it suggests that that behavior solves some basic problem for the sex that practices it. It's not that the other sex could not learn to practice it, but they usually don't without a lot of encouragement and learning.

Specifically, given that time, energy, and resources are limited, why do boys practice behaviors repeatedly that contribute to intergroup competition? Why don't they do something else instead? The answer I suggest in this book is that it must have led boys, when they grew up, to survive better. This makes sense if fights between groups are common. The historical record and modern conflicts suggest this is true.

The same holds for girls. The behaviors of girls, practicing caring for vulnerable individuals, is found in most mammalian species. It is not hard to believe that there is some innate basis for girls' greater interest in vulnerable creatures, particularly babies. A mother who found babies appealing likely would be more likely to keep her own baby alive than a mother who found babies unattractive.

That is not the whole story regarding girls, however. Because boys are much louder and less private than girls, it took me a while to begin to focus on girls' behaviors. When I did, I was quite surprised to see that the stereotypes that apply to girls' behavior around the world, such as "sugar and spice and everything nice," did not fully describe what I was actually seeing girls do. As most people agree, girls spend a lot of time talking about other people in their lives. When they are very young, they do this through pretend play, evoking mothers and babies and fathers. When they become more verbal, they discuss their family and friends. These discussions, however, are not composed simply of saying "nice" things about their family and friends. Often, they are dissecting the most negative aspects of another's behavior. As girls approach adolescence, boys increasingly become the subject of their discussions.

So I asked myself, why are girls and women spending so much of their time, energy, and resources discussing other people's weaknesses? There are so many other things they could be doing. When I looked at research reports from across diverse cultures, I found that, sure enough, the same discussions were taking place around the world.

What I suggest is that these concerns must have led girls, when they grew up, to survive better. Why would this be? The conclusion I present is that, to survive, girls need to grow up to be able to depend on others for assistance with child care. A mother who has no help from anyone else will be much less likely to stay alive herself and to keep her children alive. Talking about important others in one's life allows a girl to figure out who is helpful and who is not, and how to cement bonds with the helpful people.

Paradoxically, I also found that two girls or two women talking do not typically help one another, other than to be reassuring. In fact, two unrelated females often can become fast enemies. Because they have so much in common, they need similar physical resources, and beginning in adolescence, they may compete for the same men.

This creates an inherent conflict in unrelated human females' relations with one another. They very much want each other's support, because they worry continually about how they will accomplish their tasks in life. Because they are the same age, each knows more than anyone else what daunting tasks lie just ahead. At the same time, they must invest first and foremost in their families. How this plays out leads to some very confusing relationships.

My goal is to show that early in development, across diverse cultures, boys and girls differ in their interests and accompanying behaviors. This provides compelling evidence for an innate basis for some sex differences. An innate basis suggests that if almost every member of one sex in a species shows this behavior, then it must solve some very important problem. This problem influenced our genes' survival, so that those individuals who did not exhibit these behaviors did not survive to pass on their genetic material, the source of innate biases.

In closing, I would like to thank Richard Wrangham for his support over the past decade. Richard's brilliant contributions to primatology and his unceasing enthusiasm helped shaped the trajectory of my own career. I would not have written this book without his continued encouragement. and his inclusion of me as an associate member of the Department of Human Evolutionary Biology at Harvard University. I extend my thanks to the entire department for their generosity and warmth over the past many years. I also warmly thank Steve LeBlanc of the Peabody Museum at Harvard for reading this book and providing critical feedback and lively discussions over several years' time. I am also deeply indebted to Emmanuel College for the wonderful working conditions it has provided over the past decade. The many dedicated, enthusiastic students I have come to know so well at Emmanuel have greatly enriched my life, both in my classes and in our joint work in the field or laboratory.

I also thank Joanna Ng of Oxford University Press for believing in this book, Abby Gross, my editor, and the rest of the team at Oxford. Of course, the errors herein are all mine.

WARRIORS AND WORRIERS

CHAPTER ONE

◆

Introduction: What Is the Difference between a Boy and a Girl?

WALKING DOWN THE ORANGE DIRT ROAD, IN BARE FEET AND school clothes, the 50 children and I are thankful it's starting to rain. The scarce rain settles the dust that otherwise chokes our throats and burns our eyes. Goats, chickens, and cows saunter on the few yards of grass next to the road. Men on motorbikes pass so close their clothes brush against us. The occasional car honks loudly, and we squeeze onto the grass to avoid being run over.

I am 7,000 miles from home, in Uganda, a place totally different from anywhere I have ever lived before. I came to learn about sex differences in young children in a non-Western culture. Even before I left, I knew how dangerous it could be. Now I am beginning to learn how women and men survive. I am trying not to think about yellow fever, poisonous snakes, mosquitoes carrying malaria, unclean water, careening motorbikes, and men with rifles. Yesterday, an 8-month-old baby of one of the few schoolteachers here died during the 6-hour journey to a hospital. A young man was killed on a motorbike the day before.

The Rwenzori Mountains of the Congo stand tall and purplish gray in the distance to my right. I am grateful to be on this side of them. I know that almost 6 million people have died in the Congolese war which began in 1998. Even though the official war ended more than 5 years ago, the dying hasn't [1]. Half of those who have died are children under 5 years of age. I can't even imagine what the faces of so many children would look like, let alone the suffering of their mothers.

Three miles down the road, I enter the tiny dung and wood house of one girl. Her father and six siblings ask me how I am; her mother is too ill to come out to welcome me. I speak briefly to her father and siblings. I must leave quickly to walk the 3 miles back by myself to the school grounds where I am staying. On the way back, I again pass the tiny gray shacks housing families with seven or more young children. With the light fading, I hurry, as I have been told it would be dangerous to be out alone after dark. My goal this trip is mainly to observe and to conduct some simple studies. My observations already show some key differences in the ways that boys and girls survive here in an environment as dangerous as this.

The question of exactly what sex differences exist and whether they have a biological foundation excites a lot of people. It should. After a baby is born, a parent's first concern typically is for its physical health. The next concern is its sex. Only in the most modern societies does sex not virtually determine the future life of a new human being. In Uganda, it doesn't take long to see that in public places, there are lots of men hanging around—at the informal trading posts, in the bars, on motorbikes offering rides, and in the towns alongside the road. In contrast, almost every woman I saw had at least one child, if not several children, by her side. Even in modern societies, however, one's sex usually plays a large role in the path a life follows.

Thus, it is easy to understand why the differences between men and women hold a fascination for almost everyone. Academic scientists have published thousands of papers on the subject, with the general conclusion being that men and women are mostly the same [2], and whatever differences exist have been socialized [3]. The only exceptions are that women bear children and men are physically stronger, which leads to different behaviors in adulthood. I began my research career 30 years ago, and sometime during those years, I came to believe that the differences between men and women are more complicated than the way they are usually described. I study children, because children allow me to observe human nature before society has exerted too much of an influence. The earlier a behavior appears in children, the more likely this behavior has some biological basis. What I have found is that girls and boys behave very differently beginning in infancy and early childhood, long before girls bear children and boys become the physically stronger sex.

Preventing Dying Young

What I will suggest in the pages that follow is that men and women differ most strongly in a few behaviors that help them to avoid dying early, before they can safely pass their genes from their bodies to the bodies of their children. Many of these genes have been around for millions of years. Bodies don't last very long in comparison, and it is a person's instinctive task to stay alive long enough to ensure that his or her genes find a new home in a new body. Our genes have programmed us to do this for them.

There are many ways to die early: infectious and noninfectious diseases, starvation, choking, a fight, organ failure, falling off a cliff, fires, motor vehicle accidents, drowning, diarrhea, animal attacks, freezing, inability to care for oneself due to mental illness or physical disability, tornadoes, familial abuse, war, drugs, heatstroke, earthquakes, structural collapses, lightning strikes, and overexertion, to name a few. In Uganda, a lot of people die early. Despite the efforts of many people, almost 1 out of every 10 children dies before turning a year old [4, 5]. Across sub-Saharan African, 22% of children die before age 15 [6]. Six of 1,000 mothers who deliver healthy children die in the process [7], and for those men who make it to age 15, 39% of them will die before age 60 [6]. In hunter-gatherer populations, more than 25% of infants died in the first year of life, and 49% of children died before they reached sexual maturity [8]. We forget that our brains were formed when child mortality was 50 times what it is in modern societies.

Every one of the ancestors of people alive today managed to avoid an early death and to pass their genes to their children. Any genes that helped people reduce the chances of early death would be more likely to be passed on to their children, because any other kinds of genes would disappear: Their owners died before they could pass on their genes. Behavior that helps to prevent early death therefore must be programmed into our genetic material.

What I have come to believe is that men and women have evolved to specialize in preventing death from different causes. That way, their children had two parents who could cover more forms of danger and thus be better able to keep them alive. This has important effects on the kinds of social behavior that characterize men and women, and the way that young girls and boys behave. But before I present my ideas, I need to describe what other researchers have already discovered about sex differences.

Background: What Social Scientists Believe

Most social scientists who specialize in studying human beings have concluded that the primary difference between women and men is that women are more sociable than men. They claim that women care more about relationships, whereas men are more concerned with getting a job done [9–11]. Their evidence consists of some key, consistent findings. First, men in a psychology laboratory look as if they are more task-oriented than women. Put a group of young men in a room in a modern university and ask them to work together on a task. You'll find that they spend much more time on task than do young women in the same situation. The men focus on the job: They shout out their opinions, present competing pieces of information, jockey for talking time, disagree loudly, allow overt conflicts to erupt, and create a hierarchy in terms of speaking time. When the time is up, they cheerfully relay a solution to the experimenter.

A group of women in the same situation behaves quite differently. The women politely inquire about one another's personal backgrounds and relationships, consider thoughtfully the concerns raised by one another's lives, confirm each other's current feelings about life, and generously acknowledge the importance of each woman's perspective. All of this is accompanied by much eye contact, smiling and turn-taking, and relatively little attention to the task that the experimenter presented [10, 12–14]. It seems that the women care more about one another, whereas males care mostly about the task.

This conclusion is reinforced by differences observed in men's and women's interactions with their families and closest same-sex friends. When women are with their relatives and close friends, what do they do? They talk about what's wrong in their lives—their personal vulnerabilities and worrisome aspects of their relationships—and then they try to support one another's feelings. What do men do? They play games or watch others playing games, often not exchanging a single word [15, 16]. Women love intimate talks; men prefer some sort of activity.

Finally, women rarely physically injure other women. At all ages across almost all cultures, men beat each other up much more than women do [17, 18]. This is particularly true for extreme violence. While homicide rates differ greatly from country to country, women commit less than 10% of them everywhere [19, 20]. Surely, men must care less about others if they are willing to kill each other so much more often.

Social Scientists Miss Some Evidence

These observations underlie the idea that women are basically more sociable and caring than men. But, on reflection, this is not so clear. For example, are men really more task-oriented than women? Evidence in the real world suggests the opposite of what research in a university laboratory shows. In most cultures, women consistently work longer hours than men. Men spend more time playing sports and games with one another, and this has been true since the first written accounts of human history [21–25]. Women typically take most of the responsibility for caring for babies and older family members, and for finding and preparing food. Surely this counts as a task, one that often requires working around the clock. Add an outside job, such as teaching or running a corporation, and most women work harder than a typical man. Anecdotally, I didn't see any women in Uganda just hanging around, but I did see a lot of men doing just that.

What about women's greater intimacy and concern for friends and family? Intimacy and concern can be expressed in ways that do not require prolonged verbal discussion about personal worries. It is possible to show one's vulnerabilities and caring about another person without talking at length about them [26]. The physical closeness of men during sports, travels, or even war may surpass the deepest conversations between women in terms of intimacy. Furthermore, in Uganda as in many other non-Western countries, boys and men often walk around holding hands with a close male friend. These pairs of friends then interact in large groups together. Although my findings in Uganda show that girls spend more time than boys in one-on-one relationships [27], that doesn't mean that boys don't have friends who are just as intimate.

How about men's greater levels of violence? Men are certainly more physically violent than women. But how this is related to liking people is not clear. In most species, males are more physically aggressive than females, but in some of those species, males are the more sociable sex. For example, male chimpanzees fight like crazy to become the dominant male in the community, sometimes injuring one another along with way [28–31]. But male chimpanzees also groom one another and spend time next to one another more than female chimpanzees do. Further, male chimpanzees cooperate quite a bit. They patrol their territories together, hunt in groups, team up to help one another climb the male dominance hierarchy, share their food and even their favorite mating partner, and attack other communities as a united front [30, 32–35]. Female chimpanzees rarely, if ever, do any of these things, and if they do interact with another adult, it is more often with a male than with another female. They are busy finding food and taking care of their offspring.

Sometimes, of course, hatred causes physical violence, but often it does not. In nonhuman species, often the more two individuals depend upon one another, the more they fight and then reconcile [36]. They fight because they spend a lot of time together, which inevitably causes conflicts to erupt from time to time. They figure out how to resolve their conflicts, however, because they need one another. By doing so, their relationship can develop so that it meets both partners' needs. Paradoxically, fighting actually can be useful for the continual adjustments required to maintain a relationship. Physical aggression therefore does not mean that a person doesn't like to be with other people. The question of whether one sex is more sociable than the other is not so easily resolved, but it is an important starting point for understanding one piece of the puzzle of human nature.

Some Differences between Men and Women in Their Social Behaviors

Before trying to answer the question of which sex is more sociable, it is worth asking another one. Why should women and men differ in their social behaviors, or in any other way? This is a critical question, and one that evolutionary biologists ask. It is important because it requires thinking about what benefits and costs come with specific social behaviors. It is also important because it requires thinking about whether one sex benefits more from a specific behavior in preventing the ultimate cost: dying too early to reproduce successfully.

What I suggest here is that throughout most of human history, men and women have specialized in different behaviors necessary to ensure the survival of their children to adulthood. Thus, women who have genes that result in their dying before they have successfully raised their children will not pass on these genes. Over time, behaviors allowing women to survive long enough to produce and raise adult children will be preferentially represented in women's genomes. Behaviors, such as paying close attention to the state of one's body, avoiding conflicts, finding a reliable mate while excluding competitors, and investing a lot in children likely have been specifically useful in keeping women alive. The same process will have happened with men and the behaviors critical to their survival. Behaviors that likely have been particularly useful in keeping men alive include physical fighting, selecting friends who are strong and skilled, and competing in groups. These patterns of sex differences appear across diverse cultures and are found even in young children. It is these behaviors that I will focus on here.

Background: What Evolutionary Biologists Believe

How are genes for these specific behaviors passed from human parents to children? Obviously, and of particular interest to males, sexual intercourse is required. Most postpubertal males happily assume the initial responsibility for ensuring that their genes are transmitted. Females like to have sex too, but not as freely, frequently, or with as many partners as males do [37–40].

Sexual intercourse without ensuring care of the resulting baby accomplishes nothing however in terms of passing on genes. A dead baby doesn't help one's genes survive into the next generation. Of particular interest to women, therefore, is that sex can lead to nine months of gestation, followed generally by many years of primary responsibility for feeding and caring for children, care that sometimes lasts a lifetime. Most postpubertal females, with strong encouragement from their parents, therefore wisely exercise caution before they have sex and get stuck feeding and caring for the baby that emerges from their body. Males like to take care of babies and children too, of course, but not as freely, frequently, or intensely as females do.

Evolutionary biologists examining evidence from hundreds of mammalian species created parental investment theory to explain these sex differences in behavior [41]. In almost all mammalian species, males invest more in competing for females and initiating sex, whereas females spend more time, energy, and resources in making sure the resulting baby stays alive. In most mammalian species, including humans, children are cared for much more by females than by males.

Mammalian males focus on finding a fertile female, then figuring out how to have sex with her. A typical male mammal's strategy involves attempting to have sex whenever and with whomever he can, potentially producing more and more offspring, whose survival will depend entirely on the females he impregnates. In between matings, he must fight off other males and attract females, which can entail great risk and perhaps a little charm. Even if a male dies while fighting off other males, provided he has impregnated a few responsible females, he will have successfully transmitted his genes.

Female mammals, on the other hand, must be more careful than males, since they will bear the burden of gestating, breastfeeding, and raising any babies produced after sex. In particular, they must be selective about their mating partners and their environments. They must protect themselves. In most species, and even in humans until very recently, if a mother died, then her baby or young child died too [42]. Thus, a mother absolutely must not die. Should she die, then she is killing not only herself but also all of her dependent children. Even in modern societies, a mother who dies leaves a huge psychological mark on the children she leaves, particularly those who have not yet reached puberty [43].

A mother's first priority, then, is to stay alive long enough to care for her children. Like other female mammals, human mothers must avoid risks and take care of themselves as much as possible. She must be healthy, and stay healthy, for a long time.

Differences in Parental Investment Don't Completely Explain the Special Case of Humans

In some ways, however, humans are not just like any other mammalian species. Human babies and children require more time, energy, and resources to raise than any other mammalian offspring. Human babies arrive unusually helpless at birth [44] and remain children for a far longer time than in any other species [15]. It is only when a child is capable of having his or her own children that the mission of gene transmission has been successfully accomplished.

A human mother therefore confronts a huge task. Not only must she scrupulously take care of herself, she must do so while gestating, then breastfeeding, procuring food for, protecting, and educating each one of her children. This will help ensure that all her children can live to reproduce themselves. For human mothers, taking care of children requires a long time period, lots of near misses, and often some tragedies. UNICEF estimates that close to 9 million children under 5 years of age still die annually in the world today [45]. Millions of others live but struggle to grow up, some with serious disabilities that require lifelong care.

Human infants are so vulnerable for so long that mothers alone are not sufficient. They need help. Who is most likely to help a mother? Those who share genes with her children. This means that maintaining ties to her own mother and other members of the older generation as well as bonding with a man are invaluable to helping a human mother keep her children alive. In very few mammalian species does a nonhuman mother receive assistance with child care [46, 47]. For human mothers, however, assistance makes a huge difference to the survival and success of their children.

A human mother therefore has to do some things very differently than most female mammals. She must, if she can, maintain strong ties to her husband and to her mother or her husband's mother. Hunter-gatherer communities, which are considered the best living example of the type of environment in which humans evolved around 200,000 years ago [48], illustrate what happens. In these small communities, a mother depends strongly on others for help in raising her children. She marries the father of a new child. She raises her children with the help of her husband as long as he remains loyal to her [49]. She lives with her own mother or her husband's mother, and any other relatives who happen to be in the community at that time [50]. Although divorce and moving to a new community happen all the time, a mother depends heavily on her current husband and the grandmothers of her children to help her [51–53].

A woman who devotes a lot of her time to thinking about who can best assist her in bringing up her children benefits enormously. The consequences of this choice could not be greater for her life and the lives of her children. Should her assistants slack off or disappear, she is stuck holding the baby and caring for the rest of her children too. Relying on her own mother or choosing a good mate to start with is not enough, however, given the long time it takes to bring children to reproductive age. A woman must continuously keep tabs on others, for example, defending her mate from any other woman who might contemplate stealing him. Thus, whereas females of many species compete over food and territory and resources [54], human females must compete over mates too. Human fathers often invest more than most other mammalian males in caring for their children, but they are a variable lot [52, 55]. Around the world, fathers usually provide some resources or food or protection to the mother of their children [56], especially if they care about her [55, 57]. In almost every society, however, some fathers have more than one wife at a time; some fathers change partners frequently; and some fathers have lots of sexual partners simultaneously [58]. At the extreme, some fathers vanish completely. Even in the most modern societies, most divorced fathers eventually lose contact with their children after a few years [55]. Further, it is not easy for a modern woman to find a replacement. Men aren't so keen on caring for another man's child [59]. This makes it critical that a woman select her mate carefully—and keep an eye on him afterward to make sure he pays attention to her.

Other female competitors must be kept away. An unrelated woman, kind and reassuring and similar as she may be, nonetheless is a competitor. A mother must weigh the benefit of having a close relationship with an unrelated woman who has a lot in common with her against the cost that this other woman might steal her food or run off with her husband. As much as mothers might wish for company, to share their lives with someone who experiences the same joys and heartbreaks, this requires a complicated calculation.

Because life is so difficult for a human mother, she must carefully select not only her mate and her friends but in many societies also her children. Many mothers around the world kill their babies when they cannot take care of them [60], especially when caring for a baby would make them unable to take care of their other children. Mothers who are not healthy themselves, who have many other children, who have little assistance from others, and who have few resources must figure out how to protect themselves and their other children. Sometimes, this leads to killing, abusing, or neglecting a child. This does not mean that mothers haven't tried everything else first. Compared with other species, human mothers have a lot to think about when it comes to their relationships, and they make tough choices to change them when they have to.

Meanwhile, what is a man up to? Unlike the basic tenets of parental investment theory, generally human males are not as free as most other males to devote time to having sex with fertile females, while totally ignoring the well-being of their children. In many hunter-gatherer societies, men often help with child care. They never do as much as mothers do, though, especially when children are most in need [61]. They are not bound to children the way mothers are. Biologists' parental investment theory still applies: Compared with their wives, husbands spend a lot more time thinking about sex, though less so than before they had children [62, 63].

What makes men unique compared with other species is that they like to fight and compete as a group. No example demonstrates this better than war. Unlike most other species, men band together in solidarity to risk their lives to defeat another group [34, 64]. For many thousands of years, human males have engaged in intergroup warfare [65]. Archaeologists provide powerful evidence of warfare from every part of the globe: mass graves filled with piles of skulls, and bones pierced with arrowheads or other projectiles; shields and body armor, gates, mud-brick walls, and eventually fortresses constructed high on mountaintops with narrow slits for windows; rooms filled with every type of weapon, made from stone, bronze, and iron; vehicles designed to carry weapons, and ancient roadways constructed to carry the vehicles carrying the weapons; cave paintings depicting battles. From simple hunter-gatherer societies, horticultural and agricultural societies, complex societies headed by big men to modern states, war has been found in abundance [66–68]. Thousands of years ago, weapons and their transportation became a major focus of men's lives, and this continues to be the case [69]. While the percentage of men dying in conflicts has decreased over recorded history, a lot of time, energy, and resources remain devoted to intergroup conflicts, even in the most modern of societies. As a result, human males stand out with respect to how much time, energy, and resources they invest in one another. From early in life, boys love to play fight with one another [43]. They share their interests in enemies and weapons. They compete over everything. Later in life, they continue to enjoy their competitions.

Yet compared with other species, human males are far less aggressive. They also relish one another's competitive company. With remarkable flexibility, human males who compete for sexual partners and status turn around and cooperate in battle with those same individuals when an enemy appears. A man protects his community with the help of his fellow man. Throughout human history, unrelated men have risked their individual lives to fight off other groups of men. Together, the men ensured that their genes triumphed over the enemy's genes [65, 70, 71].

Why would a man do this? If a man wanted to stay alive, his inclinations—and genes—should keep him away from war. What would possibly push him to risk his life for his immediate competitors? The answer is that otherwise he, and all the members of his community, would die. If too many men decided not to fight, they would all end up killed by other groups. Men in communities whose genes programmed them to fight cooperatively would likely triumph over uncooperative men in other communities. They might also gain the uncooperative men's territory, wives, and children and ultimately eliminate the other men's uncooperative genetic material. Meanwhile, the victors would preserve their own territory, wives, children, and their cooperative genes, even if a few men from the victorious coalition died in the process (sometimes up to 25% of the male community members in ancient days) [67, 68]. In fact, mathematical modeling based on ancient warfare supports the contention that enough men perished in battles to tilt the advantage toward the evolution of cooperative men who occasionally sacrificed themselves for other men and their community in warfare [65].

Interestingly, although men are relatively unique in engaging in warfare, they are not the only species that does so. Of the two species currently alive that share the most genetic material with humans, one of them, chimpanzees, is the only other living primate species that engages in what looks like warfare [31, 34, 64, 72, 73]. As in many other mammalian species, chimpanzee males fight viciously for high rank. The highest-ranked alpha male then obtains the most mating opportunities [33, 74]. What makes chimpanzee males' fights for status so intriguing is that after a vicious fight, chimpanzee males turn around and reconcile their conflicts, settle their grievances, and join together in a coalition. These coalitions then proceed to engage in carefully orchestrated defensive and offensive operations against neighboring communities [72, 73, 75].

Human males behave in a similar fashion. Men of course do not cooperate only in times of war. They have a created for themselves a host of institutions, including governments, businesses, and religions, through which they also cooperate and sometimes defeat other institutions.

What this suggests is that for thousands of years, human females and males have faced different sorts of major problems and found different types of solutions. Women have taken primary responsibility for the long-term survival of vulnerable children. This happens early, and around the world. In Uganda, I frequently saw preschool-age girls carrying their baby brothers and sisters. They paid close attention. They kept their little siblings alive while they were in charge. Sometimes a young boy did the same, but not often.

In contrast, around the world, men have taken primary responsibility for fighting wars. This starts early too. In Uganda, 28,500 boys from 7 to 18 years of age helped the men of their side fight the civil war started by Idi Amin, which led to 300,000 deaths initially and another 100,000 not long after [76]. The Lord's Resistance Army continues to fight in Uganda. Very few women join.

The different problems that males and females face require different strategies to solve. It makes sense to suppose that over thousands of years, genes have guided men and women to behave in ways that have helped them to cope with their individual problems. These genes programmed each sex to specialize in surviving different forms of death. What I am specifically suggesting in this book is that human males are programmed to develop traits that are associated with becoming a *warrior*, and that human females are programmed to develop characteristics that are related to becoming a *worrier*.

Warriors and Worriers

Psychologist Carolyn Zahn-Waxler [77] was the first to describe boys who suffer from emotional or behavioral problems as warriors, and girls with problems as worriers. This does not imply that girls are not mean or aggressive or that boys never worry. What it means literally is that when boys and girls in Western societies develop serious emotional and behavioral problems, boys are more likely than girls to strike out violently while girls feel a lot more anxious and depressed and withdraw more from others. These differences in the sexes become even more pronounced after puberty, just when each sex becomes able to reproduce. What I will try to demonstrate here is that emotional and behavioral problems merely make basic differences between boys and girls more noticeable. Underneath, even boys and men without obvious problems have warrior attributes. Underneath, girls and women worry continually about their own and their family members' health.

These patterns of warriors and worriers fit what I and a number of other researchers have found through our observations, interviews, and experiments around the world. To be clear, I am not claiming that all boys or men display all the behaviors that are necessary to become a successful warrior, only that these behaviors are much more frequent in males of all ages. Even more critically, having warrior traits does not require killing anyone, unless this becomes necessary. Many of the traits that accompany interest in war, such as enjoyment of fighting, pleasure in competition, preference for allies who are strong and competent, and undying loyalty to one's own group, are useful in government, business, and other peacetime institutions. In contrast to boys and men, girls and women for the most part exhibit little interest in these behaviors. This does not prevent some women from being soldiers or showing the traits associated with being a successful warrior. However, not nearly as many women as men become warriors, and a warrior woman learns to fight the enemy differently than a man does [78].

Likewise, few girls or women display *all* the behaviors that are necessary to become a successful worrier. Further, having worrier traits is useful in contexts other than child rearing. The traits that accompany caring for vulnerable individuals over the long haul, including staying healthy and avoiding risks, maintaining relationships with families and a mate, getting rid of interfering competitors, and investing in close kin and others who can help a mother raise her children, can be used in other helping professions as well. Boys and men for the most part exhibit less interest in perpetual worrying about themselves and other individuals; many find it a waste of time. Some men do become primary caregivers to children and exhibit the traits associated with being a successful worrier. However, not nearly as many fathers as mothers care for children, especially when the children are really vulnerable. Further, a worrier father likely learns to care for children differently than a mother does [51].

Defending against an enemy attack and caring for a vulnerable child for years require different skills. When there are no wars or babies, men and women behave much more similarly to each other. Nevertheless, even without wars or babies, men and women must be genetically prepared in case either comes along. Thus, these two sex-typed patterns should produce different kinds of fears, interests, choices of social partners, organization of relationships, preferences for environments, and ultimately different decisions geared to prevent early death, even in young children, across diverse cultures.

We are not conscious of being *warriors* or *worriers*. Rather, being a warrior or a worrier is like having a special program continually running in the background of one's mind. It is through my observations of the behaviors of boys and girls over several decades that I have concluded that these different programs exist. I will start first by looking at the development of boys because that is where I began my research career.

References

1. Polgreen, L., Congo's death rate unchanged since war ended. *New York Times*, 2008.
2. Hyde, J. S., The gender similarities hypothesis. *American Psychologist*, 2005. 60(6): pp. 581–592.
3. Wood, W., and A. H. Eagly, A cross-cultural analysis of the behavior of women and men: Implications for the origins of sex differences. *Psychological Bulletin*, 2002. 128(5): pp. 699–727.
4. Republic of Uganda, M.o.F., Uganda National Report, in *United Nations Office of the High Representative for the Least Developed Countries and Small Island Developing States*, United Nations, Editor. 2005: Kampala.
5. Ssewanyana, S., and S. D. Younger, Infant mortality in Uganda: Determinants, trends and the Millennium Development Goals. *Journal of African Economies*, 2008. 17(1): pp. 34–61.
6. Murray, C. J. L., and A. D. Lopez, Mortality by cause for eight regions of the world: Global Burden of Disease Study. *Lancet*, 1997. 349(9061): pp. 1269–1276.
7. Mbonye, A., et al., Declining maternal mortality ratio in Uganda: Priority interventions to achieve the Millennium Development Goals. *International Journal of Gynecology and Obstetrics*, 2007. 98(3): pp. 285–290.
8. Volk, A. A., and J. A. Atkinson, Infant and child death in the human environment of evolutionary adaptation. *Evolution and Human Behavior*, 2013. 34: pp. 182–192.
9. Bakan, D., *The duality of human existence: An essay on psychology and religion*. 1966, Oxford: Rand McNally.
10. Parsons, T., R. F. Bales, and E. A. Shils, *Working papers in the theory of action*. 1953, Westport, CT: Greenwood.
11. Taylor, S. E., et al., Biobehavioral responses to stress in females: Tend-and-befriend, not fight-or-flight. *Psychological Review*, 2000. 107(3): pp. 411–429.
12. Aries, E., *Men and women in interaction: Reconsidering the differences*. 1996, New York: Oxford University Press.
13. Bales, R. F., *Interaction process analysis: A method for the study of small groups*. 1950, Oxford: Addison-Wesley.
14. Borgatta, E. F., and R. F. Bales, The consistency of subject behavior and the reliability of scoring in interaction process analysis. *American Sociological Review*, 1953. 18(5): pp. 566–569.
15. Kaplan, H., K. Hill, J. Lancaster, and A.M. Hurtado, A theory of human life history evolution: Diet, intelligence, and longevity. *Evolutionary Anthropology*, 2000. 9(4): pp. 156–185.
16. Winstead, B., and J. Griffin, Friendship styles, in *Encyclopedia of women and gender*, J. Worell, Editor. 2001, Boston: Academic Press. pp. 481–492.

17. Maccoby, E. E., and C. N. Jacklin, *The psychology of sex differences*. 1974, Stanford, CA: Stanford University Press.

18. Moffitt, T. E., A. Caspi, M. Rutter, and P. A. Silva *Sex differences in antisocial behaviour: Conduct disorder, delinquency, and violence in the Dunedin Longitudinal Study*. 2001, New York: Cambridge University Press.

19. Daly, M., and M. Wilson, *Homicide*. 1988, Hawthorne, NY: Aldine de Gruyter.

20. Daly, M., and M. Wilson, An evolutionary psychological perspective on homicide, in *Homicide: A sourcebook of social research.*, M. D. Smith and M. A. Zahn, Editors. 1999, Thousand Oaks, CA: Sage. pp. 58–71.

21. Craig, S., *Sports and games of the ancients*. 2002, Westport, CT: Greenwood.

22. Hochschild, A. R., and A. Machung, *The second shift*. 2003, New York: Penguin.

23. Leibs, A., *Sports and games of the Renaissance*. Vol. 4. 2004, Westport, CT: Greenwood.

24. Whiting, B. B., & C. P. Edwards *Children of different worlds: The formation of social behavior*. 1988, Cambridge, MA: Harvard University Press.

25. Kristof, N., and S. Wudunn, *Half the sky: How to change the world*. 2010, London: Virago.

26. Wright, P. H., Toward an expanded orientation to the study of sex differences in friendship, in *Sex differences and similarities in communication: Critical essays and empirical investigations of sex and gender in interaction.*, D. J. Canary and K. Dindia, Editors. 1998, Mahwah, NJ: Erlbaum. pp. 41–63.

27. Benenson, J. F., H. Markovits, and R. W. Wrangham, Girls spend more time than boys with one close friend in a Ugandan village. Manuscript in preparation, 2013.

28. De Waal, F., *Chimpanzee politics: Power and sex among apes*. 1982 Baltimore: Johns Hopkins University Press.

29. de Waal, F. B. M., The integration of dominance and social bonding in primates. *Quarterly Review of Biology*, 1986. 61(4): pp. 459–479.

30. Watts, D. P., Conflict resolution in chimpanzees and the valuable-relationships hypothesis. *International Journal of Primatology*, 2006. 27(5): pp. 1337–1364.

31. Goodall, J., *The chimpanzees of Gombe: Patterns of behavior*. 1986, Cambridge, MA: Harvard University Press.

32. Boesch, C., Cooperative hunting roles among Tai chimpanzees. *Human Nature*, 2002. 13(1): pp. 27–46.

33. Watts, D. P., Coalitionary mate guarding by male chimpanzees at Ngogo, Kibale National Park, Uganda. *Behavioral Ecology and Sociobiology*, 1998. 44(1): pp. 43–55.

34. Wrangham, R. W., Evolution of coalitionary killing. *Yearbook of Physical Anthropology*, 1999. 29(42): pp. 1–30.

35. Wrangham, R., and B. Smuts, Sex differences in the behavioural ecology of chimpanzees in the Gombe National Park, Tanzania. *Journal of Reproduction and Fertility*. Supplement, 1980. 28: pp. 13–31.

36. De Waal, F. B. M., Primates: A natural heritage of conflict resolution. *Science*, 2000. 289(5479): pp. 586–590.

37. Kinsey, A. C., W. B. Pomeroy, and C. E. Martin, Sexual behavior in the human male. *Journal of Nervous and Mental Disease*, 1949. 109(3): p. 283.

38. Clark, R. D., and E. Hatfield, Gender differences in receptivity to sexual offers. *Journal of Psychology and Human Sexuality*, 1989. 2(1): pp. 39–55.

39. Udry, J. R., L. M. Talbert, and N. M. Morris, Biosocial foundations for adolescent female sexuality. *Demography*, 1986. 23(2): pp. 217–230.

40. Udry, J. R., and B. C. Campbell, Getting started on sexual behavior. *Sexuality across the Life Course*, 1994: pp. 187–207.

41. Trivers, R., *Parental investment and sexual selection*. 1972, Chicago: Aldine.

42. Campbell, A., Staying alive: Evolution, culture, and women's intrasexual aggression. *Behavioral and Brain Sciences*, 1999. 22(2): pp. 203–252.

43. Klass, D., P. R. Silverman, and S. L. Nickman, *Continuing bonds: New understandings of grief*. 1996, New York: Taylor and Francis.

44. Lancaster, J. B., and C. S. Lancaster, Parental investment: The hominid adaptation, in *How humans adapt: A biocultural odyssey* (pp. 3366)., D. Ortner, Editor. 1983, New York: Smithsonian.

45. Black, R. E., et al., Global, regional, and national causes of child mortality in 2008: A systematic analysis. *Lancet*, 2010. 375(9730): pp. 1969–1987.

46. Pusey, A. E., and C. Packer, Dispersal and philopatry, in *Primate societies*, B. B. Smuts D. L. Cheney, R. Seyfarth, and R. W. Wrangham Editors. 1987, Chicago: University of Chicago Press. pp. 250–266.

47. Hrdy, S. B., *Mothers and others: The evolutionary origins of mutual understanding*. 2009, Cambridge, MA: Belknap Press.

48. Balter, M., Was North Africa the launch pad for modern human migrations? *Science*, 2011. 331(6013): pp. 20–23.

49. Marlowe, F., *The Hadza: Hunter-gatherers of Tanzania: Origins of human behavior and culture*. 2010, Berkeley: University of California Press.

50. Alvarez, H., Residence groups among hunter-gatherers: A view of the claims and evidence for patrilocal bands, in *Kinship and behavior in primates*, B. Chapais and C. Berman, Editors. 2004, Oxford: Oxford University Press. pp. 400–442.

51. Konner, M., *The evolution of childhood: Relationships, emotion, mind*. 2010, Cambridge, MA: Belknap Press.

52. Hewlett, B. S., and M. E. Lamb, *Hunter-gatherer childhoods: Evolutionary, developmental, and cultural perspectives*. 2005, New Brunswick, NJ: Aldine Transaction.

53. Sear, R., and R. Mace, Who keeps children alive? A review of the effects of kin on child survival. *Evolution and Human Behavior*, 2008. 29(1): pp. 1–18.

54. Clutton-Brock, T., Sexual selection in females. *Animal Behaviour*, 2009. 77(1): pp. 3–11.
55. Parke, R. D., *Fatherhood*. 1996, Cambridge, MA: Harvard University Press.
56. Brown, D. E., *Human universals*. 1991, Philadelphia: Temple University Press.
57. Belsky, J., L. Youngblade, and E. Pensky, Childrearing history, marital quality, and maternal affect: Intergenerational transmission in a low-risk sample. *Development and Psychopathology*, 1989. 1(4): pp. 291–304.
58. Betzig, L., Means, variances, and ranges in reproductive success: Comparative evidence. *Evolution and Human Behavior*, 2012. 33: pp. 309–317.
59. Daly, M., and M. Wilson, *The truth about Cinderella: A Darwinian view of parental love*. 1998, New Haven, CT: Yale University Press.
60. Hrdy, S. B., *Mother nature: A history of mothers, infants, and natural selection*. New York: Pantheon 1999.
61. Konner, M., Hunter-gatherer infancy and childhood: The !Kung and others, in *Hunter-gatherer childhoods*, B. S. Hewlett and M. E. Lamb, Editors. 2005, New Brunswick, NJ: Aldine Transaction. pp. 19–64.
62. Gettler, L. T., T. W. McDade, A. B. Feranil, and C. W. Kuzawa Longitudinal evidence that fatherhood decreases testosterone in human males. *Proceedings of the National Academy of Sciences*, 2011. 108(39): pp. 16194–16199.
63. Gray, P. B., S. M. Kahlenberg, E. S. Barrett, S. F. Lipson, and P. T. Ellison Marriage and fatherhood are associated with lower testosterone in males. *Evolution and Human Behavior*, 2002. 23(3): pp. 193–201.
64. Wrangham, R. W., and D. Peterson, *Demonic males: Apes and the origins of human violence*. 1996, Boston: Houghton Mifflin.
65. Bowles, S., Did warfare among ancestral hunter-gatherers affect the evolution of human social behaviors? *Science*, 2009. 324(5932): pp. 1293–1298.
66. Keeley, L. H., *War before civilization*. 1997, Oxford: Oxford University Press.
67. LeBlanc, S. A., and K. E. Register, *Constant battles: The myth of the peaceful, noble savage*. 2003, New York: St. Martin's Press.
68. Pinker, S., *The better angels of our nature: Why violence has declined*. 2011, New York: Viking.
69. Gabriel, R. A., *The culture of war: Invention and early development*. 1990, Westport, CT: Greenwood.
70. Alexander, R. D., *The biology of moral systems*. 1987, Piscataway, NJ: Aldine de Gruyter.
71. Darwin, C., *The descent of man and selection in relation to sex*. 1871, London: John Murray.
72. Mitani, J. C., D. P. Watts, and S. J. Amsler, Lethal intergroup aggression leads to territorial expansion in wild chimpanzees. *Current Biology*, 2010. 20(12): pp. R507–R508.
73. Watts, D. P., and J. C. Mitani, Boundary patrols and intergroup encounters in wild chimpanzees. *Behaviour*, 2001. 138(3): pp. 299–327.

74. Duffy, K. G., R. W. Wrangham, and J. B. Silk, Male chimpanzees exchange political support for mating opportunities. *Current Biology*, 2007. 17(15): pp. R586–R587.

75. Watts, D. P., M. Muller, S. J. Amsler, G. Mbabazi, and J. C. Mitani., Lethal intergroup aggression by chimpanzees in Kibale National Park, Uganda. *American Journal of Primatology*, 2006. 68(2): pp. 161–180.

76. Eichstaedt, P., *First kill your family: Child soldiers of Uganda and the Lord's Resistance Army*. 2009, Chicago: Lawrence Hill.

77. Zahn-Waxler, C., Warriors and worriers: Gender and psychopathology. *Development and Psychopathology*, 1993. 5(1–2): pp. 79–89.

78. Thomas, J. R., and K. E. French, Gender differences across age in motor performance: A meta-analysis. *Psychological Bulletin*, 1985. 98(2): p. 260.

PART I

---◆---

Warriors

CHAPTER TWO

◆

Enemy Fighting: A Man's Basic Instinct

THE WORLD IS FILLED WITH DANGERS. UNDERSTANDING THE dangers that faced early humans is critical to understanding the kinds of specific problems that men and women faced and the solutions they needed [1]. This is true even in modern societies, especially for the very young and those with vulnerabilities. Elsewhere, and not so long ago, life was a very risky business for everyone. Even if a child survived to sexual maturity, many died early from a variety of causes before they reached 65 years [2, 3]. From an evolutionary perspective, humans who died too young left no children and thus could not pass on their genes. We are the children of those who survived long enough to reproduce and care for us. If boys and girls very early in life find different problems attractive, and create different types of solutions, then this suggests an innate sex-typed guidance system for survival.

The lives of early humans were particularly complicated compared with those of most other mammals. One way in which humans differ from other animals is that we kill each other in large numbers all around the world. So to keep children alive, humans have to cope with their fellow killer humans [4]. This requires some degree of confrontation. Just staying away doesn't work well, because the enemy is likely to go after you, if not this time, then the next. Sometimes a distant community has resources or territory that will greatly improve the chances of survival for a local community's children. Immoral as it may sound, offensive action can greatly benefit the home community. An arms race develops.

Consequently, it often makes sense to fight against other groups. Of course, engaging in physical battle against another group could endanger the lives of everyone in the community. No one's genes would survive this. This problem can best be solved by delegating fighting the enemy to one specific group: young men. Women can then protect themselves and their children. Older men can supervise from a distance. Young men should fight the enemy in a location as far away as possible from everyone else. Then, between them, men and women are able to maximize the chances that their children will survive.

Boys' Fears

I believe that men and women have genes designed to confront different problems. These problems are reflected in the fears of young boys and girls [5]. Boys and men are less afraid of death than girls and women are, and they take more frequent and greater risks [6]. Parents who have both sons and daughters often learn that it's much more difficult to get their boys to worry about things such as health or hygiene, worries that are extremely useful for protecting their lives.

What do boys fear? Based upon my years of study of children and, more recently, adults, I believe that boys' and men's specialty is worrying about enemies. The enemy is their problem, and it is their responsibility to defeat it. Because the enemy is not always present, boys and men don't worry all the time. Nonetheless, I believe that confronting the problem of the enemy has allowed human males to evolve a whole suite of instinctive reactions that still exist today.

The intuitive preoccupation with enemies is so strong that when modern men fight other forms of danger, they end up recasting these as the enemy. For example, men *fight* wars on drugs; they *battle* cancer; they *attack* illiteracy; they *combat* infection; they *defeat* bad attitudes; they *assail* political beliefs; they *assault* stereotypes, and so forth. Girls and women use these terms much less spontaneously. It is the enemy who has got hold of boys' and men's attention and resources.

An excellent example of this is the reaction of the United States to the terror attacks of September 11, 2001, which killed about 3,000 people. In that same year, almost 40,000 people died in car accidents, and 16,000 or so died in gun-related incidents inflicted by community members on one another. It's no accident that the United States has spent more than $1 trillion on efforts to eradicate the enemy primarily in Iraq and Afghanistan. Only a tiny proportion of the money spent on war is used to reduce deaths from car accidents and murders by fellow Americans. Most Americans approved of this decision, at least initially, because Iraq and Afghanistan could provide a training ground for future enemies who could come to the United States and kill Americans. While some people may have thought this decision unwise or unbalanced, no leader of a country can govern if he or she is perceived as weak on the enemy. Weak on helping the underprivileged, weak on battling unemployment, weak on protecting citizens' health, weak on attacking the sources of global warming, but not weak on defeating the enemy. In fact, it is difficult to imagine an individual of either sex supporting a leader of a band, tribe, chiefdom, or state who did not appear capable of or committed to vanquishing all enemies. While women often support men in this, they expect men to make these decisions and send young men to fight the enemy.

Does this focus on the enemy appear only under direct threat? Absolutely not; one must be prepared *before* the threat arrives. The organization Global Day of Action on Military Spending (GDAMS), devoted to reducing military spending, estimates that just 20% of the amount spent on military operations around the world could meet all the UN's eight Millennium Development Goals (MDGs) [7]. That is, in US dollars, $1.531 trillion was spent on the military in 2009, while annually it would take $102 billion to eradicate poverty and hunger (Goal 1); $7.2 billon to achieve universal primary education and promote gender equality (Goals 2 and 3); $10 billion to reduce child mortality and improve maternal health (Goals 4 and 5); $14.2 billion to combat HIV/AIDS, malaria, and other diseases (Goal 6); $155.6 billion to ensure environmental sustainability (Goal 7); and $40 billion to promote global partnership and development (Goal 8). Although member countries ratified the UN's millennium goals, fighting enemies represents by far the biggest allocation of most countries' resources. According to one UN official speaking in 2011 [8]:

> 2 April 2011—The money spent by countries to achieve targets such as eliminating poverty, educating all children and providing decent health

care is still only a fraction of what they spend on arming themselves, a senior United Nations disarmament official warned today.

Sergio Duarte, the UN High Representative for Disarmament Affairs, marked the Global Day of Action on Military Spending by calling on governments to re-orient their spending and thinking and devote more resources towards the Millennium Development Goals (MDGs).

In a statement Mr. Duarte noted that military spending has soared by half over just the past five years, with total expenditure now estimated at more than $1.2 trillion worldwide.

"Less than one tenth of annual military expenditures would be enough to achieve our agreed development goals, lifting all people out of extreme poverty by 2015," he said.

When traveling, one can appreciate why this is so. When I landed at Entebbe airport in Uganda, I was relieved to be surrounded by United Nations trucks. While Uganda has its problems, its neighbors, particularly the Congo and South Sudan, have even more. Millions of people have been killed in East Africa in the last two decades. If the enemy kills you, then there's really nothing else left to spend money on.

There is no one I admire more than the undergraduate students in my course on warfare who are planning to enter the US armed forces. They stand up in front of my class and profess with deep humility and dignity their willingness to die for all of us, to die to keep the United States and its allied countries free from the enemy. Should an enemy attack, my life and the lives of every person I love depend on these young, proud, brave, mostly male future combatants.

The clearest evidence that this represents an intuitive, biological reaction comes from research with young children. Enemy fighting requires a combination of intuitive reactions. A boy's brain seems to propel him to enjoy play fighting. Combine his enjoyment of play fighting with a fascination with enemies, and the recipe for enemy fighting begins to take shape. Add in boys' love of competition, and investment in other boys, and a combination of conditions arises that makes human warfare possible. These are biological ingredients that permit groups of males to engage in group warfare against another group that I call the enemy. The enemy is not a group of people, with their own personalities. They are one: the enemy. I will discuss each of these ingredients in turn based on what I have learned.

Pleasure in Play Fighting

Most little boys enjoy play fighting. Play fighting is often called "rough-and-tumble play" in the objective wording of the biological and psychological literatures. This of course disguises its basic quality: fighting and loving it. In fact, the only way to distinguish play fighting from real fighting is the laughter and lack of anger that accompany the "play" version. By the time little boys are old enough to interact enjoyably with one another, toward the end of infancy, play fighting is one of their favorite activities [9]. Even boys who do not feel comfortable with actual play fighting because they are less sociable, smaller, or less coordinated than other boys still enjoy observing it from a distance or engaging in it virtually through computer or video games, or in former days, books. The enjoyment that play fighting provides continues well into adolescence and even in some places into adulthood [10, 11]. Adult males indulge in forms of play fighting such as wrestling, which has been popular for thousands of years [12, 13]. In contrast, females rarely engage in this form of play. While girls may chase each other and sometimes engage in mock blows, they almost never wrestle and tumble on the ground. Watching girls engage in their version of "rough-and-tumble play" does not bring to mind fighting.

This same basic pleasure in play fighting has been found in most existing hunter-gatherer tribes in South America and Africa. Yumi Gosso and her colleagues [14] have shown that, in these societies, boys' play includes lots of mock fighting, against one another and against small animals. In South America, many young boys play with bows and arrows and slingshots, which they get from their fathers. They rehearse hunting behaviors in their play. Girls rarely participate in these activities.

In fact, boys have been reported to frequently engage in play fighting in early childhood through adolescence in many diverse societies and cultures [15]. Long-term studies in England, Scotland, and Ireland in the 1800s confirm the prevalence of play fighting and the pleasure it gives young boys [16]. As any adult knows who has watched boys freely playing outside of school away from the eyes of their adult supervisors, nothing has changed. Brian Sutton-Smith [17], an expert in young children's play, concluded that at least 70% of boys take part in games that include attack, defense, chase, escape, and capture. The attraction of play fighting is so great that even when boys are not actually fighting, they often are dreaming up different ways of engaging in fighting. In contrast, girls hardly ever engage in or imagine play fighting.

A study with 6- to 9-month-old infants in Boston clearly shows just how primitive these reactions are in boys [18]. Infants at this stage cannot talk and certainly don't understand which sex they are and what proper male and female behavior is. They can sit in their mothers' laps and watch pairs of video clips however. In each pair of video clips, on one side, an adult model hit a balloon; on the other, an adult cuddled the same balloon. Only the boys looked more at the adult hitting the balloon, even if the adult was a female. After watching the adult models, boys started hitting their balloons much more than girls did. These tiny infant boys derived great pleasure from learning to hit—and they learned it fast.

In one of the most primitive of all present-day hunter-gatherer communities, the Hadza who live in Tanzania give boys their first bow and arrows by 2 to 3 years of age. Every single boy, in every Hadza community owns his own bow and arrow by age 5 [19]. While this shows clear evidence of the effect of socialization, it does not explain why boys, and not girls, are given weapons. Men hunt larger animals, but women hunt too. Both sexes require protection. I believe part of the reason boys are given weapons is because they like them, particularly projectile ones, more than girls do.

By 3 years of age, boys can throw much farther, faster, and more accurately than girls can [20]. There is no other physical activity early in life at which boys excel so greatly compared with girls. By middle childhood, across diverse cultures, boys are practicing their unique skill by throwing sticks, rocks, balls, and whatever else is nearby. In adolescence, boys have increased threefold in how much better they are than girls at throwing. At this point, boys also become much better than girls at short- and long-distance running, vertical and horizontal jumping, catching, sit-ups, balance, and grip strength. Puberty causes boys to grow so much heavier, taller, and more muscular than girls that there is almost no overlap between the two sexes in these physical skills. Before adolescence, boys differ little from girls in their height, weight, muscle mass, and physical skills, except of course for throwing. The difference in throwing force and velocity occurs even in the tiniest hunter-gatherer communities [21].

Throwing is a uniquely human behavior [1a]. Although males in most mammalian species engage in play fighting much more than females do, they don't throw. It is difficult to throw when one is balancing on four feet.

Chimpanzees, one of human's closest living genetic relatives, are somewhat of an exception [22]. Though they don't do it often, both in the wild and in captivity, male chimpanzees sometimes do throw, especially adolescents. Only a few female chimpanzees have ever been observed to throw. Further, male chimpanzees demonstrate a hand preference when they throw, usually using their right hands [23]. Not only that, but they stand up on two feet when they throw. They also aim at moving targets, such as a human passerby at a zoo or an annoying baboon in the wild. They rarely throw an object at another chimpanzee, however, and they don't throw at the enemy. And their throws carry little force.

Whereas other animals prefer their own group to another group [24], there is no evidence to show that they actively contemplate the destruction of the enemy. Of course, male chimpanzees, with their regular territorial patrols and proven obliteration of all members of a neighboring community [22, 25], may resemble humans. They may have an enemy. What seems clear, however, is that human males are fairly unique in having a category that goes beyond simple differentiation of their own group from another group. The enemy can be conceptualized and localized: It seeks to destroy one's own group. It comes not only in human form but in other forms too.

It would make sense to see boys' play fighting simply as biological practice for climbing the dominance hierarchy and outperforming their fellow males. If so, then young boys would be expected to target only nearby boys who will be their future regular competitors. They would dream merely of outperforming their peers. They would worry about only their own superiority. They don't. Their fears go beyond those of defeating another boy. Instead, they also create a category called the enemy. The enemy constitutes a different beast entirely. The enemy wakes people in the night. The enemy lives to destroy you and all that you love. It is human males' job to stop it.

What attracts males to enemies and young men to fighting the enemy is the strong belief that some beings are just evil and will stop at nothing to destroy good people. The enemy is irrational, responding to nothing, not logic, reason, empathy, or shared feelings; the enemy's only goal is to destroy everything and everyone. At least, this is the way my teaching assistant Ryan Dolen and his friend Matt Palumbo, both of whom are joining the US military, jointly explain their view of the enemy and their pride in their willingness to combat it to keep us all safe.

Enemies and Weapons

It is surprising how quickly enemies become a target of young boys' play fighting. Of course, when a real enemy appears, he takes center stage in everyone's life. But nothing shows as strongly how much little boys are attracted to enemies as when there is no actual enemy. When there are no real enemies, boys invent them. By 3 years of age, boys living in modern, peaceful societies regularly play out superhero roles in which they combat enemies, while the girls are playing house [17]. Of course, society gives enemies names, so boys often simply ingest the content of what they hear from the media. Girls don't. Girls simply do not take to enemies the way boys do. Informally, I have asked a number of parents of boys and girls whether they encourage their sons, but not their daughters, to become enemy-fighting superheroes. Not one parent was aware of doing so. Quite the opposite: They claimed never to have done so.

Boys' enemies often consist of evil fantasy figures whose sole aim is to destroy mankind. Often, these evil figures are not borrowed from other sources but are made up on the spot by the boys themselves. When boys are creating enemies, their imaginations compare with those of the best Hollywood movie moguls [26]. Further, when enemies are afoot, weapons become invaluable. Boys' fascination with enemies goes hand in hand with their captivation with weapons [27].

It seems to me that boys are intuitively attracted to enemies. Boys and girls cannot even identify their own sex until they reach 2 or 3 years of age. Even then, they don't know exactly what gender means [28, 29]. In fact, until around age 6 or 7, in Western cultures with their own idiosyncratic dress codes, children believe that they can change sexes simply by cutting long hair or changing into a dress [30]. However, well before this age, boys already prefer playing with weapons and with transportation vehicles, whereas girls do not [28, 31]. In one experiment [26], 20-month-old toddlers were shown a person rocking a doll, banging a hammer, wearing a bracelet, and shooting a gun. When they were given a choice of these toys, boys played more with the gun, and girls with the bracelet, even though none of these boys owned a toy gun at home. Two-year-old boys enjoy playing with tanks, planes, toy guns, and male military figures, even when alone [32]. It is highly improbable that all over the world, parents have socialized only boys to like enemies and have succeeded in doing so when their children are still infants.

Further, war play against the enemy begins around the same time as boys' attraction to weapons. Peter Smith [33] interviewed parents of boys in England and Italy about their children's play. Parents reported that their sons' greatest attraction was to weapons; after this, boys liked playing with combat figures, such as toy soldiers or Star Wars or Transformer figures, and acting out superhero roles. In both countries, parents reported that their sons began war play by 2 or 3 years of age [34, 35]. Even in Germany, where talk of war is politically incorrect, German boys show the same order of interests [27]. Thus, boys appear to be born with a specialized monitoring system for enemies. Their interest in weapons is connected to their efforts to repel them. As Vivian Gussin Paley [36], a veteran kindergarten teacher, concluded after many years of thinking otherwise: "Let the boys be robbers, then or tough guys in space. It is the natural, universal, and essential play of little boys" (Paley, 1984, p. 116).

As most people know, construction also fascinates young boys [14]. This fascination with construction also can be related to war play. Studies from hunter-gatherer societies to modern ones show that while girls enjoy constructing figures, weaving baskets, and building homes and furniture, boys enjoy constructing weapons, forts, and railways. The connection between construction and war is even more clear when I watch what happens after the boys have finished a construction. What pleasure they get from destroying their creations. Destruction depends on construction.

I, personally, have never met a boy who wasn't spellbound by a gun or anything that resembled it. In fact, in a recent American study, 93% of children between 2 and 14 years who accidentally killed someone with a gun were boys [2a]. Cars and trucks are a close second. The excitement that weapons or vehicles generate leads boys to create them from materials that bear no resemblance whatsoever. In many American preschools, for example, in order to discourage the development of aggression, the policy is to not allow children to play with any type of weapon. The idea is that *adults* cause children to learn to become aggressive, not that aggression is something that occurs in all species, including humans. Despite parents' and teachers' best intentions, every one of the more than 50 preschool teachers I have met has described boys' shooting bullets out of a doll's head, transporting ammunition in baby carriages, or tying up enemies with jump ropes. If the right materials and tools are unavailable, then a boy must rely on his imagination to perform his duties. As Paley commented during her preschool teaching days, [36] "Even in nursery school, the boys pick up any loose item and shoot" (Paley, 1984, p. 81).

Historical evidence shows that this attraction to weapons and war has been around for a very long part of human history. Miniature toy soldiers and their tiny weapons have been excavated in archaeological digs in diverse areas of the world and date back thousands of years. Warlike figures have been found in Syria, Egypt, the Mediterranean, and Asia and all around Europe [34]. Although many adults would prefer to believe that boys like weapons and fighting enemies because they are pressured into it by society, the evidence suggests this is not true. In an attempt to examine the honest preferences of young boys, without any parents or teachers present, my students and I interviewed more than 200 children between 4 and 9 years of age in Plymouth, England [37]. Each child was brought individually to a corner of a large room and was told that he or she could say what he honestly felt and that no one ever would know what was said. We asked the boys, and some girls too, to list their three most favorite toys and explain what they did with each of them. The youngest boys, at 4 years of age, some of whom were quite timid, already showed great pleasure in targeting enemies with physical violence. More than half the boys, at all ages, spontaneously reported that they used one or more of their three favorite toys to physically aggress against an enemy. Some of the smallest and shyest boys described with glee the destruction they enjoyed wreaking on imaginary enemies.

Here is a list of these British boys' favorite things to do with their toys that included physical aggression against a living being:

fighting enemies on Play Stations, drawing pictures of bow-and-arrow battles, swinging Bionicles at their stuffed animals, making their knights fight enemies, watching other kids fight each other on television, playing Pokemon cards to battle one another, destroying Yu-Gi-Oh! cards with monsters on them, making Action Man and Power Rangers kill baddies and hit people, Ninja Turtles swinging swords, shooting and killing vampires, throwing cars on baddies then jailing them, firing cannons on pirates, Action Man trapping bad animals in nets, Game Boy players squashing animals, Power Rangers bashing other Power Rangers with their horns and killing enemies with their swords and guns, shooting toy guns, Action Man killing passing people, Dexter shooting robots, Army man fighting enemies, Winnie-the-Pooh shooting baddies, the Hulk smashing others, soldiers fighting wars, Captain Hook fighting people with his hook,

Spiderman killing a three-armed monster, bashing others with bricks, a Ninja Turtle falling on, then shredding the baddies, using army tanks to shoot at others, Bayblades battling and ripping others, T-rex killing with his claws, throwing a sister's doll down stairs to break it, He-man killing bad guys with blades, destroying dinosaurs and watching dinosaurs eat meat, whipping brother with snakes, crocodiles eating animals, chopping off bad guys' heads on Play Station, watching Scooby Doo kill living beings, wrestling toys, killing robots on Play Station, and Rayman fighting baddies.

After asking boys to list their favorite activities, each boy was asked to rate how much he liked enemy fighting versus playing going to the moon or putting out fires. After all, soldiers, astronauts, and firemen are all traditional male favorites with ingenious and colorful vehicles to ride, such as tanks, rocket ships, and fire engines. The winner was enemy fighting. Fighting the enemy is simply even more fun than landing on the moon or putting out a fire.

Of course, there were many other uses to which boys put their toys, and many toys were used in nonaggressive ways. The following are nonaggressive uses of toys by these same boys:

driving cars, pirate ships, lorries, tractors, trucks, police cars, and buses; making buildings, playing hide-and-seek with an animal, kicking and hitting punching bags, riding bikes and scooters, making airplanes, bouncing and kicking balls, jumping, hitting drums, drawing animals, taking teddy on a picnic, making up stories with Thomas the Tank Engine and his friends, helping Bob the Builder to fix things, making a dog into Father Christmas, Piglet visiting other toys, playing on structures in the playground, folding origami, playing with spaceships, putting on a show in the Jungle Book theater, walking the dinosaur, playing with Hot Wheels and remote-controlled cars, watching Action Man rollerblade, getting Spiderman stuck in his web, building ships and houses and castles with Legos and K'nex, blowing up rocks on a computer program, spinning Bayblades, fishing, reading stories in bed, dressing up like Harry Potter or Peter Pan, playing in bed with teddy bear, putting lion to sleep and cuddling him, playing board games, painting pictures, racing cars or playing golf on the Play Station, casting spells like Harry Potter, playing football and basketball and baseball, playing music on the stereo, crashing cars, blowing bubbles, playing marbles, playing with Play Doh, jumping in boxes, performing magic tricks, drawing figures from *Lord of the Rings*, making airplanes fly, swinging Bionicles, spinning and launching Bayblades, play-ing pinball, driving cars into slime, pulling Stretch Man, smashing towers or playing or building with Transformers, walking and caring for horses, pretending to be robots, making the toy bird from the *Lion King* fly, find-ing hiding dogs, playing monkeys, watching Power Rangers on television, playing with magnets, dressing up as a fireman, playing with fire engines, building cars from kits, making sharks swim, playing with putty, spinning tops, bouncing on pogo sticks, playing songs on the guitar, skateboarding, playing with swords, sleeping with rabbits, playing with sand, playing with panda in the woods, solving puzzles, sliding, making up songs, watching worms wiggle, playing with boats in the bathtub, shooting water pistols at people, playing with a game cube, and playing Tetris.

Even some of these suggest aggression.

Contrast these aggressive and nonaggressive activities with those of girls. Almost none of the girls suggested using their toys to fight enemies or mentioned physical aggression at all. The following is a complete list of the girls' favorite things to do with their toys:

playing catch, adopting cats and dogs in a computer game, pretending to be teenagers, watching Rug Rats cartoons on television, dressing up, and feeding and taking shopping and walking and putting to sleep dolls and pretending they are real, curing sick animals, enjoying picnics with, cuddling, walking, carrying, playing with, sleeping with, dressing up and petting stuffed animals; playing the piano, riding bikes, pretending to shop, playing school, dancing, playing with balloons and puppets, putting on makeup and dressing up, making a film, giving tea parties, playing with trains, pretending to run a pet shop, building houses from bricks, making food from Play Doh, playing hula-hoops, playing with Diva stars, giving Bratz dolls surprise birthday parties and trips to the hairdresser and dressing them up, running a farm, skipping rope, walking on stilts, feeding their MicroPets, arranging dates between Action Man and Barbie, fixing Barbie's hair and dressing her and letting her play in her castle and with her cars; dressing Baby Annabel, sending bad animals to bed alone and sleeping with good animals, playing cat's cradle with string, arranging clothes on actual and video game figures, playing on the swings, play-ing Twister, playing with K'nex, playing cards, reading books, making Spirograph pictures, watching fish in an aquarium, racing bikes, playing hide-and-seek with animals and dolls, playing tennis, solving jigsaw puzzles, drawing pictures, making cakes from sand, playing with pretend fairies, pretending to be a veterinarian, playing Kerplunk, taking care of Care Bears or Fizz, playing Downfall, building Lego castles, taking bear to church, playing dominoes, helping Scully the monster build houses, playing board games like Scrabble, dancing with a Princess doll, watching Tweenies on videos, letting Bob the Builder fix the house, kissing bunny toys, listening to Thomas the Tank engine make train noises, playing with a doctor's kit, and finally some exceptions: using Action Man to kill baddies, and using Play Station to play Grand Theft Auto and kill people.

No wonder social scientists conclude that human females are more sociable than males. Only a very small percentage of girls' ideas regarding toy play concerns harming another living being.

Similar evidence for boys' spontaneous, early interest in fighting enemies comes from Ageliki Nicolopoulou, another American preschool teacher [38]. She systematically recorded stories told by the 10 boys and 8 girls in her class in western Massachusetts. She found that more than 90% of boys' stories included aggressive violence against an enemy target. By 4 years of age, every single boy's story consisted of fighting a violent enemy.

As an example, Nicolopoulou provides the following prototypical story verbatim:

Once upon a time there was a monster and Mummyman came. And Mummyman squished poison out of his nose. And then G.I. Joe came and the G.I. Joe had a gun. At the part where it shooted a yellow light, shot out poison at the monster, and the monster died. And Cutman cut a house and it fell on Mummyman and he got squished. And Mummyman's tushy fell off. And Superman was seeing this and it didn't look funny. And Superman put Mummyman back together. And Mummyman squirted poison out of his nose at Superman and then Mummyman squirted lava and fire out of his nose and killed Superman. Then Mummyman shot poison out of his nose at Cutman and Cutman died. And then Cutman came alive again. And Cutman and G.I. Joe became friends. Then Mummyman squirted lava out of his nose holes onto the wall and it bounced onto a tree and the tree fell down. And it broke the mountains and the mountains said "Why did you fall on me?" but the tree ignored him. And Superman was standing on the ground and Cutman looked at Superman and said,

"Hey! What's going on with my eyes?" And Superman said, "I put poison in your eyes to make me look like a ton of Supermans." And the poison came out of Cutman's eyes and Superman looked like one plain Superman. Then Cutman cut off Superman's head. The G.I. Joe said, "What a show!" (Ethan, Seth, Zachary, Jacob). (Nicolopoulou, 1997, p. 178)

Mummyman is quite an enemy. Although he is an individual, he is not a fellow peer from the preschool. He is larger than life, and not of Hollywood's creation.

Vivian Gussin Paley [36], a preschool and kindergarten teacher, also noted the great significance of monsters and superheroes to boys between the ages of 3 and 5 years. She too concluded that young boys have an intuitive fascination with them. Here is another story, this one recounted by a 5-year-old boy in her Chicago kindergarten classroom based on the popular *Star Wars* movie:

Once there was Luke Skywalker, and Darth Vader cut off his hand. Then IG88 froze Han Solo. Then Luke killed the storm troopers. Then Hammerhead shot Han Solo, but he was not dead, only bleeding a lot. (Paley, 1984, p. 21)

A final example shows how much time boys spend considering the problem of, and solutions to, enemies. John Gottman [39], a careful investigator of human behavior, recorded the conversations of boys and girls in a midwestern American preschool. As he tells it, boys and girls suffer from different fears and fixate on different anxieties. From early in life, boys' attention is drawn to lethal enemies that can destroy them and their families. Here is a conversation between a 3-year-old boy, Jonathan, and a 4-year-old boy, Billy, that Gottman recorded:

J: I didn't want to have any [soap] when I was a baby.
B: Yeah, like kryptonite hurts Superman? And that's poison.
J: Yeah.

Later,

B: And rattlesnakes are poison.
J: Ark!

B: Yes, they are.

J: No, they rattle their tail before they bit people.

B: Yeah, that makes them sick.

J: Or a person shot the snake. The snake would be hurt.

B: Yeah, 'cause I hate snakes.

J: Yech!

Which continues with:

B: And I hate sharks. But I love to eat sardines.

J: I love to eat shark.

B: Yeah, but they're so big!

J: But we can cut their tail.

B: Yeah, what happens if we cut them to two?

J: It would bite us, it would swim, and we would have to run. Run very fast, run to our homes.

B: Yeah, but ummm...

J: By the trees. Mr. Shark bited the door down and we would have to run way in the forest.

B: Yeah, but...but if he bited all the trees down...

J: And then we would have to shoot him. Yeah, and the shark is poison.

B: But pink is. Red is, yellow is.

B: Yeah, but people are too. What happened if the shark ate us?

J: We would have to bite him in, on his tongue.

B: Yeah, what happened if we bite him so far that we made his tongue metal?

J: Yeah.

B: Then he couldn't have breaked out of metal.

J: He can eat metal open. Sharks are so strong they can even bite metal.

B: Yes.

J: How about concrete? Concrete could make it.

(Gottman, 1986, pp. 160–161)

For boys, confronting an enemy with no weapons is frightening. I can illustrate this best with the following anecdote. As most Americans know, Scooby-Doo is a popular cartoon TV show aimed at young children; it depicts a skinny, disheveled, and frightened young man named Shabby and his enormous, equally fearful dog, Scooby. Shabby and Scooby are accompanied by two women and one well-dressed man, who exude maturity and common sense. They solve mysteries in which they track ghostly evildoers who turn out to be just ordinary human enemies.

One day a 5-year-old boy explained to me shyly that he was too scared to watch this show with his female cousins. When I asked why, he replied that Shabby and Scooby had no weapons. Tracking an enemy without a weapon obviously is foolhardy and dangerous. Upon further inquiry, I learned that many little boys shared this one's opinion. Unbeknownst to me, Scooby-Doo may have greater appeal to little girls. Little girls aren't afraid of enemies, as long as there are mature adults around. Boys realize that mature adults are no match for a real enemy, unless the adults have weapons.

This brings out another important aspect of boys' relationship to the enemy. At some level, boys understand intuitively that even the most devoted mother is useless against someone who wants to kill you. So many women and children die directly or indirectly because of enemies. Fighting the enemy requires serious male resources. Because most young boys are still unaware of the armies deployed by their country to stop enemies, a little boy finds himself in dire straits. Nothing in his world can effectively fight an enemy, except...a superhero. How else to explain the magnetic attraction of boys to superheroes? I have observed the sheer delight of a young boy as he discovers his first superhero. What a relief to know that even if you are by yourself with no weapons, Superman or Batman or Action Man can come to the rescue. Older boys and young men around the world leave their families regularly to fight enemies and become superheroes to their communities and nations.

The Halloween costumes on sale for boys further demonstrate the continuing appeal of the superhero-enemy theme. Halloween allows children to choose costumes solely according to their real interests and pleasures. Of course, someone makes these to attract boys, and they make money by selling a lot. As most websites selling Halloween costumes show, however, boys buy costumes for superheroes—and their arch enemies: supervillains. The highly successful Japanese Pokemon card series presents another example, with cards with names such as Enraged Muka Muka, Infernal Incinerator, Creeping Doom Mantra, Malice Doll of Demise, Indomitable Fighter Lei Lei, Cyber Archfiend, Terrorking Salmon, Tribe-Infecting Virus, Nightmare's Steelcage, Invitation to a Dark Sleep, Mad Sword Beast, Dark Driceratops, Gross Ghost of Fled Dreams, Pitch-Black Warwolf, and Dragon Zombie. Through trading and negotiating, a boy lives and dies on a daily basis as he combats others using his Pokemon cards. Few girls are attracted to Pokemon cards unless they want to play with the boys.

Growing boys' increasing self-sufficiency and experience do not decrease their interest in enemies. Video games illustrate this well. Many contain enemy fighters, weapons, and extreme violence. Who plays these games? Boys and men, alone and together [31, 40]. For example, *World of Warcraft* by Blizzard Entertainment is the most popular of the multiple-player games, with its expansions titled *The Burning Crusade, Wrath of the Lich King*, and *Cataclysm*. It has grossed billions. Girls and women rarely spontaneously play violent video games unless they are joining a boyfriend, brother, or male classmate.

Likewise, Hollywood specializes in war movies, Westerns, horror films, crime stories, courtroom dramas, action and adventure themes, doomsday scenarios, spy movies, and prison stories, filled to the brink with men fighting enemies. The movie and video game industries specialize in the creation of evilness [41], just as young boys do. According to Dolf Zillmann [41], who studies the film industry, what excites the competitive instinct most is the idea that another animate being, be it animal, man, or alien, desires to inflict harm on oneself or one's group. When such an enemy does not exist, girls and women don't think about it. But boys and men will create one. They make and watch the movies. Fighting provides pleasure, but not enough to sustain a whole movie. It is the enemy that captures the interest of male moviegoers. The ability to watch others killing enemies generates billions and billions of dollars. Since filmmaking began more than a hundred years ago, violence always has had its appeal. Films by the Japanese director Kurosawa, Mexican revolutionary movies, Chinese leftist films, Indian Don films, and Soviet propaganda movies show that disparate cultures share the American penchant for watching violence unfold.

Another organization that understands this basic fact about men is the military. The United States military works closely with toy and entertainment companies so that the latest weapons and army heroes are available in toy stores, and in video games, and hence in boys' living rooms [42]. The US government initially produced video games designed to provide simulations of war only for those entering the military. Then, the US Department of Defense expanded its audience and developed games for everyone's use, such as *Desert Storm, America's Army, Full Spectrum Warrior*, and *Full Spectrum Combat*. Massively multiple online role-playing computer games, such as the hugely popular *World of Warcraft*, allow many players armed only with a computer to cooperate from around the world to hunt down and kill one another, team against team, in completely realistic contexts using the latest weaponry available. *Kuma War* replicates actual battles from and tactics used in current conflicts in which the United States is involved.

Advanced technology permits the reality of war to come even closer to home for boys and men not involved in the actual fighting. All of these games hone reflexes and increase knowledge of combat conditions in children, adolescents, and adults. Players do not even need to leave their chairs, let alone set foot on the battlefield [43]. The emotional high that fighting enemies generates is now available to anyone who wants it. Increasingly, of course, actual wars can be fought remotely as well.

Neuroscience has begun to provide evidence that men get unique pleasure from punishing an enemy [44]. In a recent study, men and women were asked to play a game against a person who played either fairly or unfairly. They then entered an fMRI scanner, which recorded which part of their brain was activated. While in the scanner, they could see the hands of the fair player and the unfair player, as well as their own hands. Painful electrical shocks then were delivered to everyone's hands.

When the fair player received a painful shock, the empathy center of both men's and women's brains lit up. When the unfair player was shocked, women's empathy centers lit up, but men's did not. In fact, when the unfair player was shocked, men's *pleasure* centers were activated. Not only did men not feel empathy, they actually enjoyed the experience of taking revenge on someone who cheated them.

Over several million years, those men whose brains specialized in detecting and fighting enemies were more likely to survive to pass on their genes to their sons. It is not that socialization is unimportant; it is critical to actual fighting. Given the young age at which boys' fascination with enemies begins across diverse cultures, it is apparent that biology plays a role. Even when no fighting is occurring, young boys across the world show the same fascination with and responsibility for defeating the enemy. Of course, while actually attacking enemies might be useful for an adult, it would be lethal for a child. Biology, however, tries to protect young boys from actual fighting. What keeps a young boy who is fascinated with the enemy and fighting it from attacking a real life enemy? One novel theory is fear. The period between early childhood and adolescence is marked by the activation of adrenal hormones. Some researchers think that these hormones induce fearfulness in young boys [45]. This means that before puberty, most boys are afraid to attack a real-life enemy. Little boys, like young girls, like to cuddle with stuffed animals, run to their mothers for comfort, and stay close to home. For many boys, these desires slowly wane with age. When boys enter puberty, the level of adrenal hormones decreases, diminishing boys' fearfulness. Thus, most male adolescents are much less fearful and ready to physically attack the enemy if one is around. Being raised in a stressful environment, however, must accelerate this process [3a]. The youngest boys in actual combat are between 7 and 10 years of age [46]. Tens of thousands of child soldiers, virtually all boys, when separated from their families, can become quite effective fighters against an enemy when older men demand it.

It is more well established that puberty for males is marked by a large increase in the level of testosterone. One of the effects of increased testosterone is a heightened sensitivity to challenges. This has the effect of reducing the threshold for perceiving someone to be an enemy [47]. Combined with their large increase in strength, coordination, and endurance, and of course throwing ability, males are biologically capable now of successfully attacking and defeating an enemy. Young men are better physically equipped to defeat the enemy than anyone else [48]. Furthermore, by the time they reach adolescence, they have psychologically readied themselves for more than a decade.

It is no surprise, then, that fighting wars and administering punishments to the enemy is practiced most by individual males in their late teens and early 20s. All countries send their youngest, strongest, and bravest men to fight first. Only when the supply runs out do they recruit older men or young boys, and women. Physical aggression is not limited to the battlefield, of course. Around the world, adolescent and young adult males physically fight more than anyone else [49]. At the extreme, homicide statistics collected in Chicago from 1965 to 1990, England and Wales from 1977 to 1990, and Canada from 1974 to 1990 demonstrate that men murder the most when they are between the ages 18 and 25 [49].

Culture determines the social acceptability of murder. For example, there are more than 10 times as many murders per capita in the United States as in England, two cultures that are quite similar in other respects. What doesn't change, however, is the sex ratio [49, 50]. Across the most diverse cultures, men murder other people, particularly unrelated same-sex people, 10 times more often than women do.

As men get older, they become physically weaker, and thus less effective fighters. The gradual reduction of testosterone in men that begins in the late 20s simultaneously slowly reduces men's willingness to attack the enemy [49]. A 30-year-old, less strong now than a 20-year-old, will enjoy a fight, but from a distance. He can supervise combat operations. Having survived war until now, he is better positioned to provide expertise than his stronger but less experienced 20-year-old male peers. A 50-year-old man, too weak to actually fight and too removed from fighting to provide much expertise, can train the younger generation of males to fight. Fighting enemies is fascinating to men of all ages, but hormonal, neuronal, and environmental changes influence the probability that a man will actually physically combat the enemy. Biology plays its role by ensuring that the men who are most likely to attack are the ones who are the most likely to succeed.

Young men not only defend societies from enemies but also start wars. The ratio of young men (15–29 years) to older men (30+ years) in a country predicts quite accurately war-related fatalities. In their study of 88 countries from all over the world, Christian Mesquida and Neil Wiener [51] showed that as this ratio of young to older men increases, the number of fatalities during conflicts increases enormously. Controlling for the country's wealth (GNP), its developmental status, and even the type of political regime did not change the strength of these findings. A concentration of physically strong young men who lack fear and are primed to retaliate against enemies, with few older men ready to control them, greatly increases the probability of warfare.

Fighting Strength and Fluid Intelligence

Being a good fighter requires being not only strong and fast but also smart, at least in certain ways. A fighter who was strong and fast, but who lost track of others or couldn't figure out appropriate tactics and plan strategies in advance would probably not have survived for long. Although this is more speculative, there is some evidence that biology helps produce males who think in ways that might be particularly useful when fighting.

Perhaps the greatest cognitive advantage men hold over women is their ability to mentally rotate objects in space [52]. This difference is present even in young infants [53], but it increases dramatically with puberty [52]. What advantage would this form of spatial intelligence provide to a man?

Imagine being on a battlefield with enemies and friends all around, where you must constantly move. A fighter who lost track of where his enemies were might find them in the wrong place, at the wrong time. Or if he needed help from friends but had lost track of them in the heat of battle, he would clearly face a disadvantage. Keeping track of the relative positions of enemies and friends even when one is moving in space is a critical component to fighting well. In fact, in one study, when adults were informed of the social connections between individuals, then given spatial information about their whereabouts men were much better than women at recalling the spatial positions of allies, which would correspond to the kind of rapid tracking that a battlefield situation would require [54].

Fighting also requires strategic thinking. This is of course quite clear on a real battlefield, but we can also see it in the kinds of games that are attractive to men. Chess is explicitly patterned as a form of war-based strategy game. Strategy is a key ingredient of most group sports, including soccer, baseball, and football. Tactics are rehashed repeatedly not just by players but by male observers and reporters too. In each of these, not only are the good players celebrated for their physical prowess, but so are the coaches and players who have a good sense of when to do things. Similarly, knowing who is good in what kinds of situations is also useful when fighting. Maybe it is no accident that there are boys and men who can't add two numbers without making a mistake but who can tell you what the batting average is for every player on their favorite teams for the last 20 years [4a].

More generally, during late adolescence and the early 20s, when men are physically strongest and fighting enemies is most common, a specific type of cognitive ability, named fluid intelligence, peaks. Fluid intelligence refers to the ability to think fast about highly abstract and novel ideas, often involving pattern formations [55, 56]. The greatest discoveries of brilliant mathematicians and scientists occur to them when they are in their late teens or early 20s. This doesn't mean that many other discoveries don't occur later in life, but simply that the most creative ideas occur during the same period in which men are maximally physically fit and quick. These types of problems require finishing patterns, rearranging puzzles, transforming mathematical relationships, and following logical arguments without any physical basis. Critically, it is not just the most brilliant abstract thinkers who exhibit their greatest discoveries during this period. All individuals, men and women, think and move fastest when they are between 18 and 25 years of age [55].

Why should such fast, abstract reasoning about novel patterns be best when people are so young? What task requires it? Perhaps young men and young women need this ability to find a mate, but it is unclear how this would help. Furthermore, many men marry after this ability has already begun to decline [57], and many women excel in other types of reasoning, such as verbal abilities and memory for faces and places [52, 58]. How about hunting? The problem here is that the best hunters are older than 25 [59].

Although there is no specific evidence for this, one explanation for why fluid intelligence is greatest when men are simultaneously physically strongest and fastest is because it increases victory in warfare. Abstract conceptualization of the enemy's battle formations, strategic planning of future moves, rapid execution of complicated tactics, alongside maximal physical prowess and speed, seems like a good recipe for winning a war. Men with these heightened physical and cognitive skills may have defeated more enemies, and passed the genes for these traits to their sons. After their physical skills waned, fluid intelligence and speed became less critical to survival, so they diminished too.

Regardless of the truth of this proposition, these days a major problem preoccupying educators is the difficulty that many boys have in acquiring academic skills. The idea that fighting wars requires a fairly high level of thinking could be valuable. Educators could use males' innate attraction to fighting enemies as a tool. Skills could be learned in the context of defeating the enemy. Calculating points won and lost would make mathematics more real. Geographical knowledge would be essential to establishing territorial boundaries. History would provide real-life examples of warfare, politics, and changing national boundaries. Morality could be broached through the generation of competitive rules. Clothing considerations could include evolution and camouflage of animals in differing environments. Physical education on the playground could take its playbook from military exercises. The importance of naps and eating right to basic training could be stressed. As the boys grow, the incredible scientific advances that the military has produced in technology, medicine, and engineering could be introduced. Fluid intelligence could be co-opted as a means to win battles, even if it didn't originally evolve for this purpose. As strange as this may sound, I have met many nonviolent boys whose interest in learning was inspired by war.

Competition as the Ultimate Form of Entertainment

Play fighting and defeating enemies are fun, but nothing beats one-on-one competition. The superhero beats everyone. In most mammalian species in which females care for the young, males are very competitive with one another. Both social scientists and evolutionary biologists concur that males, whether human or nonhuman, are the less sociable sex because they are so competitive. Males spend a lot of time fighting each other to gain higher status, better resources, and more females to inseminate. Human males are much more overtly competitive than females. According to one of the most universally used psychological scales, the Bem Sex-Role Inventory, masculinity *means* scoring high on competitiveness, assertiveness, aggressiveness, dominance, and similar attributes [60].

The quest to dominate other males begins as early as children begin to interact [61]. Very young boys, when put together, will start competing very quickly and will soon sort themselves out into a dominance hierarchy. The biggest and most aggressive child can beat the second-biggest and aggressive child who beats the third-biggest and most aggressive child, and so forth. It starts in toddlerhood with struggles over valued objects, territorial rights, play fighting, and even speech forms and continues to interactions with make-believe enemies.

Language provides a perfect example. When Carol Gilligan [62] titled her seminal work on sex differences *In a Different Voice*, she almost surely meant voice in the figurative sense: men and women have different concerns. However, as early as children learn to speak, boys and girls really do talk differently. This difference appears so early that it is hard to believe it is anything but innate. Then, it becomes stronger with much practice.

When speaking to one another, young boys issue directives, command others, insult them, tell jokes at others' expense, ignore what someone else just said, disagree with another's point, call one another names, brag, tell stories highlighting their own accomplishments, curse, threaten others, use direct statements, and generally behave in a domineering fashion toward one another [61, 63–65]. In the conversations of children in a working-class African American neighborhood in southwest Philadelphia in the 1970s, Marjorie Harkness Goodwin [66] found that one of the activities the boys most enjoyed was competition—over anything. They competed over making slingshots and paper airplanes, playing with yo-yos, driving go-carts, bending hangers, performing the best dance steps, and everything else they seemed to enjoy.

The same sex differences appear in a wealthier environment. Boys talk tough, and girls try to get what they want while being perfectly polite. Amy Sheldon [67] recorded the conversations of upper-middle-class, primarily white nursery school children in the midwestern United States as they played in a housekeeping center she created. She brought in three same-sex children at a time to a room with a kitchen that included a play pickle that was particularly attractive.

Here is how boys attempt to get the pickle:

KEVIN: (at the table) Pickle. (takes the pickle)....

NICK: I'm cutting- I'm cutting- No, I have to cut that! (*Nick tries to take pickle back from Kevin*)

KEVIN: No, I cut it.

NICK: No! No, no, <u>no</u>! You're the children!

KEVIN: No, I'm not!....

NICK: (screams) Kevin, but the, oh, I <u>have</u> to cut! I want to cut it! I want to cut it! It's mine!

(Sheldon, 1990, p. 22)

Here is how girls attempt to get the pickle. Note that what they are doing and what they are saying are not the same:

SUE: And strawberries for dinner, right?

MARY: And the- this for dinner. (*Mary puts the pickle in a pot on the stove*)

SUE: And the pickle. Do you like pickle? (*Sue takes the pickle out of the pot*)

MARY: And this (*the hamburger*) is for dinner. (*Mary pulls the hamburger and pickle out of Sue's hand and puts them back in pot*)

SUE: No, they aren't for dinner, no, Lisa wants pickles. (*Sue tries to grab the hamburger and pickle back from Mary but she holds on and put them back in the pot*)....

SUE: No, Lisa wants pickle. (*Sue tries to grab the pickle again*)

MARY: She gots (*unintelligible*)....

SUE: You want pickle, Lisa?

LISA: Mmmhm. (*Mary brings the pickle over to Lisa at the table*)

SUE: Lisa says she wants pickle.

(Sheldon, 1990, p. 17)

Although the girls are fighting over the pickle, you wouldn't know it from listening to them. As early as 3 years of age, children have learned how to speak like boys or like girls, suggesting that forms of speech have a biological basis.

But learning plays a big role too. A female student of mine listening to my lecture on sex differences in speech interrupted me to describe her experience. She had been brought up with four older brothers and had learned to "speak boy," as she put it. When she started school, none of the girls wanted to play with her, so she spent her time with the boys. As she grew older, however, the boys preferred to play with the other boys, and she became lonely. She consciously described struggling to learn the language of the girls so that they would not reject her. She learned to apologize for any pretense of being superior. When she won a game, received a higher grade, had an extra friend, or was chosen by the teacher for an honor, she wouldn't talk about it. Instead, she would explain that she really did not deserve the recognition. In order to reassure her friends that she was no better than they were, she would talk about one of her weaknesses.

By middle childhood, when a boy's team beats another team, the winners never let the losers forget the outcome [68, 69]. Their pitiless comments and denigrating humor paint a picture for all school inhabitants to see of the rankings of both teams and pivotal members of the winning and losing teams. Girls don't want any conflict, so they try to make everyone equal. They forget who won or lost.

I have heard these very differences while walking past many a tennis court. In a men's game, the winner of a shot will brag loudly about his winning shot. The winner of a point has no qualms about insulting his opponent whose ball went over the fence, under the net, or into the adjacent court. It is not only the opponent's tennis playing skill that is criticized; nothing is safe. The loser of the point replies with his own calculations regarding the winner's dim future prospects. Both players also acknowledge one another's good shots when the shots truly reflect superior skill. In the ideal matchup, each man appears to believe that he is just a bit better than his opponent, but that his opponent is actually very good, ensuring, of course, that he himself is even better.

Contrast that with the language used by two women tennis players. If a woman hits a winning shot, she apologizes to her opponent. She then attributes her winning shot to any one of a number of external factors: good luck, an accident, the wind, a poorly hit shot that went awry, or hours on hours of practice. The loser replies by praising to the hilt the quality of the winning shot and the winner's skill, and follows this up by apologizing for her own poor performance. No matter the actual skill level of either player, neither wants to be perceived as better than the other, and so they agree that neither is very good. From infancy through old age, human males get pleasure from overtly competing against their male peers. Girls and women don't.

Language of course is not required to compete. One of my favorite examples of sex differences in enjoyment of competition comes from a simple game that my student Rosanne Roy and I created [70]. Four children at a time, all boys or all girls, played our bead collection game. Each child was given a thin wooden stick with a bright red line painted almost at the top. The object of the game was to collect as many beads as possible on the stick until the beads reached the red line. Each of the four children alternated rolling a die that indicated how many beads they could collect on a turn. A child could take beads either from a bowl filled with beads or from one of the other players by removing the beads from that player's stick. We created two versions of the game. In the competitive version, the child whose beads touched the red line first received a prize. In the noncompetitive version, all children who reached the red line before the time expired received a prize. Only in the competitive version of the game did it pay to remove beads from another player's stick. In the noncompetitive version, taking the beads of another player was useless.

Both boys and girls took beads from their opponents when this was useful (in the competitive version). But, strikingly, boys also took beads from the others in the noncompetitive version. When I asked them later why they did this, the boys looked puzzled. One boy explained that the game would be "no fun at all" if he didn't take his friends' beads. When I relayed this to some of my male students and colleagues, they too looked at me with puzzled expressions. They could not understand why anyone would bother playing either version of the game without taking the other players' beads. The girls could. They almost never took another girl's beads in the non-competitive version. The historical record confirms that males have always played competitive games across the most diverse cultures. Men living in Africa between A.D. 500 and A.D. 1600 played a variety of competitive sports, including wrestling, archery, the *Rungu* (a type of projectile club) throw in which the goal was to excel at hitting a stationary or moving target from a specified distance, swimming, running, canoeing, rowing, climbing, horse and oxen racing, high jump, tug-of-war, stick fighting, and dancing and gymnastic activities. Often, boys and men competed in tournaments, with the best athlete admired by the whole community. Other times, they competed directly against one another. Across Asia, physically competitive sports, including archery, wrestling, and martial arts competitions, were derived directly from warfare as well as to promote success as a soldier [13]. The Olympics, which began in Greece in 776 B.C., included a large variety of competitive sports. Competition is and always has been an important motivation for men's behavior.

Competition presents a major problem for warfare. If males are busy fighting one another, how can they fight the enemy? Men spend much of their time competing with other for status, resources, territory, and women. What happens when these same men meet the enemy? How does a man join a competitor to fight a common enemy if he has to constantly watch his back in case the other man wants his land, his wife, or even his life?

This presents a paradox. The constant male struggle to figure out who is better, faster, smarter, or otherwise more skilled could severely strain or even destroy a friendship. No female would put up with it. If it did strain the relationship, the competitors wouldn't be able to join forces to defeat the enemy. Cooperation is essential to defeating the enemy. One of the most fascinating aspects of male competition, however, is the relative ease with which boys and men can integrate competition and conflict into their friendships. In the most extreme case, they can even switch partners, so that an enemy becomes a friend.

My male students have told stories of themselves and a male friend destroying each other's property, hitting one another, and even causing serious injury when competing for status or resources. In every such case, the two have ended up forgetting their conflicts soon afterward, sometimes just hours later. One young man reported being stabbed by his teammate, one of his closest friends, during football practice. His friend, who was momentarily enraged at how forcefully my student had tackled him, pulled out a knife and stabbed my student in the stomach. The two boys reconciled less than 3 weeks later, shortly after my student was released from the hospital. Listening to this story, my female students were astounded. Never would they continue a friendship with someone who had stabbed them.

The same thing occurs between tribes all over the world. Two tribes and their leaders can be enemies sworn to the death, yet a year later they have become allies against a common enemy. Countries, too, fight horrible wars against each other, but some years later, when their interests converge, they team up as allies. The North Atlantic Treaty Organization (NATO) is just one example of this kind of alliance.

What allows two competitive males to become allies after they have fought? The process of reconciliation seems to be the key. Primatologist Frans de Waal [71] created the "valuable relationships hypothesis" to explain why in species in which individuals depend on one another for survival and reproductive success, conflicts must be resolved. There is no choice, or both individuals will suffer. A relationship that helps an animal survive or reproduce is too valuable to be destroyed just because some conflict arose, no matter how severe. Conflicts are inevitable, after all, especially when two individuals spend a lot of time together.

Yet after a serious fight, former allies find some way to signal that the hostilities are over; they reconcile. Chimpanzees actually kiss, embrace, and squeeze one another's genitals [72], and then it's back to business as usual.

We know less about reconciliation in humans. It is difficult to record behavior during a serious fight. Based on interviews with individuals in middle childhood [73], adolescence [74], and adulthood [75], however, compared with girls and young women, boys and young men state they are more willing to resolve a conflict with their same-sex friend. Girls and women report they would rather find a replacement than reconcile with someone who hurt them badly.

In an attempt to observe reconciliation without provoking an actual conflict between friends, my students and I recently asked 40 young men and 40 young women individually to imagine they had just argued with and been punched in the nose by their close same-sex friend. Everyone reported becoming enraged. Their heart rates surged. Then, we asked them to pretend that the same-sex experimenter who was outside the door was actually their friend who had punched them in the nose. They confronted the experimenter. Sure enough, despite the cursing and occasionally even thwarted attempts to punch the experimenter back, the young men afterward stated that they would be more likely than the young women to forgive their friend. Not only that, but the males' heart rates calmed down faster and their adrenal glands released more cortisol, suggesting that their bodies were preparing to invest more in a reconciliation attempt [76].

One of the most remarkable aspects of male biology is men's willingness to set aside their competitive instincts in order to cooperate to defeat the enemy. Not only can boys and men engage in friendly but serious competition without destroying their friendship, but they can even try to kill one another, then make up later. Competition does not interfere with friendships in the way that it does for females.

That play fighting, targeting enemies, and competing for dominance occur so early in male life and across so many cultures suggests that these behaviors are partly innate. These behaviors would be invaluable ingredients for fighting.

But they would not be enough. Warfare is composed of more than just one-on-one fights. It requires strong alliances between individuals. It requires intricate coordination and cooperation within a large group. When it comes to war, men must invest their time, energy, and resources in one another. Men must be sociable.

References

1. Gigerenzer, G., and R. Selten, *Bounded rationality: The adaptive toolbox.* 2002, Cambridge, MA: MIT Press.
1a. Roach, N. T., et al., Elastic energy storage in the shoulder and the evolution of high-speed throwing in Homo. *Nature*, 2013. 498(7455): pp. 483–486.
2. Gurven, M., and H. Kaplan, Longevity among hunter gatherers: A cross cultural examination. *Population and Development Review*, 2007. 33(2): pp. 321–365.
2a. Luo, M. and M. McIntire, *Children and guns: The hidden toll*, in *New York Times* September 29, 2013: New York.
3. Hill, K., A. M. Hurtado, and R. S. Walker, High adult mortality among Hiwi hunter-gatherers: Implications for human evolution. *Journal of Human Evolution*, 2007. 52(4): pp. 443–454.
3a. Ellis, B. J., et al., The evolutionary basis of risky adolescent behavior: Implications for science, policy, and practice. *Developmental Psychology*, 2012. 48(3): pp. 598–623.
4. Wrangham, R. W., Evolution of coalitionary killing. *Yearbook of Physical Anthropology*, 1999. 29(42): pp. 1–30.
4a. Baumeister, R. F., Is there anything good about men?: How cultures flourish by exploiting men 2010, New York: Oxford University Press.
5. Gottman, J. M., and J. G. Parker, *Conversations of friends: Speculations on affective development.* 1986, New York: Cambridge University Press.
6. Byrnes, J. P., D. C. Miller, and W. D. Schafer, Gender differences in risk taking: A meta-analysis. *Psychological Bulletin*, 1999. 125(3): pp. 367–383.
7. GDAMS, Fact sheet: Military spending vs. MDGs, in *Global Day of Action on Military Spending*. 2011. http://demilitarize.org/contact/
8. UN, Military spending levels remain out of control, UN official says, in *UN News Service*. April 12, 2011.

9. DiPietro, J. A., Rough and tumble play: A function of gender. *Developmental Psychology*, 1981. 17(1): pp. 50–58.

10. Pellegrini, A. D., and J. D. Long, A longitudinal study of bullying, dominance, and victimization during the transition from primary school through secondary school. *British Journal of Developmental Psychology*, 2002. 20(2): pp. 259–280.

11. Fry, D., Rough-and-tumble social play in humans, in *The nature of play*, A. Pellegrini and P. K. Smith, Editors. 2005, New York: Guilford. pp. 54–85.

12. Leibs, A., *Sports and games of the Renaissance*. Vol. 4. 2004, Westport, CT: Greenwood.

13. Craig, S., *Sports and games of the ancients*. 2002, Westport, CT: Greenwood.

14. Yumi Gosso, E. O., Maria de Lima Salum e Morais, Fernando Jose Leite Ribeiro, and Vera Silvia Radd Bussah, Play in hunter-gatherer society, in *The nature of play*, A. Pellegrini and P. K. Smith, Editors. 2005, New York: Guilford. pp. 213–253.

15. Whiting, B. B., and C. P. Edwards *Children of different worlds: The formation of social behavior*. 1988, Cambridge, MA: Harvard University Press.

16. Gomme, A. B., and D. Webb, *The traditional games of England, Scotland, and Ireland*. 1894, London: Thames and Hudson.

17. Sutton-Smith, B., J. Gerstmyer, and A. Meckley, Playfighting as folkplay amongst preschool children. *Western Folklore*, 1988. 47(3): pp. 161–176.

18. Benenson, J., R. Tennyson, and R. Wrangham, Male more than female Infants imitate propulsive motion. *Cognition*, 2011. 121(2): pp. 262–267.

19. Marlowe, F., *The Hadza: Hunter-gatherers of Tanzania: Origins of human behavior and culture*. 2010, Berkeley: University of California Press.

20. Thomas, J. R., and K. E. French, Gender differences across age in motor performance: A meta-analysis. *Psychological Bulletin*, 1985. 98(2): pp. 260–282.

21. Cashdan, E., F. W. Marlowe, A. Crittenden, C. Porter, and B. M. Wood Sex differences in spatial cognition among Hadza foragers. *Evolution and Human Behavior*, 2012. 33, pp. 274–284.

22. Goodall, J., *The chimpanzees of Gombe: Patterns of behavior*. 1986, Cambridge, MA: Harvard University Press.

23. Hopkins, W. D., J. L. Russell, and J. A. Schaeffer, The neural and cognitive correlates of aimed throwing in chimpanzees: A magnetic resonance image and behavioural study on a unique form of social tool use. *Philosophical Transactions of the Royal Society B: Biological Sciences*, 2012. 367(1585): pp. 37–47.

24. Mahajan, N., et al., The evolution of intergroup bias: Perceptions and attitudes in rhesus macaques. *Journal of Personality and Social Psychology*, 2011. 100(3): pp. 387–405.

25. Wilson, M. L., and R. W. Wrangham, Intergroup relations in chimpanzees. *Annual Review of Anthropology*, 2003. 32(3): pp. 363–392.

26. Fein, G. G., Pretend play in childhood: An integrative review. *Child Development*, 1981. 52(4): pp. 1095–1118.

27. Wegener-Spohring, G., War toys and aggressive play scenes, in *Toys, play and child development*, J. H. Goldstein, Editor. 1994, New York: Cambridge University Press. Pp. 85–109.

28. Huston, A. C., The development of sex typing: Themes from recent research. *Developmental Review*, 1985. 5(1): pp. 1–17.

29. Zosuls, K. M., et al., The acquisition of gender labels in infancy: Implications for gender-typed play. *Developmental Psychology*, 2009. 45(3): pp. 688–701.

30. Kohlberg, L., and E. E. Maccoby, A cognitive-developmental analysis of children's sex-role concepts and attitudes, in *The development of sex differences*, E. E. Maccoby and R. G. D'Andrade, Editors. 1966, Stanford, CA: Stanford University Press. pp. 82–173.

31. Goldstein, J. H., *Toys, play, and child development*. 1994, New York: Cambridge University Press.

32. Almqvist, B., Age and gender differences in children's Christmas requests. *Play and Culture*, 1989. 2: pp. 2–19.

33. Smith, P. K., The war play debate, in *Toys, play, and child development*, J. H. Goldstein, Editor. 1994, New York: Cambridge University Press. pp. 67–84.

34. Goldstein, J., Aggressive toy play, in *The future of play theory: A multidisciplinary inquiry into the contributions of Brian Sutton-Smith*, A. Pellegrini, Editor. 1995, Albany, NY: State University of New York Press, Albany. pp. 127–147.

35. Smith, P. K., Social and pretend play in children, in *The nature of play: Great apes and humans*, A. Pellegrini and P. K. Smith, Editors. 2005, New York: Guilford. pp. 173–212.

36. Paley, V. G., *Boys and girls: Superheroes in the doll corner*. 1984, Chicago: University of Chicago Press.

37. Benenson, J. F., H. P. Carder, and S. J. Geib-Cole, The development of boys' preferential pleasure in physical aggression. *Aggressive Behavior*, 2008. 34(2): pp. 154–166.

38. Nicolopoulou, A., Worldmaking and identity formation in children's narrative play-acting, in *Sociogenetic perspectives on internalization*, B. D. Cox and C. Lightfoot, Editors. 1997, Mahwah, NJ: pp. 157–187.

39. Gottman, J. M., The world of coordinated play: Same- and cross-sex friendship in young children, in *Conversations of friends: Speculations on affective development*, J. M. Gottman and J. G. Parker, Editors. 1986, New York: Cambridge University Press. Pp. 139–191.

40. Goldstein, J., Immortal Kombat: War toys and violent video games, in *Why we watch: The attractions of violent entertainment*, J. H. Goldstein, Editor. 1998, New York: Oxford University Press. Pp. 53–68.

41. Zillmann, D., The psychology of the appeal of portrayals of violence, in *Why we watch: The attractions of violent entertainment*, J. H. Goldstein, Editor. 1998, New York: Oxford University Press. Pp. 179–211.

42. Leonard, D., Unsettling the military entertainment complex: Video games and a pedagogy of peace. *SIMILE: Studies in Media and Information Literacy Education*, 2004. 4(4): pp. 1–8.

43. Campbell, B., Adrenarche in comparative perspective. *American Journal of Human Biology*, 2011. 23(1): pp. 44–52.

44. Singer, T., et al., Empathic neural responses are modulated by the perceived fairness of others. *Nature*, 2006. 439(7075): pp. 466–469.

45. Benenson, J. F., T. A. Antonellis, B. J. Cotton, K. E. Noddin, & K. A. Campbell Sex differences in children's formation of exclusionary alliances under scarce resource conditions. *Animal Behaviour*, 2008. 76(2): pp. 497–505.

46. Bellamy, C., *Adult wars, child soldiers*. New York: UNICEF, 2002.

47. Mazur, A., and A. Booth, Testosterone and dominance in men. *Behavioral and Brain Sciences*, 1998. 21(3): pp. 353–363.

48. Tanner, J. M., Growth and maturation during adolescence. *Nutrition Reviews*, 1981. 39(2): pp. 43–55.

49. Daly, M., and M. Wilson, An evolutionary psychological perspective on homicide, in *Homicide: A sourcebook of social research*, M. D. Smith and M. A. Zahn, Editors. 1999, Thousand Oaks, CA: Sage. Pp. 58–71.

50. Archer, J., Sex differences in aggression in real-world settings: A meta-analytic review. *Review of General Psychology*, 2004. 8(4): pp. 291–322.

51. Mesquida, C. G., and N. I. Wiener, Male age composition and severity of conflicts. *Politics and the Life Sciences*, 1999. 18(2): pp. 181–189.

52. Kimura, D., *Sex and cognition*. 2000, Cambridge, MA: MIT Press.

53. Moore, D. S., and S. P. Johnson, Mental rotation in human infants. *Psychological Science*, 2008. 19(11): pp. 1063–1066.

54. Markovits, H., and J. F. Benenson, Males outperform females in translating social relations into spatial positions. *Cognition*, 2010. 117(3): pp. 332–340.

55. Salthouse, T. A., The processing-speed theory of adult age differences in cognition. *Psychological Review*, 1996. 103(3): pp. 403–428.

56. Horn, J. L., Organization of abilities and the development of intelligence. *Psychological Review*, 1968. 75(3): pp. 242–259.

57. Betzig, L. L., *Despotism and differential reproduction: A Darwinian view of history*. 1986, New York: Aldine.

58. Herlitz, A., and J. Rehnman, Sex differences in episodic memory. *Current Directions in Psychological Science*, 2008. 17(1): pp. 52–56.

59. Kaplan, H., K. Hill, J. Lancaste, A. M. Hurtado A theory of human life history evolution: Diet, intelligence, and longevity. *Evolutionary Anthropology Issues News and Reviews*, 2000. 9(4): pp. 156–185.

60. Bem, S. L., The measurement of psychological androgyny. *Journal of Consulting and Clinical Psychology*, 1974. 42(2): pp. 155–162.

61. Maccoby, E. E., Gender and relationships: A developmental account. *American Psychologist*, 1990. 45(4): pp. 513.

62. Gilligan, C., *In a different voice: Psychological theory and women's development*. 1982, Cambridge, MA: Harvard University Press.

63. Brown, P., and S. C. Levinson, *Politeness: Some universals in language usage*. Vol. 4. 1987, New York: Cambridge University Press.

64. Eckert, P., and S. McConnell-Ginet, *Language and gender*. 2003, New York: Cambridge University Press.

65. Maltz, D. N., R. A. Borker, and J. A. Gumperz, A cultural approach to male-female mis-communication, in *Language and social identity*, L. Monaghan, J. E. Goodman, and J. M. Robinson, Editors. 1982, Marblehead, MA: Wiley. pp. 195–216.

66. Goodwin, M. H., *He-said-she-said: Talk as social organization among black children*. 1990, Bloomington, IN: Indiana University Press.

67. Sheldon, A., Pickle fights: Gendered talk in preschool disputes. *Discourse processes*, 1990. 13(1): pp. 5–31.

68. Lever, J., Sex differences in the complexity of children's play and games. *American Sociological Review*, 1978. 43(4): pp. 471–483.

69. Lever, J., Sex differences in the games children play. *Social Problems*, 1976. 23(4): pp. 478–487.

70. Roy, R., and J. F. Benenson, Sex and contextual effects on children's use of interference competition. *Developmental Psychology*, 2002. 38(2): pp. 306–312.

71. de Waal, F. B. M., The integration of dominance and social bonding in primates. *Quarterly Review of Biology*, 1986. 61(4): pp. 459–479.

72. de Waal, F. B. M., and A. Roosmalen, Reconciliation and consolation among chimpanzees. *Behavioral Ecology and Sociobiology*, 1979. 5(1): pp. 55–66.

73. MacEvoy, J. P., and S. R. Asher, When friends disappoint: Boys' and girls' responses to transgressions of friendship expectations. *Child Development*, 2012. 83(1): pp. 104–119.

74. Whitesell, N. R., and S. Harter, The interpersonal context of emotion: Anger with close friends and classmates. *Child Development*, 1996. 67(4): pp. 1345–1359.

75. Benenson, J. F., et al., Males' greater tolerance of same-sex peers. *Psychological Science*, 2009. 20(2): pp. 184–190.

76. Benenson, J., et al., Males prepare more than females to reconcile with a same-sex peer. Human Nature, in press.

CHAPTER THREE

◆

Male Friends: Recruiting a Fighting Force

WHAT COULD BE MORE SOCIABLE THAN WAR? LIVING FOR months with unrelated men, many of whom exhibit unfamiliar, unpredictable, and often unpleasant behaviors and emotions, all of whom reek from not having washed for weeks on end, requires an extremely high level of social tolerance [1]. Embedment in a fighting unit demands levels of loyalty, trust, self-sacrifice, and tolerance unknown in other spheres and in other species. At the extreme, a fighting man will die to save the lives of his brothers in arms. They are an army of one: united to vanquish the enemy and to preserve their community and nation. In pursuit of victory, a man must care more about his unit than his own life.

No better allies exist than other young men. Between 18 and 25 years of age, men are at the height of their physical strength and athletic prowess. They run faster, jump longer and higher, and throw farther [3]. They can think and react faster [4]. Their ability to identify new spatial pattern formations is at its peak [5]. While having a mother or father or child fighting by a young man's side might sound reassuring, they wouldn't be very effective. Not to mention that a man fights in part to preserve his genetic material, which would be safer the farther it was from the battlefield. While a few young women of the same age might overlap with men in terms of their physical skills, generally women are not as physically powerful or skilled as men [6]. In the heat of an actual battle, other young men provide the greatest support.

This places a premium on getting along with other young men—but how do men come to depend on unrelated men for their survival? I believe that growing up male requires making the transition from reliance on families to dependence on unrelated peers.

All children need adults to keep them alive. Parents usually are the adults willing to invest most heavily in a child. Biology ensures that the child responds by forming strong emotional attachments to the people who give the child the most help [7]. This attachment ensures that young children stay physically close to the person most likely to keep them alive.

But as boys develop and become more self-sufficient, they need to move away from their parents emotionally and physically. From the perspective of warfare, it makes sense to head toward other males of the same age, leaving parents, siblings, and relatives of a different age and sex behind.

In my research and observation, I have found that young boys' biology propels them toward other young boys. They learn to trust other young males more than any other members of their community, including parents. Together, they will grow up and reach the height of their physical strength and skills. Together, they will make the most effective fighting force and maximize not only their own but also their families' and their whole community's chances of survival.

If a boy is genetically programmed to practice behaviors that will help him fight wars, he will need to begin early to identify and cultivate effective allies. He should favor male peers over anyone else. This is what the evidence shows.

Informally, one of the easiest ways to see the way boys break away from adults is to visit a school just before outdoor play time. Large clumps of boys will begin emerging from the doors. As fast as possible, they distance themselves from the school and the teachers and the girls. Then, they start play fighting, enemy enactments, or group-based competitive sports and games. In contrast, girls often linger in the classroom talking with the teachers, female relatives of different ages, or one or two selected friends. Western schools force girls into age-segregated classes, with often preoccupied adults abandoning girls. Many girls are stuck figuring out who will be their social partners for the day.

Meanwhile, the boys are off having a great time playing with other boys. Despite stereotypes to the contrary, my observations suggest that it is the boys who invest more time, effort, and energy in their relations with one another [8], while girls are trying to figure out their roles. From early in life, boys possess highly social tendencies that permit rapid formation of relationships with other boys.

My students and I tested this. We created three identical circular houses. Each house contained identical gift-wrapped boxes arrayed in identical positions containing the identical puppets, stickers, paper and markers and crayons, funny hats, sunglasses, and other fun materials in each box. The only difference between the three houses was that one also contained a randomly chosen same-sex peer from the child's classroom, a second contained a friendly adult, and the third contained only the boxes and play materials. A new child then was brought to the center of these three houses, shown the inside of each one, and told to play wherever she or he wanted. Sure enough, the 3-, 4-, and 5 year-old boys spent more time with the same-sex peer than the girls did [9]. One genetic ingredient of successful warfare is the intuitive attractiveness and loyalty among boys in any organization.

Fighting versus Mothers

Early in life, the existence of male peers will incite conflict for a boy. Families, particularly mothers and other caregivers, promote order and peace. But boys want to play fight and compete against enemies. Vivian Gussin Paley's book *Boys and Girls: Superheroes in the Doll House* [10] vividly describes this conflict. She points out the mayhem that the smallest of boys inflict on girls and teachers alike in the confined space of Western preschool classes. Boys spend their time chasing and wrestling one another; fighting predators, villains, and aliens; and competing against each other. They invariably trample the girls who are cooking, caring for babies, dressing up as princesses, and following teachers' directives.

Traditional agricultural societies deal with this conflict by allowing boys to roam far from home, while girls help their mothers with housework and child care [11]. In larger hunter-gatherer communities with enough boys of the same age, boys roam farther from their families [12]. Boys are less likely than girls to follow adult rules. They are more likely to disrupt the lives of the keepers of the ordered family world, such as mothers, teachers, and even female peers [13]. But they delight in one another's company.

Young boys thus inhabit a dual world. In one world are mothers and other caregivers, who ensure their survival and restrain tendencies to aggression. In the other world are male peers, who share a very different agenda. As Eleanor Maccoby [14] pointed out, the more boys there are, the more the conflict grows between the civilian world of mothers and other caregivers, and the military world of play fighting, enemies, and competition.

This was probably Freud's most famous insight: Boys must break away from their mothers if they want to become traditional men and practice warfare-like behaviors [15]. When boys spend more time with mothers, they are restrained in their play fighting, enemy targeting, and intergroup competitions. To gain the freedom to practice fighting, targeting enemies, and competing, they have to spend time with each other. This requires physically and psychologically separating themselves from caregivers, particularly mothers and other women. The farther a boy distances himself from adults, the more experience he has with male activities.

The socialization of a young boy therefore must play a critical role in determining where a boy positions himself between his mother and his male peers. In safe communities, a mother of a young boy can keep him close and protect him from danger. Where an enemy threatens, however, a boy's community needs to ensure he spends time with his male peers practicing the skills needed for war [16]. In the end, a young man will sacrifice his life, most immediately for the other young men in his group who are standing right next to him in battle. That is what his emotions tell him [1, 17, 18]. That is what I believe allows his genes to survive. If he survives, his genes will be more likely to be passed down to his children. If he dies but his community survives, then at least some of his genes, those residing in his closest family members, will be passed down to his nieces and nephews. Those genes are safe, far away from the battlefield. In the short term however, he is fighting for the genes standing next to him on the battlefield that do not belong to him. It's an incredible shared sacrifice between fictive brothers in arms.

A problem can arise however when sons separate from mothers and spend lots of time with other boys. They can start fights inside the community. Unrestrained groups of young men practiced in group competition and without a real enemy can wreak havoc.

It is likely that socialization from the community sends signals to mothers, who relay these to their sons regarding the presence of an enemy. When things are going well for a community, adults, especially mothers, will have more time and resources to devote to their children. Life will be less stressful, and family structures will remain more intact. When an enemy looms, everything changes. Life becomes stressful for everyone. Time and resources must be rerouted. Children are left more on their own. As a result, boys have more access to other boys and fewer constraints on their play fighting, enemy targeting, and intergroup competitive play.

Boys seem highly sensitive to these different environmental cues. For example, an isolated, single mother generally cannot invest as much time and energy in her son as can a mother with more social support. Boys raised by single mothers become especially aggressive [19, 2]. Poverty works the same way. A stressed mother without resources and support invests less in her son by definition. Impoverished boys accordingly exhibit much higher rates and intensities of aggressive behavior than their richer counterparts [20–22]. Male child soldiers constitute an extreme case; they fight far away from their families [23]. Across the world, boys with few resources are far more likely to join fighting forces. While this may be due partially to their greater availability, it is likely that these boys are better prepared physically and psychologically for the life of the fighter.

This suggests that a human male's brain comes prewired to exhibit behaviors critical to victory in battle that can be modified by the environment depending on the community's needs. Just as a man's testosterone levels diminish when he marries a woman and diminish even further when he has children [24], the same process may occur with young boys. Testosterone predisposes males to respond to challenges with physical aggression [25]. When men spend time with women and children, and away from other males, this predisposition to violence decreases. Although this has not been studied with young boys, who have much lower levels of testosterone, I venture something similar happens. With a strong maternal presence, possible when the level of environmental stress is low, testosterone levels are reduced. Remove maternal protection and add male peers, and testosterone activates the male brain. In extreme circumstances where a mother plays no role in her son's life, her son will gravitate to the ubiquitous male peer–militaristic world. He will then join this world as a child soldier, gang member, mercenary, member of a militia, or, if he is lucky, a well-resourced military unit.

In other words, boys will practice play fighting, enemy detection, and one-on-one competition with their male peers unless they are restrained by the presence of caring and relatively stress-free mothers or other relatives or caring adults. Both socialization and biology likely together determine to what extent a boy becomes a part of the civilian versus military life. Nonetheless, some boys seem more ready to join their male peers in play fighting, enemy targeting, and intergroup competitions regardless of the environment [26]. Levels of testosterone almost surely play a role. Young girls born with unusually high levels of testosterone display many of the same behaviors as young boys [27].

In Western cultures, it is no surprise that boys sent to day care behave more aggressively than those under the watchful eye of female relatives. This is a primary finding of an extensive project examining the effects of day care on children. The National Institute of Child Health and Human Development Study of Early Child Care and Youth Development (NICHD SECCYD) was begun in 1991 in 10 cities around the United States. It was designed to respond to many adults' fears that putting young children into day care could harm their development. Results from this study indicated that children who were put into a center-based day care had higher rates of aggression and disruptiveness when they started primary school [28–31]. As they progress through primary school, however, children who attended day care become indistinguishable from children who were raised in more maternal environments.

This seems reassuring initially, but the real story is more complicated. What happens is that when children who have been in day care enter primary school, the other children in the class become more aggressive. In fact, the more children there are in a primary school classroom who have been in center-based day care, the more aggressive *everyone* in the class becomes [28]. While aggression increases in both boys and girls, boys are so much more physically aggressive than girls by the end of infancy [26, 32] that their aggression is far more noticeable and disruptive. By 24 months, it is easy to see that boys are more aggressive than girls with same-sex peers [33].

Even boys from very stable families become more aggressive if they go to preschool [34]. The same effect occurs with older boys. When well-intentioned psychologists attempted to reduce aggression by partnering aggressive boys with nonaggressive boys, the study backfired: All the boys came out more aggressive [35]. Male aggression blossoms around male peers if no adult counters their influence.

The idea of the male brain being genetically prepared to become activated by other males, and potentially deactivated by a strong maternal presence, helps to explain why boys raised in Israeli group homes (kibbutzim) are such effective fighters [36]. In former times, Israeli children in kibbutzim were raised from infancy through adolescence in a group home with other children, away from their parents. A female nurse cared for all the children. Boys raised on kibbutzim were more likely to participate in the riskiest and most violent aspects of military service. A full 54% of them volunteered for units with fighting requirements, whereas only 16% of boys raised with their own families did so. Boys raised on kibbutzim also displayed the most valor in battle. It is no accident that these were boys who were raised with other boys and away from their mothers.

Anthropologists have similarly found that separation from mothers and closeness to male peers are key ingredients for warfare across diverse cultures. In several cultures, the conflict between maternal care and preparation for fighting is patently obvious. In some societies mothers remain close to their sons throughout childhood, often sleeping with them at night [37]. In these societies, boys are subject to severe hazing and other initiation rituals at adolescence. This is not an accident. These rituals serve to loosen the control that mothers have over their sons and free the sons to become aggressive young men. This would be absolutely critical when societies were engaged in warfare. In fact, the most brutal male rituals, including cutting, tattooing, and scarification, are performed on male adolescents in societies where warfare is most frequent [38]. Hazing produces physical marks that identify a young man as a reliable ally to other members of his community. More important, hazing allows boys to escape the protective world of maternal care and enter the world of male peers and warriors.

I propose that over the course of evolution, human genes have been selected to create males who are efficient cooperative fighters. Genes accomplish this by instilling intuitive interactive styles in boys and men that girls and women don't have. Boys and men like interacting in ways that will allow them to quickly form a group of fighters.

What kinds of social intuitions might these be? Three core tendencies stand out. The first is that a boy should separate himself from parents and other adult caretakers. The second pushes a boy to select male over female peers. The third promotes interaction with boys who would make valuable fighting allies and rejection of boys who would not. Parents in societies where warfare seems distant often bemoan the faithfulness with which most boys follow these three principles. But these social preferences allow the formation of efficient bonds between boys who will be most able to cooperate successfully to defeat an enemy. I believe that in the past, and even now, this has meant the difference between survival and death of a community.

Principle 1: Escape with Your Peers

Literature, as is often the case, provides a colorful window into this first principle. What happens to boys and girls when their parents are missing? Books that describe the lives of young orphaned boys are much more lively and interesting than books that describe orphaned girls. An orphaned girl is a lonely individual confronting tough times. Madeline, in Ludwig Bemelmans's charming French stories, is probably the most famous orphaned girl. She lives in an orphanage run by nuns with rigid rules and almost no social interaction. In Bemelman's first classic book, Madeline has her appendix removed [39]. In the second, she is rescued from drowning by a dog [40]. These are frightening stories about a vulnerable girl.

Contrast that with *The Adventures of Tom Sawyer* [41]. Tom lives with his aunt, half-brother, and cousin. He goes from one exciting episode to another with his closest friend, Huckleberry Finn. In doing so, he meets a host of other boys and one wicked murderer. The stories are about an enterprising and courageous boy.

There are many books like this. In *James and the Giant Peach*, James escapes his horrid aunts in a giant peach [42]. The peach fills with exotic and friendly characters who fight off angry sharks and men in the clouds and eventually winds up as a beautiful mansion in New York City. Harry Potter finds himself at Hogwarts surrounded by close friends and one unspeakably evil enemy [43]. Orphaned boys live the ideal life: no parents, just other boys, a distant caregiver, and one or more unmistakably evil enemies. At the end of these books, no one feels sorry for the orphan. Quite the contrary, many wish they too could live his life. Surrounded by friends, with clear enemies, life sounds idyllic. No one is worried about rupturing an appendix or drowning—or being lonely.

What literature suggests, anthropology has confirmed around the world. Universally, boys prefer to remain with boys of the same age and away from others, especially adult caregivers [44]. In many traditional societies, boys herd animals, hunt small game, or simply play together in fields, forests, or playgrounds, while girls are typically found helping their mothers with child minding and household responsibilities [11, 45]. Adolescent boys often create their own separate games and activities. In some societies, they live in separate houses [44].

Even married men in some traditional societies up until recently lived apart from their wives in the men's house, the center of the community [46]. Women were forbidden from entering. Not surprisingly, men's houses were more common in cultures where warfare occurred frequently. Girls and women don't have the same desire to escape their families. Margaret Mead [47] reported in Samoa and New Guinea that even when girls play with a close friend, they play near adults, frequently inside their homes, a neighbor's house, or a school.

Even where gender roles are quite egalitarian [48], such as in Western societies, the same pattern arises. School-age boys play farther away from the school and its teachers than girls do, and boys roam farther from their homes than girls do [49, 50].

This desire to escape one's family begins early. In the study I described previously with the three identical houses, even boys who had just turned 3 spent more time with another boy compared with girls, who preferred to play near the adult or alone [9]. In a more naturalistic study of 3- to 5-year-old children in preschools, observers found that the more peers who were present, the more the boys moved farther away from the adults [51]. The opposite was true for the girls. Likewise, when 4- and 5-year-old children were placed in a room with their mothers and some toys, the boys moved farther away from their mothers than the girls did [52]. Even at summer camp, boys spend their time farther away from their counselors, whereas girls jockey to get closer [53].

The preference that boys show for escaping their families and other adults has been observed around the world. This occurs in the simplest of hunter-gatherer societies in Tanzania [45]. In agricultural communities in Kenya, Guatemala, Japan, Mexico, the Philippines, Liberia, India, and Peru, boys move farther away from home than girls. Girls stay close to adults, especially their mothers and other female relatives [11]. This sex difference is not confined to childhood. Cross-cultural research shows that young adult men also go farther from home than young women do [54], that is, unless a woman is marrying into her husband's family's home, which then becomes her new home. That young boys display this preference so early suggests that genes may have programmed boys more than girls to escape their families. The environment of course can change genes' directives, but the initial push for boys to break away may be biologically based.

Part of the reason may be that boys rely on peers more than girls do. To determine whether they do, my colleagues and I asked Belgian children, adolescents, and adults whether family or friends are better sources of help [55]. At every age, compared with girls and women, boys and men thought that friends would be more useful than parents. In contrast, girls and women thought that parents would be just as helpful as friends.

We next wanted to learn what kind of help males receive. So we asked young men and women from Montreal to describe personal experiences of when they actually needed help. Again, compared with the women, the young men reported that their same-sex friends had been more helpful than their parents both with specific tasks and with meeting their social and emotional needs. In contrast, the young women reported that parents had been at least as helpful as their same-sex friends.

From early in life through at least young adulthood, boys and young men are comfortable relying on same-sex friends, as much as or more than parents. This brings them together, which furthers their learning to trust in one another. If they have to work together, they know whom to trust. If they need to fight, they have gained invaluable knowledge about one another's strengths and limitations.

This makes it particularly important for boys to fit in with their peer group. In fact, a boy who has trouble following the rules of his peer group is likely to have real problems. Since the 1980s, many researchers have tried to figure out why some children cannot get along well with their peers. No one knows for sure. Some early findings suggest, however, that for many troubled boys, their problems stem from difficulties following the rules of their peers.

In an intriguing study, 164 boys from Minnesota who as children had had problems severe enough to have been treated at a child guidance clinic were followed up by researchers. These boys all fought in World War II as adults [56]. The researchers first identified a subset of these boys who had engaged in bad conduct during their military service. They then identified another subset of those boys who had attained a grade of sergeant or higher without any disciplinary or mental health troubles. Both of these groups of men had been treated in the clinic as children, so all had fairly serious problems as children.

What distinguished those who engaged in bad conduct in the military from those who did well? It turned out that the key difference was how well they got along with the other boys in school. Those boys who later engaged in bad conduct in the military were described as not listening to their peers, being mean and hurtful, and showing explosive behavior toward other boys. Whether they behaved respectfully toward teachers didn't make a difference. In contrast, those boys who as men served with honor in the military had gotten along well with the other boys in school, despite their other problems. In fact, how well a boy gets along with his male peers even predicts other types of severe psychological problems that develop in the military [56, 57].

Separating himself from his family is a prerequisite for successful military engagement. If young men are responsible for fighting the enemy, they need to do so far away from their families. Seeking out male peers and learning to rely on one another is an important facet of boys' social lives that predicts success in the military and likely in other organizations too. Boys rely on peers more than family members, but they also rely on same-sex peers more than other-sex peers compared with girls. This leads to the second principle of boys' social interactions.

Principle 2: No Girls Allowed

Most young primates, when they are capable of play with others, prefer to spend time with others of the same sex [58]. Humans are no exception: Segregation by sex starts very early in life. In traditional societies like those in Liberia, Kenya, India, Mexico, the Philippines, and Okinawa, where little formal schooling exists, young boys spend more time with other boys than with girls [11, 59]. In Japan, China, and Bali, among Australian Aborigines and the Navajo and Hopi in Arizona, and even in a school for the blind in the United States, children segregate themselves by sex as early as age 2 [60]. The same occurs in hunter-gatherer societies, like the !Kung bushmen or the Hadza, as long as enough play partners of the same sex are available [12, 61].

Girls also end up playing with girls. But sex segregation is much stronger for boys. Boys really want to play with other boys; girls like to play with both girls and boys. The same asymmetry holds for men and women, unless sexual relations are involved [13, 62–65]. Men share more leisure activities with one another than women do [66], just as they always have played sports together more than women have [67].

What drives this difference? One of the most immediate causes is simply that boys get so much pleasure from playing with other boys. This is much less so for girls. To look at this objectively, my students and I went to preschool and kindergarten classrooms and created groups of six children of the same sex. All the children in each group told us they were friends with each other. The children were free to play however they wished. Later, we asked some neutral observers to watch the videotapes of the children's play and rate how much pleasure each group seemed to have. The observers rated the boys' groups as enjoying themselves more than the girls' groups [68]. They pointed out the spontaneity, enthusiasm, and sheer delight in one another's company exhibited by the boys. The girls, in contrast, appeared nervous and uncomfortable, seemingly waiting for an adult to appear to organize a structured task.

I believe that girls need to be really close friends, almost like family, in order to relax in one another's company. Boys enjoy themselves more easily, even when they are not close friends. Thus, in my study with the three identical houses, when we chose a random same-sex peer from the classroom, boys were more likely than girls to play with the peer [9].

In modern, technologically based societies, women bear fewer children and are able to take part in many activities previously reserved for men. Nonetheless, the asymmetry in same-sex preferences persists [13]. This can be difficult to see in Western schools because all the children are forced into the same age-graded classrooms. But during free time, girls are far more likely than boys to offer to help the teacher erase the board or grade papers or run an errand. They are much more likely to volunteer to remain inside and forgo recess or gym altogether. The boys have disappeared out the door before the girls even have a chance to excuse themselves from activities with other girls.

Unfortunately, many boys go further than simply preferring the company of other boys over girls. Across the world, starting at about 5 years of age, boys start consciously insulting and physically assaulting girls simply because they are girls. This same form of harassment often continues throughout adulthood. As an example, in Western societies, boys often accuse girls of harboring polluting diseases such as cooties, a disease that, according to their male classmates, afflicts many American girls [50]. Cooties fortunately can be combated with a cooties' shot (often a dot in the middle of a forearm), but its effects wear off rapidly. In many cultures around the world, women's menstruation serves the same function as cooties. It too is considered a disease that can contaminate men who come too close [69].

Boys and men not only stay away from girls and women, and often insult and assault them, but also dominate them. In fact, in most species of mammals, males generally outrank females. This is true for humans also. This difference in status begins in toddlerhood, even in the most modern of cultures. In one study, two unfamiliar toddlers together dressed in gender-neutral clothing came to a psychology laboratory with their mothers. Right from the start, the young boys were rough and paid little attention to young girls. Often, a male toddler literally ran over a female toddler in his rush to get a toy. Boys didn't pay attention, even when asked something by a young girl. The female toddlers actually ran away from the male toddlers [70]. By age 4, in another study, groups of two boys and two girls playing with the same attractive movie viewer encountered very different experiences depending on their sex. The movie viewer, designed by psychologists William Charlesworth and Peter Lafreniere, is operated by having one child turn a crank and a second child push a light, so that a third child can watch movies through a peephole. The fourth child is simply a bystander. To watch the movies, a child has to persuade the other three peers to not only forgo watching the movies themselves but also work to ensure that the child can see the movies. The result was that boys got to see a lot more movies than girls did [71].

Boys remain dominant as they grow older, even when physical force is not an issue. Strikingly, there is evidence that boys will outperform girls in competitive athletic and academic activities—even when girls are more talented. In a classic study of 9- to 11-year-old African American children from Chicago playing in a dodgeball tournament, the researchers divided the children into four teams based on their dodgeball skills: highly skilled boys, highly skilled girls, low-skilled boys, and low-skilled girls. The boys always beat the girls. Even the least-skilled boys beat the most-skilled girls [72]. Because the researchers thought that the highly skilled female dodgeball players may simply have been afraid of the boys' physical strength, they repeated the study with another set of girls and boys and had them compete in a spelling bee. The results were identical. When the highly skilled girls faced the poor-spelling boys, the boys still won. In modern societies with laws protecting girls, girls now outperform boys in schoolwork. Nonetheless, it remains difficult for a female to beat a male in a head-to-head competition.

Recent studies on bullying show the same pattern of intimidation of girls by boys. A study in the US Midwest found that bullying followed a predictable pattern. High-status boys bullied low-status boys. In turn, low-status boys bullied high-status girls [73]. This pattern continued into adolescence.

Dan Olweus [74] began the study of bullying in primary and secondary schools across Norway. He estimated that one out of seven students were involved in a bullying episode, as either the bully or the victim. Overall, boys were more likely to be bullied than girls, but when girls were bullied, they were much more likely to be bullied by boys than by other girls. The reverse was not true, however. No matter how it was measured, girls rarely bully boys. This same pattern of bullying was found in Sweden, Finland, England, the Netherlands, Japan, Ireland, Spain, and Australia.

In adulthood, men are higher-ranked than women in virtually every society that has been studied. This is true for the most egalitarian hunter-gatherers, the Hadza of Tanzania, where the women are highly independent [12]. It is even true for societies with matrilineal inheritance, where property gets passed down from mother to daughter, not from father to son as is usually the case. In these matrilineal societies, it's not the women who have the highest status in the community, however, but their brothers. Men generally hold higher-status occupations, hold higher-status positions within the same occupation, and receive more pay for the same position [75–77].

Adult males not only outrank adult females but they continue the same pattern of abuse found in younger children. When they get older, husbands regularly physically attack their wives. Only in the most egalitarian societies with strict laws protecting women do wives retaliate against their husbands [48]. In a study of almost 25,000 women from Bangladesh, Brazil, Ethiopia, Japan, Namibia, Peru, Samoa, Serbia, Thailand, and Tanzania, the World Health Organization (WHO) found that the proportion of husbands who physically hurt their wives ranged from a low of 15% in Japan to a high of 71% in Ethiopia. In the European Union and United States, estimates are that 20% to 25% of husbands physically abuse their wives (www.nytimes.com/2006/10/06/world/06violence).

The higher rank and power of men around the world does not play out only in direct physical intimidation. It also is codified in many nations' formal and traditional laws. Women confront discrimination through marital laws that give more power to husbands than to wives [78]. Workplaces pay women lower salaries than men receive for the same job [79] and promote women more slowly than men in nations that prohibit discrimination on the basis of sex [75, 80]. Even in the most modern of media, such as video games for young people, women are portrayed in inferior positions to men [81]. While this is slowly changing, it requires muscular laws that are enforced, and men are needed to enforce these laws. Thus, male dominance begins at age 2 years and continues throughout adulthood in every society.

Boys will accept girls under a few conditions. First, girls who can pass for boys are tolerated. Boys will accept tomboys. These girls often prefer the company of boys over girls, enjoy direct competition, and might even fight physically [13, 82, 83]. While they still are likely to be relegated to inferior roles, they can take part in boys' activities.

Second, boys also will play with girls when they have little other choice. This often happens in sparsely populated neighborhoods [84] or in small communities with few children, such as hunter-gatherer bands [61, 85]. The same holds for men. A woman who is willing to play by men's rules can work closely with men or even run a company. Likewise in the military, when few male recruits are available, as in Israel with its small population or the United States after compulsory military service ended, women can join.

Third, in very rich and liberal Western classrooms where teachers may demand that children of both sexes engage in the same activities, boys show greater tolerance of girls [50]. I suggest this is because the adults in these communities don't expect their sons to need to fight a war. In such a case, it is probably true for men as well. When military service is unlikely, and wives demand that their husbands share child care and household responsibilities, men almost certainly show greater tolerance of women. When the possibility of serving in the military looms, however, I would guess that the basic pattern reappears.

As problematic as this is, if boys who will grow into young men want to form the most effective fighting force, exclusion of girls, and later young women, makes sense. A military unit composed of all young men will be physically stronger than one that contains women too [6]. There are reasons for including women in military roles, but from a purely physical standpoint, men are far bigger, stronger, more athletic, and more energetic. Further, the intuitive camaraderie that brings boys together early allows them to build experience negotiating with and relying on one another for support. Unless a girl is a tomboy and has been allowed to practice with the boys, not only will she almost certainly be less physically strong, but she also will have much more difficulty learning how to get along with others. This would be detrimental to success. A military unit must be cohesive or it will lose.

One puzzle remains. Why do high-ranked boys bully lower-ranked ones, and lower-ranked boys bully girls? This leads me to one final principle that I believe underlies boys' social interaction.

Principle 3: Military Material Only, Please

It's not enough to assemble a group of like-minded boys, far from their families and girls, in order to create an efficient fighting force. The fighting force must be the best it can be. Some discrimination is necessary to maximize the chances of success. What characteristics in a boy make him a good fighter? It is precisely those characteristics should appeal most to boys when they select their male friends.

Physical Toughness
Few traits are more valuable in a physical fight than being big, strong, athletic, and energetic. Even before they are born, boys are bigger [86] and more energetic [87] than girls. Still, sex differences in size, strength, and athletic skill are relatively small before adolescence, with one huge exception: throwing [88]. After adolescence, adolescent boys are superior to girls across a wide range of physical skills that require strength, coordination, and energy [3].

Boys and young men are attracted most to boys who exhibit just the skills that would be invaluable in a fighter [89, 90]. Little boys, older boys in middle childhood, and adolescent boys prefer to be friends with the physically strongest, tallest, and most athletic boys around [91–93]. This preference continues throughout life and across the world. As anyone who has attended Western elementary, junior high, and senior high schools knows, the tallest, strongest, most athletic boys are respected not only by the girls but also by the other boys [94]. Tall, strong men are admired most by other men even in the simplest of hunter-gatherer societies [95]. In the most modern societies, men are more likely to employ physically taller and more energetic male peers over shorter and less energetic ones [96]. As education increases and the need for physical skills decreases, the value of physical strength diminishes, but even then it doesn't disappear.

What makes boys' and men's preference for physically strong male peers so fascinating is that these are just the peers who provide the most competition. Why should boys and men be so attracted to peers who might be superior to them? Don't boys and men want to dominate everyone else?

The only answer that makes sense to me is that boys and men desire to form the physically strongest group possible. That way, they can have the best chances of defeating another group. One physically strong and nimble group member can determine the outcome for the whole group.

This desire to associate with the physically toughest males makes human males unique compared with males of other species, and compared with human females. Few girls or women care how physically strong their female friend is. Yet, a boy or man, given the chance, will stick closely to the strongest and most athletically talented male around.

Emotional Toughness

What other traits might aid in the war effort? Emotions have been studied around the world. And, around the world, men express emotions less often and with less intensity than women do. This is especially true for fear and sadness. The only exception is anger, which is typically associated with aggression. However, there is no evidence that boys or men actually feel angrier than girls or women [97, 98].

Why should men be so emotionally cool? Emotions communicate feelings to others. They also affect our own behavior. If you're fighting an enemy, communicating evaluations about progress to oneself or others are both potential weaknesses when things are not going well. Fearing death or mourning a lost comrade during an attack can be lethal emotions to transmit, or even to feel [6]. A person who loses control of his emotions cannot think clearly about what is happening around him. Revealing to the enemy that one feels scared or sad would be even worse. A man cannot change the course of war through his emotions, only through his motivation to win and his behavior. While anger likely helps provide a shot of adrenaline, emotional cool is critical to fighting well.

Fear is the worst emotion to feel when fighting. Fear makes people shy away from dangerous situations, such as war. Unsurprisingly, around the world men experience less fear than women [99–101]. Who is more likely to pick up a poisonous snake and get bitten [102, 103]? Who is more likely to be strangled by their pet python? Who enjoys riding motorcycles most? Who is more likely to fall off the edge of a cliff? Who is more likely to hit a tree during a skiing accident? Whose bungee cord is more likely to break? Who is more likely to shoot themselves with a handgun they found in a secret hiding place? Who is more likely to be swept away during a hurricane that was predicted by the weather service? The statistics are clear. At every age, males take many more risks than females do. And they are much more likely than girls or women to die from risky behaviors. Insurance companies know this and charge men higher premiums. Males take greater risks than females because they are less afraid [104].

This sex difference in fearfulness begins in the first few weeks of life. Infant girls show fear earlier than infant boys do [105]. Later in infancy, when faced with long, dark tunnels, robots that activate themselves spontaneously, or a stranger unexpectedly entering a room, young boys approach much faster than young girls [106]. By adulthood, men continue to express fear less frequently and with less intensity than women, and this is true across diverse cultures [107–109].

These same sex differences occur with sadness. If an infant in a newborn nursery begins crying, newborn boys show less distress than newborn girls [110, 111]. By 14 months of age, when infants see an adult have an accident, infant boys show less concern than infant girls [112]. Men exhibit less sadness than women around the world [113].

Authors know the importance of being cool when battling the enemy. James Bond embodies the British battle against the enemy. Of all his positive qualities, his cool stands out. From my many observations, even the youngest male toddlers do not like their male peers to become too upset. Emotional "cool" is a big draw even before a boy can explain what type of peer he most respects.

Boys and men greatly prefer other boys and men who don't let their emotions show. They don't expect the same of girls and women, from whom uncool displays of emotion are tolerated. But boys naturally show less emotion than girls. Ross Buck showed this in an ingenious way [114, 115]. He asked 4- to 6-year-old children to view slides showing pleasant and unpleasant pictures. Observers who were in another room and who could not see the slides tried to guess just from the children's facial expressions which kind of slide a child was watching. This was relatively easy with the girls. But the observers found it very hard to read the boys' facial expressions. The older boys showed even less emotion than the younger ones. When the study was replicated with adults, the sex difference was even stronger. Men's expressions were much more difficult to read than women's. Men actually moved their facial muscles less than women did.

Boys expect each other to be emotionally muted. By age 6, they value other boys who are emotionally cool [93]. Even in early childhood, boys who cannot control strong emotions are often insulted by being called girls or gay—two inferior types in boys' minds [116–119]. Being cool is an important part of boys' intuitive measuring stick for manliness. I suggest that "manliness" means the type of individual one would want next to you when the enemy attacks.

Certainly, emotional cool is highly valued by boys living in difficult environments [120]. But this intuition is so strong that it is even shared by advantaged boys who live far from the possibility of war. This was brought home clearly by a recent study that looked at adolescent boys in a private school in the liberal, generally antiwar northeastern United States who were interviewed about how they dealt with personal difficulties [121]. They all agreed that openly expressing their feelings was just not a useful way of coping with problems. Expressing emotions decreased their status with the other boys. Their preferred response was being stoic, not showing emotion, even when dealing with something as painful as the death of another person. If a boy did show his emotions, his male friends would react by making fun of him, telling jokes, or ignoring or distracting him. The victim of these attacks appreciated this: Being made fun of helped him to calm down. According to these boys, this type of reaction showed that their friends cared about them. Many boys taunt one another not to bully each other but to help each other out, to teach each other how to deal with the world most beneficially. The only exception these boys made was when a relative died. Only then was some expression of pain permissible.

A little boy needs to express fear and sadness when he is in danger. This signals to caregivers that he needs help and may keep him alive. But as he grows older and more able to take care of himself, emotions are less helpful. This is especially so in the context of battle.

On the surface, the one exception would appear to be anger. Anger makes people more aggressive and can make other people back down. However, too much anger is detrimental. An enraged man, wildly gesticulating and shouting at his target, might prove effective in the civilian world. In the military however, real anger can produce bad decisions in the heat of the moment that could endanger the whole unit [97, 98, 122]. An angry man is erratic and undependable.

It is thus not surprising that when girls and women become angry, they stay that way longer, and they often experience more intense anger than males do [123, 124]. The reason that everyone thought women didn't get angry is that anger is the one emotion that girls and women hide better than boys and men. Thus, boys and men look angrier than girls and women and also act on their anger more frequently; careful analysis shows, however, that in general, they become angered much less easily.

Physical and emotional toughness are important traits in a fellow fighter. So is self-confidence.

Self-confidence

I am always impressed by the style of boys or men when they are speaking to an audience. They make confident, clear, and indisputable declarations. They present themselves in the most positive manner possible, speaking loudly with a stern intonation accompanied by forceful gestures. Their self-assured posture is guaranteed to persuade listeners of the brilliance of the speaker's accomplishments and the truth of his message. Male presentation styles surely inspire more confidence than the way many women communicate. A woman's talk often comes peppered with self-deprecatory descriptions and gestures. She often begins her talk apologizing for some failing. Her posture indicates uncertainty and subordination. She speaks with wavering, halting rhythms, and with so many qualifications that the listener questions not only the woman's message but her whole character, even when her talk is brilliant.

The advantages of communicating self-confidence to oneself, one's group, and the enemy cannot be overestimated [125]. Fighting is not just physical force. A critical part of being an effective fighter is feeling and projecting confidence. This works in two ways. People who feel confident are in fact more effective. Projecting confidence to the enemy signals that maybe you are stronger than he thought. In contrast, any hint of insecurity or vulnerability could be fatal. Supreme self-confidence can take individuals in any endeavor much further than they would have gone otherwise. The very definition of masculinity in fact rests heavily on projected self-assurance. According to the most well-established assessment of gender identity, men who exhibit signs of self-doubt, lack of certainty, low self-esteem, or indecisiveness are not fully masculine [126]. Self-confidence is critical to winning any contest, and winning competitions is critical to being a man. I suggest that being a man means knowing deep down that you will be able to defeat the enemy. No doubt is allowed.

Men score higher than women on even the simplest measures of self-esteem. For example, Rosenberg's popular self-esteem scale asks respondents to indicate whether they agree or disagree with 10 statements rating their evaluations of themselves. Men repeatedly and universally score higher than women on this scale. Men appear to be born believing that they are of high ability, whereas women do not easily assimilate the idea that they are as good as others. Hundreds of studies show this effect and suggest that men just feel better about themselves than women do. Men feel particularly good about themselves in domains such as athletic ability, appraisal of their personality, and overall satisfaction or happiness with themselves. Women in contrast rate their behavioral and moral conduct as more socially acceptable to their societies than men do [127]. In other words, men just feel good about who they are, whereas women feel good about being moral. This starts very early in life. Even 7-year-old boys have more self-confidence than 7-year-old girls [128].

Boys and men value self-confidence in their friends. They are attracted to other boys who perform well [129]. Girls actually prefer other girls who share their own problems and don't have high levels of self-esteem. To test this systematically, my students and I asked some adolescents and young adults what they thought their closest same-sex friends would think if they did something really well (got good grades, performed well in a sport, made a good friend, or found a loving romantic partner). The males responded that their friends would think more positively of them. The females didn't. In fact, many females even described being afraid that if they were too successful, their friends would abandon them.

I believe that males value high self-esteem in themselves and their male peers because it increases the probability of beating the enemy. High self-esteem can make someone with poor abilities do well; low self-esteem can make someone with excellent abilities do poorly. In warfare, where getting the best out of everyone is critical, having allies with high self-esteem is invaluable. The more one's allies have high self-confidence, the more intimidating they are; the greater the likelihood the enemy will retreat. This seems to be an excellent strategy for winning. Of course, this may occasionally incite wars based on overconfidence [125]. Better to be overconfident than underconfident and surrender before you even begin.

Physical and emotional toughness and self-confidence in a male peer are highly attractive to boys and men. Those with high levels of these traits would strengthen any fighting force. But a war is not won by an individual. Boys and men need to know that an individual is dependable and worth including in a group.

Obedience to Rules

From early in life, boys drive teachers crazy. Many cannot sit still; they talk out of turn; they run around the school building; they shout and curse and laugh and shriek incessantly; they injure themselves frequently; they fight openly; they spend as much time away from adults as possible; they perpetually require excitement and movement to stave off boredom. In traditional societies without formal schools, mothers attempt to force their sons to help with household chores but eventually end up letting them roam as far from home as they will go. Boys so easily forget or overtly disobey their mothers' directives that their mothers turn instead to their more reliable daughters for assistance [11].

Amazingly, these same boys show an incredible reverence for rules: not rules created by women or other authorities but rules created by the boys themselves. From early childhood, boys begin to generate rules, to negotiate changes in rules, to argue over broken rules and appropriate penalties. They ignore the rules of women and girls but follow their own rules to the letter [117]. Men playing informal sports spend money to hire a male referee, just to ensure that the rules are followed. Some female teams in modern societies also hire referees—but these are mostly male. As one frustrated coach of a female sports team patiently explained to me, female referees sometimes feel so sorry for a player, they don't apply the rules fairly.

Rules are critically important to humans. No group can exist without them. Rules create a social system. They generate scripts that permit a disparate group of individuals to function as a whole. They allow people who are physically distant to coordinate their activities. They ensure that the same standards are applied to everyone, so that fairness reigns and individuals choose to remain rather than jump ship. To some, rules form the essence of morality. Jean Piaget [130], one of the founders of developmental psychology, declared, "All morality consists in a system of rules, and the essence of all morality is to be sought for in the respect which the individual acquires for these rules" (Piaget, 1932, p. 13).

Most social primate species instinctively follow many rules. These regulate vital aspects of life, including who ranks highest, holds territory, mates with whom, forms an alliance, begins and ends conflicts, or can join the community and must leave, to name just a few [131]. These rules are not written down but are followed because primates' genes have created biological instincts that lead them to behave in certain ways. Primate rules remain fairly static and nonnegotiable throughout animals' lives. Although individuals' roles may change from infancy through old age, the basic rules of life don't change.

Humans, on the other hand, continually generate new rules, revise old ones, and attempt to circumvent those they deem unfair. They rebel against rules they dislike and sacrifice their lives to uphold rules they consider superior. This may be one of the most distinctive aspects of being human. Rules, however, have been a primarily male occupation. For thousands of years, males have constructed the rules that underlie religions, governments, economic systems, businesses, educational structures, and of course judicial courts and the military [132]. Since ancient times, games with rules created by boys and men have predominated all over the world [133, 134]. Even men who break established rules often end up adhering to an alternate set of rules such as those found in criminal gangs or militias. Men and boys who join rule-bound systems prosper when they follow the rules of other boys and men.

What is fascinating is that even young boys play games with complex rules. Jean Piaget [130] studied Swiss boys as young as 4 years of age who were playing marbles. Every aspect of the game, from who made the first move to how to determine whether to play again, was codified by the boys. Tens or even hundreds of rules governed every game. According to Piaget, "The game of marbles, for instance, as played by boys, contains an extremely complex system of rules, that is to say, a code of laws, a jurisprudence of its own" (Piaget, 1932, p. 13). Girls show no interest.

Typically, young boys learn the rules of a game from older boys. They then negotiate local revisions and demand respect for their version of the "sacred" laws. Marble games contain infinite variants, local customs, and generational changes. These function in the same way as the rules for today's more popular Yu-Gi-Oh! and Pokemon card games, or any board game or physical sport. Individual marbles or cards differ in their roles and power. Adherence to these rules allows fair competition. Breaking the rules invites social ostracism and expulsion from the game. Obedience to the rules elicits honor and respect. Gallantry is much admired as victors offer to play again to provide losers a chance to redeem themselves. Players can modify rules at any moment, if they can get the others to agree. An individual player must always be ready to contribute to rule making, or the other players will leave him out in the cold.

Janet Lever [135], a sociologist who spent a lot of time on the playgrounds of American elementary schools, described the critical part that rules play in boys' games in middle childhood in Western societies. When boys are left to roam freely on the playgrounds, they choose to engage in activities that contain many rules. When a dispute regarding the rules arises, boys will negotiate new rules or will call on respected peers to settle disputes. All of this effort is made simply to maintain the rules. The many sports played around the world from ancient to modern times, in traditional and advanced societies, contain rules for boys and men but seldom for girls and women. According to Lever's observations, the few games that girls play, typically turn-taking games, do not involve many rules. If an individual girl does not follow the rules of the game, such as continuing to jump rope or play hopscotch after having tripped, the girls simply end the game. Negotiations are rare. Even when boys and girls play together in the same game, boys stick much more closely to the rules than the girls. Girls often shake their heads at what seems to them a bizarre emphasis on enforcing the rules at the expense of other more important concerns, such as someone's feelings.

You might think that paying attention to other players' feelings would make it easier to play together than sticking to a set of fairly rigid rules. But you would be wrong. One of the more interesting things noted by Lever [136] was that boys' games lasted much longer than girls' games. Lever reported, "Boys' games lasting the entire period of 25 minutes were common, but in a whole year in the field, I did not observe a single girls' activity that lasted longer than 15 minutes" (Lever, 1976, p. 482). Although boys quarreled more frequently than girls, the boys enjoyed the conflict, especially those over the rules. According to the physical education teacher at Lever's school, "His boys seemed to enjoy the legal debates every bit as much as the game itself. Even players who were marginal because of lesser skills or size took equal part in these recurring squabbles" (Lever, 1976, p. 482). In fact, much of modern Western education until recently was based on the idea that physical sports with rules prepared boys to fight wars as men [137]. In contrast, girls often prefer practicing gymnastics and dance, which contain few rules and often require little cooperation with others.

Of course, following rules should not be confused with moral behavior. Carol Gilligan [138], a well-known psychologist, quite reasonably claimed that women have a moral sense that does not depend on following rules. Before that, men were considered more moral simply because they were more rule-oriented [139]. Gilligan's research shows that when people are given hypothetical scenarios and asked to make moral judgments about them, males refer to rules more than females, who emphasize responsiveness to personal relationships [140]. Kay Johnston [141], a colleague of Gilligan's, used the following Aesop's fable to explore boys' and girls' solutions to moral challenges:

> It was growing cold, and a porcupine was looking for a home. He found a most desirable cave but saw it was occupied by a family of moles.
>
> "Would you mind if I shared your home for the winter?" the porcupine asked the moles. The generous moles consented and the porcupine moved in. But the cave was small and every time the moles moved around they were scratched by the porcupine's sharp quills. The moles endured this discomfort as long as they could. Then at last they gathered courage to approach their visitor. "Pray leave," they said, "and let us have our cave to ourselves once again."
>
> "Oh no!" said the porcupine. "This place suits me very well." (Johnston, 1988, p. 71)

Adolescents from the Boston area then were asked to describe the problem presented in the fable and to offer a solution. Boys were much more likely to respond with a rule rather than a reference to maintaining harmony, whereas girls were more evenly divided. Examples of rule-based solutions included "The porcupine has to go definitely. It's the mole's house." "Send the porcupine out since he was the last one there" (Johnston, 1988, p. 53). Girls were more likely to attempt to maintain a harmonious relationship with responses such as "Wrap the porcupine in a towel" or "The both of them should try to get together and make the hole bigger" (Johnston, 1988, p. 53). These differences illustrate clearly the use of impersonal rules versus the desire to respond to one individual's personal problem.

According to Gilligan, rules ensure fairness, equality, and justice, a major concern of boys who are less invested in one particular individual's plight [142]. Because every individual's situation is unique, however, general rules rarely apply to interpersonal conflicts. No one would maintain a relationship with another person who responded to all interpersonal conflicts by citing a rule. Gilligan's keen clinical skills allowed her to uncover a basic difference in the concerns of the two sexes. Each form of responsiveness, rules that ensure justice for as many as possible as well as responsiveness to unique individual needs, has its place.

Boys' and men's concern with rules nevertheless serves a critical function for coordinating a community. One cannot provide extra investment in one individual at the expense of others without some recourse to rules, or everyone else in the group will rebel. If too many people get special breaks, the whole community will break down. In fact, large-scale organizations, such as businesses and governments, use much the same tactics that boys learn on the playing fields in childhood. Adherence to fixed rules, revision of outdated ones, and adoption of new ones are necessary. Learning to negotiate rules is invaluable for running a group. If there is no group, however, then rules downright interfere. Girls and women do not benefit from practicing negotiating impersonal rules in their interpersonal relationships.

Athletic ability, emotional cool, and self-confidence in a fellow fighter provide an individual advantage to that person and his group. Rules serve the group's interest. Rules permit allies to coordinate their efforts. Rules permit distinguishing friends from the enemy. Rules increase the impact of learning. Rules permit synchronization of attacks from distant posts. Rules are essential to group fighting. Males' love of rules suggests that boys and men are not simply interested in beating their individual competitors, as in most other primate species. They want to beat them according to the rules. They want to cooperate too.

This love of rules is so strong that rules are applied even in one-on-one competition. The strange notion of fighting fair requires following rules. Otherwise, a man loses the respect of other men. Duels fought by gladiators and bullfighters, wrestlers, and boxers occur according to specified man-made rules. On the surface this seems bizarre. Why should two men fighting to the death follow any rules at all? Yet, throughout history men have generated rules for the most brutal of conflicts. Girls and women don't follow any rules in their fights, and this often makes female fights all the more interesting because the drama is so much less predictable.

Expertise

There is one more trait that boys and men especially value in their peers: expertise. Human males specialize. They recognize and respect individual expertise, and they organize their groups in order to capitalize on the abilities of each of their allies. Expertise comes in many forms: physical prowess, emotional cool, self-confidence, leadership skills, social savvy, as well as a host of physical, engineering and other skills that might benefit the group. In fact, men value proficiency in just about any activity that could potentially contribute to a war effort. It is worth remarking again just how extraordinary this is. Organizing groups in this way involves getting highly competitive individuals to acknowledge that other individuals have more skills in some specific areas than they do. Not only that, but the same competitive individuals will defer to the opinion of the more skilled one.

I suggest that valuing another's superior expertise so highly occurs because the inferior individual feels that he too will benefit from his ally's skill. In war, the most effective fighting force should maximize each member's potential. But it is a two-way street. A male who is inferior in one way has to be good in another way. Otherwise, the group won't value him. That means that whether he is skilled at throwing a ball, leading a company, or making his peers laugh, his peers respect him. Males will suffer great hardship, sometimes in the form of extreme hazing in their groups, to prove that they are worthy of a group's respect. Obtaining the respect of the group is a great feeling. The result is that males defer to those who are more skilled and expect others to respect their own area of expertise. The whole group benefits.

Males' reverence of other males' skills begins early. During the year and a half she spent in a working-class African American neighborhood in southwest Philadelphia in the 1970s, Marjorie Harkness Goodwin [143] recorded the conversations of the neighborhood children. Her recordings confirm the respect that boys accord expertise, regardless of its content. For example, Goodwin describes an episode in which the boys have constructed a go-cart, then proceed to argue about who is the best driver. All agree that the best driver is Malcolm; they then go on to discuss others' levels of driving expertise in terms of rank order:

MALCOLM: I'm the *dr*iver.
TONY: He's the driver.//You know he drives it.
MALCOLM: I know what//that-Ossie can't **dr**ive that good.
OSSIE: See- I'm number *three* driver. I'm number *three* driver.
MALCOLM: And *Dave* can't drive that good,=
TONY: I'm number//*two* driver.
OSSIE: I'm number *three* driver.
(Goodwin, 1990, p. 41 // signifies overlapping speech with the next
    person; = signifies that the next turn begins immediately after the prior
    one finished; bold italics indicates emphasis.)

Other forms of expertise also merit admiration among these same boys. Goodwin provides examples of the type of skills on which these boys rank themselves:

While playing with yo-yos

CARL: I do it experience! I do it **bet**ter than **Os**sie. Watch. I'll win again!
Discussing whose slings are better
VINCENT: All mines is better than y'alls.
WILLIAM: I could walk on my hand better than anybody out here. Except him. And Freddie. *Thom*as can't walk.
Practicing original dance steps
JIMMY: I'm the best what you call, best step maker *out* here. *While making paper model airplanes*
FREDDIE: Ossie I'm a show you a *b*ad plane boy. Bad plane. Bad plane. It go-it glides anywhere. It's **bet**ter **than** any airplane you know. (Goodwin, 1990, p. 40)

These boys acknowledge when others are better than they are. Meanwhile, the girls in this neighborhood were not discussing their skills but rather who was friends with whom.

Boys respect their peers' expertise in a way that girls don't. This became clear to me after individually interviewing 9- to 11-year-old working-class children from the Boston area [144]. I brought each child one at a time to a quiet room and asked them to describe every one of his or her same-sex classmates. Boys made more refined judgments than girls did. Many of these boys' judgments reflected candid appraisals of other boys' expertise and willingness to work hard. Boys described the other boys in their class in terms of their academic ability, their athletic ability, and their specific interests and hobbies. They mentioned how hard the other boys worked, how willing they were to abide by or break rules of authority figures, how much they made fun of others, how goofy they were, as well as how strange and good or bad they were. Girls rarely did so. The only two characteristics used more often by girls than boys were whether the classmate was nice and whether she reciprocated nice actions.

Other studies have found this same difference. For example, one researcher [145] interviewed college students in Missouri about the ideal traits they would wish for in same-sex friends. Young men wanted their friends to be intelligent, athletic, creative, socially connected, capable of financial success, and imbued with a sense of humor, much more than young women did. Young women did not mention specific areas of expertise. It is a testament to the sociable nature of boys and young men that they so value a male peer's expertise.

Expertise is critical from early in life because across diverse cultures, boys' and men's friendships are based on shared activities [146]. Even very young boys are attracted to one another because they both enjoy wielding weapons, racing trucks, constructing fortifications, or chasing aliens around the room. By early childhood, boys fight happily with other boys who share their fantasies regarding potential invasion by enemies. In middle childhood, the importance of a boy's competitive team begins to take precedence over most other activities in his life. By adulthood, much of men's interactions with one another occur during work or leisure time and revolve around concrete activities. According to Swain [147], 75% of men report common activities as the most important part of their relationship with same-sex friends and that men's friendships mostly consist in providing assistance to one another during an activity. In contrast, women spent their time talking with friends about relationships they have (or had) with third parties.

The Strange Case of Males' Attitude Toward Homosexuality

The desire to have peers who are potential allies in a group targeting the enemy may increase understanding of one of the more difficult parts of males' social behavior—their instinctive aversion to feminine boys, and by extension to homosexuality. Many nonhuman male primates will scapegoat or displace their aggression onto the weakest males, but there is no evidence that weak males are excluded as long as they defer to stronger ones. But boys taunt and even bully their less masculine peers [148]. Even in the most politically correct environments, boys will often insult or attack boys who behave like girls. What is it about a boy who behaves like a girl that males don't like? A boy who behaves like a girl does not like play fighting, targeting enemies, or one-on-one competition. He might even enjoy domestic activities.

Babies can differentiate male from female faces by 3 months of age [149]. By 17 months, boys and girls begin to use language to label their own and others' gender [150]. Between 2 and 3 years of age, children become increasingly conscious that there are two sexes [151, 152]. By 5 or 6 years, they become confident that their gender identity will remain constant forever [153, 154]. If you ask children who are younger than 5 or 6 whether a person can change from one sex into the other, they will respond affirmatively. After this age, they think the question is ridiculous. No researcher has managed to persuade a child older than 5 or 6 years that simply changing the length of one's hair or one's clothing will transform a child of one sex into the other sex.

But that's not how boys, or men, actually behave. They seem to believe that some boys (or men) can indeed turn into girls. If a boy in Western society grows waist-length hair and wears frilly dresses to school, most boys believe that he has essentially become a girl, no matter how old they are when you ask them. Most men do too. Feminine boys can readily be identified by males of any age. Feminine boys may not enjoy play fighting, enemy detection, or engaging in direct competition. They may prefer to cook in the kitchen, care for baby dolls, or dress up as attractive young women [116, 117].

Most boys do not like feminine boys and tease them or try hard to change them into "real" boys. Around the world, boys expend much more effort and time than girls in assessing the extent to which a boy is a "real boy" [155]. Just like being manly seems to mean being ready to join a fighting force, being a real boy does too. Early in life, long before boys understand what homosexuality or transgender categories are, boys seem to share a picture of what it takes to be a boy. No such thing as a "tomgirl" exists; feminine boys are sissies or fake boys. What makes this so striking is the contrast with girls, who do not have a "real girl" or a womanly scale. Girls are much more tolerant in their definition of a girl or woman. For the most part, girls exhibit little interest in the degree to which a girl believes she is a girl, in whether a girl plays exclusively with girls, or in the activities a girl prefers. The only attribute by which a girl measures another girl is in terms of her attractiveness to boys, and this concern does not emerge strongly until adolescence. Boys and men seem to come equipped with a universal boy-measuring stick that they use to measure degree of boyishness and manliness, whereas girls don't have a female equivalent.

These intuitive male scales might explain the reason that between three and six times as many boys as girls in Western societies find themselves visiting a gender identity disorder (GID) clinic. Boys with GID experience many more difficulties getting along with their peers. They receive more teasing and are less liked than girls with GID, and this holds true across a number of societies including both Canada and the Netherlands [156], which are highly tolerant of transgendered individuals and homosexuality in adults.

The definition of a boy is much narrower than that of a girl. The characteristic that towers above the others in defining a male is that of enemy fighter. A man who cannot fight is by definition not a man. According to military historians, a man's prime fear when entering the military is that he will not be able to fight and will be revealed as not truly a man [6]. While there are gradations in boyishness and manliness, the prototypical male cannot be mistaken, and boys understand this before they turn 5. While pretty girls may embody the ideal girl, other girls are real girls too. A girl is accepted as a girl regardless of her feelings about being a girl, her play partners, or her sex-role behaviors; even a boy can be a girl if he wants to be. To be a boy requires fitting through a much narrower filter.

Men in many countries treat effeminate men the same way that preschool-age boys treat feminine boys [157–159]. One of the chief ways that this plays out is in attitudes toward homosexuality. Men dislike homosexuality much more than women do, especially homosexual men [160]. Why is this? There is evidence that men's dislike of homosexuality is more about fear of effeminate male behavior than fear of actual homoerotic behavior.

Homoerotic behavior is commonplace among males. Many of the most prototypical boys from toddlerhood through adolescence engage in quasi-sexual behavior with one another, as they continually make physical contact. Being jumped on, hit, sat on, rolled over, run into, slapped, hugged, and pushed all the time occur in every known culture between young boys [44]. Sexual relations between males in other primate species occur routinely in the juvenile period [161]. In cultures with frequent warfare such as ancient Greece or Rome, men regularly practiced homosexuality [162, 163]. In fact, in some cultures homosexual relations between boys are encouraged as a means of cementing male bonds. As a dramatic example, in Melanesian cultures, young boys are required to commit fellatio on young men who then go off to fight wars. Likewise, in ancient Greece, boys practiced homosexuality with men until the boys were ready to go off to war. Although there are no reliable figures for modern societies, given the general social stigma associated with sex between males, there is some evidence that the proportion of males who are not self-identified as gay who nevertheless have had sexual relations with men, especially in adolescence, is not insignificant [164, 165].

Because manliness seems defined by warfare, homosexuality may be fine as long as it does not interfere with men's roles in fighting enemies. Many homosexual men are excellent warriors. For example, Julius Caesar is believed to have had many homosexual lovers, but he was a great general, so no one minded.

Only some homosexual men dislike warfare and instead like activities that are more typically associated with women. It probably is not really homosexuality, therefore, that young boys fear but femininity or "girlieness." Specifically, feminine boys' unwillingness to share most boys' favorite activities and to cooperate with them likely constitutes the basic problem.

The primary reason soldiers give for their willingness to sacrifice their lives is their allegiance to their "band of brothers" [17, 18]. Should a man prove disloyal because of his lack of commitment to the band, to being a warrior, then the whole enterprise of warfare is jeopardized. Fighting boys and men cannot accept someone who won't get with the program. If they did, their side would lose. No wonder the American military has tied itself up in knots trying to figure out how not to discriminate against homosexual men.

Little boys' brains are wired to identify and eliminate boys who could not perform as trusted allies in times of war. The key problem with homosexuality from the male perspective lies in the subset of homosexual males who do not enjoy play fighting, targeting enemies, and one-on-one competition [166]. Boys who display blatantly feminine behavior in early childhood by wishing to be girls, by preferring to associate with girls, and by engaging in girls' activities generally do not enjoy male activities. Thus, I suggest that it is not homosexuality per se that threatens boys and men; rather, it is deep concern about some boys' lack of commitment to the cooperative venture of fighting enemies.

I believe that young boys follow the principles of distancing themselves from caregivers, from girls, and from boys who would not be good allies in a war instinctively. They do it because there is a partial genetic basis for their likes and dislikes. That their social preferences appear so early in life, and across so many diverse cultures, strongly suggests that genes may be guiding these preferences. Certainly, such preferences would combine in young adulthood to maximize the chances the young men could form an effective fighting force [16]. Critically, when no enemy looms, these same social preferences would facilitate success in many other pursuits. What boys may be programmed to learn easily does not have to be used to fight the enemy. Successful cooperation in any activity would result. The key is that young boys prepare early to function as part of a group of allies.

References

1. Junger, S., *War.* 2010, New York: Hachette Book Group.
2. Côté, S., Vaillancourt, T. LeBlanc, J. C., Nagin, D. S., and Trembly, R. E. The development of physical aggression from toddlerhood to pre-adolescence: A nation wide longitudinal study of Canadian children. *The Journal of Abnormal Child Psychology*, 34(1), pp. 71–85.
3. Tanner, J. M., Growth and maturation during adolescence. *Nutrition Reviews*, 1981. 39(2): pp. 43–55.
4. Salthouse, T. A., The processing-speed theory of adult age differences in cognition. *Psychological Review*, 1996. 103(3): pp. 403–428.
5. Horn, J. L., Organization of abilities and the development of intelligence. *Psychological Review*, 1968. 75(3): pp. 242–259.
6. Browne, K., *Co-ed combat: The new evidence that women shouldn't fight the nation's wars.* 2007, New York: Penguin.
7. Bowlby, J., *Attachment.* 1969, New York: Basic Books.
8. Douvan, E. A. M., and J. Adelson, *The adolescent experience.* 1966, New York: Wiley.
9. Benenson, J., A. Quinn, and S. Stella, Boys affiliate more than girls with a familiar same-sex peer. *Journal of Experimental Child Psychology*, 2012. 113, pp. 587–593.
10. Paley, V. G., *Boys and girls: Superheroes in the doll corner.* 1984, Chicago: University of Chicago Press.
11. Whiting, B. B., and C. P. Edwards *Children of different worlds: The formation of social behavior.* 1988, Cambridge, MA: Harvard University Press.
12. Marlowe, F., *The Hadza: Hunter-gatherers of Tanzania.* 2010, Los Angeles: University of California Press.
13. Maccoby, E. E., *The two sexes: Growing up apart, coming together,* 1998. Cambridge, MA: Belknap Press/Harvard University Press.
14. Maccoby, E. E., Gender and relationships: A developmental account. *American Psychologist*, 1990. 45(4): p. 513.
15. Freud, S., *Group psychology and the analysis of the ego.* 1921/1990, New York: Norton.
16. Zurbriggen, E. L., Rape, war, and the socialization of masculinity: Why our refusal to give up war ensures that rape cannot be eradicated. *Psychology of Women Quarterly*, 2010. 34(4): pp. 538–549.
17. Bourke, J., *An intimate history of killing: Face to face killing in twentieth century warfare,* 1999. London: Granta Books.
18. Marshall, S. L. A., and S. L. Atwood, *Men against fire: The problem of battle command in future war.* 1978, New York: Peter Smith.
19. Chodorow, N., *The reproduction of mothering.* 1999, Berkeley: University of California Press.
20. Farrington, D. P., The family backgrounds of aggressive youths. Book supplement to the *Journal of Child Psychology and Psychiatry*, 1978(1): pp. 73–93.

21. Farrington, D. P., Predictors, causes, and correlates of male youth violence. *Crime and Justice*, 1998. 24: pp. 421–475.

22. Rutter, M., H. Giller, and A. Hagell, *Antisocial behavior by young people.* 1998, New York: Cambridge University Press.

23. Eichstaedt, P., *First kill your family: Child soldiers of Uganda and the Lord's Resistance Army.* 2009, Chicago: Lawrence Hill.

24. Storey, A. E., C. J. Walsh, R. L. Quinton, and K. E. Wynne-Edwards Hormonal correlates of paternal responsiveness in new and expectant fathers. *Evolution and Human Behavior*, 2000. 21(2): pp. 79–95.

25. Mazur, A., and A. Booth, Testosterone and dominance in men. *Behavioral and Brain Sciences*, 1998. 21(3): pp. 353–363.

26. Baillargeon, R. H., et al., Gender differences in physical aggression: A prospective population-based survey of children before and after 2 years of age. *Developmental Psychology*, 2007. 43(1): pp. 13–26.

27. Hines, M., *Brain gender.* 2005, New York: Oxford University Press.

28. Dmitrieva, J., L. Steinberg, and J. Belsky, Child-care history, classroom composition, and children's functioning in kindergarten. *Psychological Science*, 2007. 18(12): pp. 1032–1039.

29. Belsky, J., et al., Are there long-term effects of early child care? *Child Development*, 2007. 78(2): pp. 681–701.

30. Belsky, J., War, trauma and children's development: Observations from a modern evolutionary perspective. *International Journal of Behavioral Development*, 2008. 32(4): pp. 260–271.

31. Belsky, J., Early child care and early child development: Major findings of the NICHD Study of Early Child Care. *European Journal of Developmental Psychology*, 2006. 3(1): pp. 95–110.

32. Maccoby, E. E., and C. N. Jacklin, *The psychology of sex differences.* 1974, Stanford, CA: Stanford University Press.

33. Hay, D. F., et al., The emergence of gender differences in physical aggression in the context of conflict between young peers. *British Journal of Developmental Psychology*, 2011. 29(2): pp. 158–175.

34. Patterson, G. R., R. A. Littman, and W. Bricker, Assertive behavior in children: A step toward a theory of aggression. *Monographs of the Society for Research in Child Development*, 1967. 32(5): pp. 1–43.

35. Dishion, T. J., J. McCord, and F. Poulin, When interventions harm: Peer groups and problem behavior. *American Psychologist*, 1999. 54(9): pp. 755–764.

36. Snarey, J., and L. Son, Sex identity development among kibbutz-born males: A test of the Whiting hypothesis. *Ethos*, 1986. 14(2): pp. 99–119.

37. Whiting, J. W. M., R. Kluckhohn, and A. Anthony, The function of male initiation ceremonies at puberty, in *Readings in social psychology*, E. E. Maccoby, T. Newcomb, and E. Hart, Editors. 1958, New York: Holt, Rinehart and Winston. pp. 359–370.

38. Sosis, R., H. C. Kress, and J. S. Boster, Scars for war: Evaluating alternative signaling explanations for cross-cultural variance in ritual costs. *Evolution and Human Behavior*, 2007. 28(4): pp. 234–247.
39. Bemelmans, L., *Madeline*. *1939*. 1967, New York: Penguin Putnam.
40. Bemelmans, L., *Madeline's rescue*. 1953, New York: Viking.
41. Clemens, S. L., M. Twain, and R. Rodgers, *The adventures of Tom Sawyer*. 1933, New York: Three Sirens Press.
42. Dahl, R., *James and the giant peach*. 1988, New York: Puffin Books.
43. Rowling, J. K., S. Fry, and C. De Wolff, *Harry Potter and the philosopher's stone*. 1997, London: Bloomsbury.
44. Schlegel, A., and H. Barry III, *Adolescence: An anthropological inquiry*. 1991, New York: Free Press.
45. Marlowe, F., *The Hadza: Hunter-gatherers of Tanzania: Origins of human behavior and culture*. 2010, Berkeley: University of California Press.
46. Whiting, J. W. M., and B. B. Whiting, Aloofness and intimacy of husbands and wives. *Ethos*, 1975. 3(2): pp. 183–207.
47. Mead, M., *Sex and temperament in three primitive societies*. 2007, New York: HarperCollins.
48. Archer, J., Cross-cultural differences in physical aggression between partners: A social-role analysis. *Personality and Social Psychology Review*, 2006. 10(2): pp. 133–153.
49. Bryant, B. K., The neighborhood walk: Sources of support in middle childhood. *Monographs of the Society for Research in Child Development*, 1985. 50(3): p. 122.
50. Thorne, B., and Z. Luria, Sexuality and gender in children's daily worlds. *Social Problems*, 1986. 33(3): pp. 176–190.
51. Fabes, R. A., C. L. Martin, and L. D. Hanish, Young children's play qualities in same, other, and mixed sex peer groups. *Child Development*, 2003. 74(3): pp. 921–932.
52. Benenson, J. E., D. Morash, and H. Petrakos, Gender differences in emotional closeness between preschool children and their mothers. *Sex Roles*, 1998. 38(11–12): pp. 975–985.
53. Huston, A. C., The development of sex typing: Themes from recent research. *Developmental Review*, 1985. 5(1): pp. 1–17.
54. Troll, L. E., Gender differences in cross-generation networks. *Sex Roles*, 1987. 17(11): pp. 751–766.
55. Benenson, J. F., C. Saelen, H. Markovits, and S. McCabe Sex differences in the value of parents versus same-sex peers. *Evolutionary Psychology*, 2008. 6(1): pp. 13–28.
56. Roff, M., Childhood social interactions and young adult bad conduct. *Journal of Abnormal and Social Psychology*, 1961. 63(2): pp. 333–337.
57. Roff, M., Preservice personality problems and subsequent adjustments to military service: The prediction of psychoneurotic reactions, in *USAF School of Aviation Medicine, Report*. 1957. pp. 57–136.

58. Conradt, L., Could asynchrony in activity between the sexes cause inter-sexual social segregation in ruminants? *Proceedings of the Royal Society of London. Series B: Biological Sciences*, 1998. 265(1403): pp. 1359–1368.

59. Wenger, M., Work, play, and social relationships among children in a Giriama community, *Children's social networks and social supports*, D. Belle, Editor. 1989, New York: Wiley. pp. 91–115.

60. Freedman, D. G., *Human infancy: An evolutionary perspective*. New York. 1974, Wiley.

61. Draper, P., Social and economic constraints on child life among the!Kung. *Anthropology Faculty Publications*, 1976. 13: pp. 200–217.

62. Gurven, M., and K. Hill Why do men hunt? A reevaluation of man the hunter and the sexual division of labor. Commentary. *Current Anthropology*, 2009. 50(1): pp. 51–74.

63. Marlowe, F. W., Hunting and gathering. *Cross-Cultural Research*, 2007. 41(2): pp. 170–195.

64. Mehta, C. M., and J. N. Strough, Sex segregation in friendships and normative contexts across the life span. *Developmental Review*, 2009. 29(3): pp. 201–220.

65. Rubin, K. H., G. G. Fein, and B. Vandenberg, Play, in *Social, emotional, and personality development*, N. Eisenberg, Editor. 1983, New York: Wiley. pp. 693–774.

66. Popham, F., and R. Mitchell, Leisure time exercise and personal circumstances in the working age population: Longitudinal analysis of the British household panel survey. *Journal of Epidemiology and Community Health*, 2006. 60(3): pp. 270–274.

67. Standlee, L., and W. Popham, Participation in leisure time activities as related to selected vocational and social variables. *Journal of Psychology: Interdisciplinary and Applied*, 1958. 46(1): pp. 149–154.

68. Benenson, J. F., and K. Alavi, Sex differences in children's investment in same-sex peers. *Evolution and Human Behavior*, 2004. 25(4): pp. 258–266.

69. Abu-Lughod, L., *Sentiments, honor and poetry in a Bedouin society*. 1986, Berkeley: University of California Press.

70. Jacklin, C. N., and E. E. Maccoby, Social behavior at thirty-three months in same-sex and mixed-sex dyads. *Child Development*, 1978. 49(3): pp. 557–569.

71. Charlesworth, W. R., and P. La Freniere, Dominance, friendship, and resource utilization in preschool children's groups. *Ethology and Sociobiology*, 1983. 4(3): pp. 175–186.

72. Cronin Weisfeld, C., G. E. Weisfeld, and J. W. Callaghan, Female inhibition in mixed-sex competition among young adolescents. *Ethology and Sociobiology*, 1982. 3(1): pp. 29–42.

73. Rodkin, P. C., and C. Berger, Who bullies whom? Social status asymmetries by victim gender. *International Journal of Behavioral Development*, 2008. 32(6): pp. 473–485.

74. Olweus, D., Victimization by peers: Antecedents and long-term outcomes, in *Social withdrawal, inhibition, and shyness in Childhood*, K. H. Rubin and J. B. Asendorpf, Editors. 1993, Hillsdale, NJ: Erlbaum. pp. 315–341.

75. Eagly, A. H., and S. J. Karau, Role congruity theory of prejudice toward female leaders. *Psychological Review*, 2002. 109(3): pp. 573–598.

76. Quinn, N., Anthropological studies on women's status. *Annual Review of Anthropology*, 1977. 6: pp. 181–225.

77. Rosaldo, M. Z., L. Lamphere, and J. Bamberger, *Woman, culture, and society*. 1974, Stanford, CA: Stanford University Press.

78. Oppermann, B., Impact of legal pluralism on women's status: An examination of marriage laws in Egypt, South Africa, and the United States. *Hastings Women's Law Journal*, 2006. 17: pp. 65–92.

79. Blau, F. D., and L. M. Kahn, *Gender differences in pay*. 2000, National Bureau of Economic Research., Cambridge, MA (Working Paper #7732) http://www.nber.org/papers/w7732

80. Eagly, A. H., and L. L. Carli, Women and the labyrinth of leadership. *Harvard Business Review*, 2007. 85(9): pp. 62–71.

81. Dill, K. E., and K. P. Thill, Video game characters and the socialization of gender roles: Young people's perceptions mirror sexist media depictions. *Sex Roles*, 2007. 57(11): pp. 851–864.

82. Coie, J. D., and K. A. Dodge, Aggression and antisocial behavior, in *Handbook of Child Psychology*, W. Damon and N. Eisenberg, Editors. 1998, Hoboken, NJ: Wiley. pp. 779–862.

83. Huston, A. C., In P. H. Mussen, Editor, Handbook of Child Psychology Vol. 4 Socialization, personality, and Social development (E. M. Hetherington Vol. Ed.) Sex-typing. *Handbook of Child Psychology*, 1983. pp. 387–467.

84. Gottman, J. M., The world of coordinated play: Same- and cross-sex friendship in young children, in *Conversations of friends: Speculations on affective development*, J. M. Gottman and J. G. Parker, Editors. 1986, New York: Cambridge University Press. pp. 139–191.

85. Harkness, S., and C. M. Super, The cultural context of gender segregation in children's peer groups. *Child Development*, 1985. 56(1): pp. 219–224.

86. Tanner, J., and A. Thomson, Standards for birthweight at gestation periods from 32 to 42 weeks, allowing for maternal height and weight. *Archives of Disease in Childhood*, 1970. 45(242): pp. 566–569.

87. Eaton, W. O., and L. R. Enns, Sex differences in human motor activity level. *Psychological Bulletin*, 1986. 100(1): pp. 19–28.

88. Thomas, J. R., and K. E. French, Gender differences across age in motor performance: A meta-analysis. *Psychological Bulletin*, 1985. 98(2): pp. 260–282.

89. Strayer, F., and J. Strayer, An ethological analysis of social agonism and dominance relations among preschool children. *Child Development*, 1976. 47(4): pp. 980–989.

90. Weisfeld, G. E., Social dominance and human motivation, in DR Omark, FF Strayer, DG Freedman *Dominance relations: An ethological view of human conflict and social interaction*, New York: Garland Press, 1980, pp. 273–286.

91. Tuddenham, R. D., Studies in reputation: I. Sex and grade differences in school children's evaluation of their peers. II. The diagnosis of social adjustment. *Psychological Monographs*, 1951. 333: pp. 1–39.

92. Weisfeld, G. E., C. C. Weisfeld, and J. W. Callaghan, Peer and self perceptions in Hopi and Afro American third and sixth graders. *Ethos*, 1984. 12(1): pp. 64–84.

93. Adler, P. A., S. J. Kless, and P. Adler, Socialization to gender roles: Popularity among elementary school boys and girls. *Sociology of Education*, 1992. 65 (July): pp. 169–187.

94. Closson, L. M., Status and gender differences in early adolescents' descriptions of popularity. *Social Development*, 2009. 18(2): pp. 412–426.

95. Apicella, C. L., F. W. Marlowe, J. H. Fowler, and N. Christakis Social networks and cooperation in hunter-gatherers. *Nature*, 2012. 481(7382): pp. 497–501.

96. Judge, T. A., and D. M. Cable, The effect of physical height on workplace success and income: Preliminary test of a theoretical model. *Journal of Applied Psychology*, 2004. 89(3): pp. 428–441.

97. Potegal, M., and J. Archer, Sex differences in childhood anger and aggression. *Child and Adolescent Psychiatric Clinics of North America*, 2004. 13(3): pp. 513–528.

98. Kring, A. M., Gender and anger, in *Gender and emotion: Social psychological perspectives.*, A. H. Fischer, Editor. 2000, New Yor: Cambridge University Press. pp. 211–231.

99. Fredrikson, M., P. Annas, H. Fischer, and G. Wik Gender and age differences in the prevalence of specific fears and phobias. *Behaviour Research and Therapy*, 1996. 34(1): pp. 33–39.

100. McLean, C. P., and E. R. Anderson, Brave men and timid women? A review of the gender differences in fear and anxiety. *Clinical Psychology Review*, 2009. 29(6): pp. 496–505.

101. Davey, G. C. L., Self-reported fears to common indigenous animals in an adult UK population: The role of disgust sensitivity. *British Journal of Psychology*, 1994. 85(4): pp. 541–554.

102. Omogbai, E. K. I., et al., Snake bites in Nigeria: A study of the prevalence and treatment in Benin City. *Tropical Journal of Pharmaceutical Research*, 2002. 1(1): pp. 39–44.

103. Currie, B. J., S. K. Sutherland, B. J. Hudson, and A. M. Smith An epidemiological study of snake bite envenomation in Papua New Guinea. *The Medical Journal of Australia*, 1991. 154: pp. 266–268.

104. Campbell, A., Staying alive: Evolution, culture, and women's intrasexual aggression. *Behavioral and Brain Sciences*, 1999. 22(2): pp. 203–252.

105. Nagy, E., et al., Different emergence of fear expressions in infant boys and girls. *Infant Behavior and Development*, 2001. 24(2): pp. 189–194.
106. Robinson, J. L., J. Kagan, J. S. Reznick, and R. Corley The heritability of inhibited and uninhibited behavior: A twin study. *Developmental Psychology*, 1992. 28(6): pp. 1030–1037.
107. Hall, J. A., J. D. Carter, and T. G. Horgan, Gender differences in nonverbal communication of emotion, in *Gender and emotion: Social psychological perspectives*, A. H. Fischer, Editor. 2000, Cambridge: Cambridge University Press. pp. 97–117.
108. Brody, L. R., and J. A. Hall, Gender and emotion in context, in *Handbook of emotions*, M. Lewis, J. M. Iavailand-Jones, and L. F. Barrett, Editors. 2008, New York: Guilford. pp. 395–408.
109. Brody, L. R., and J. A. Hall, *Gender and emotion*. 1993, New York: Guilford.
110. Simner, M. L., Newborn's response to the cry of another infant. *Developmental Psychology*, 1971. 5(1): pp. 136–150.
111. Sagi, A., and M. L. Hoffman, Empathic distress in the newborn. *Developmental Psychology*, 1976. 12(2): pp. 175–176.
112. Zahn-Waxler, C., J. A. L. Robinson, and R. N. Emde, The development of empathy in twins. *Developmental Psychology*, 1992. 28(6): pp. 1038–1047.
113. Mirowsky, J., and C. E. Ross, Sex differences in distress: Real or artifact? *American Sociological Review*, 1995. 60(3): pp. 449–468.
114. Buck, R., Nonverbal communication of affect in children. *Journal of Personality and Social Psychology*, 1975. 31(4): pp. 644–653.
115. Buck, R., A test of nonverbal receiving ability: Preliminary studies. *Human Communication Research*, 1976. 2(2): pp. 162–171.
116. Emmerich, W., and K. Shepard, Development of sex-differentiated preferences during late childhood and adolescence. *Developmental Psychology*, 1982. 18(3): pp. 406–417.
117. Fagot, B. I., Beyond the reinforcement principle: Another step toward understanding sex role development. *Developmental Psychology*, 1985. 21(6): pp. 1097.
118. Garvey, C., *Play.* 1977, London: Fontana.
119. Huston, A. C., Chess, S. and Thomas, A. The development of sex typing: Themes from recent research, in W. L. Licamele (editor) *Annual progress in child psychiatry and child development, 1986.* 1987, Philadelphia: Brunner/Mazel. pp. 168–186.
120. Staff, J., and D. A. Kreager, Too cool for school? Violence, peer status and high school dropout. *Social Forces*, 2008. 87(1): pp. 445–471.
121. Oransky, M., and J. Marecek, I'm not going to be a girl. *Journal of Adolescent Research*, 2009. 24(2): pp. 218–241.
122. Brebner, J., Gender and emotions. *Personality and Individual Differences*, 2003. 34(3): pp. 387–394.

123. Campbell, A., Sex differences in direct aggression: What are the psychological mediators? *Aggression and Violent Behavior*, 2006. 11(3): pp. 237–264.
124. Campbell, A., and S. Muncer, Intent to harm or injure? Gender and the expression of anger. *Aggressive Behavior*, 2008. 34(3): pp. 282–293.
125. Wrangham, R., Is military incompetence adaptive? *Evolution and Human Behavior*, 1999. 20(1): pp. 3–17.
126. Bem, S. L., The measurement of psychological androgyny. *Journal of Consulting and Clinical Psychology*, 1974. 42(2): pp. 155–162.
127. Gentile, B., et al., Gender differences in domain-specific self-esteem: A meta-analysis. *Review of General Psychology*, 2009. 13(1): pp. 34–45.
128. Kling, K. C., J. S. Hyde, C. J. Showers, and B. N. Buswell Gender differences in self-esteem: A meta-analysis. *Psychological Bulletin*, 1999. 125(4): pp. 470–500.
129. Benenson, J. F., and J. Schinazi, Sex differences in reactions to outperforming same-sex friends. *British Journal of Developmental Psychology*, 2004. 22(3): pp. 317–333.
130. Piaget, J., *The moral development of the child*. 1932, London: Kegan Paul.
131. Smuts, B. B., D. L. Cheney, R. Seyfarath, and R. W. Wrangham *Primate societies*. 1987, Chicago: University of Chicago Press.
132. Tiger, L., *Men in groups*. 2005, Piscataway, NJ: Transaction.
133. Craig, S., *Sports and games of the ancients*. 2002, Westport, CT: Greenwood.
134. Leibs, A., *Sports and games of the Renaissance*. Vol. 4. 2004, Westport, CT: Greenwood.
135. Lever, J., Sex differences in the complexity of children's play and games. *American Sociological Review*, 1978. 43(4): pp. 471–483.
136. Lever, J., Sex differences in the games children play. *Social Problems*, 1976. 23(4): pp. 478–487.
137. Paxson, F. L., The rise of sport. *Mississippi Valley Historical Review*, 1917. 4(2): pp. 143–168.
138. Gilligan, C., *In a different voice: Psychological theory and women's development*. 1982, Cambridge, MA: Harvard University Press.
139. Kohlberg, L., *The philosophy of moral development: Moral stages and the idea of justice*. 1981, New York: Harper and Row.
140. Jaffee, S., and J. S. Hyde, Gender differences in moral orientation: A meta-analysis. *Psychological Bulletin*, 2000. 126(5): pp. 703–726.
141. Johnston, D. K., Adolescents' solutions to dilemmas in fables: Two moral orientations—two problem solving strategies, in *Mapping the moral domain: A contribution of women's thinking to psychological theory and education*, C. Gilligan, J. V. Ward, J. M. Taylor, and B. Bardige Editors. 1988, Cambridge, MA: Harvard University Press. pp. 49–71.
142. Gilligan, C., and G. Wiggins, The origins of morality in early childhood relationships, in *Mapping the moral domain: The emergence of morality*

*in young children,*in. C Gilligan, J. V. Ward, J. M. Taylor, and B. Bardige, Editors. 1987, Cambridge, MA: Harvard University Press. pp. 277–305.

143. Goodwin, M. H., *He-said-she-said: Talk as social organization among black children.* 1990, Bloomington: Indiana University Press.

144. Benenson, J. F., Gender differences in social networks. *Journal of Early Adolescence,* 1990. 10(4): pp. 472–495.

145. Vigil, J. M., Asymmetries in the friendship preferences and social styles of men and women. *Human Nature,* 2007. 18(2): pp. 143–161.

146. Winstead, B., and J. Griffin, Friendship styles, in *Encyclopedia of women and gender,* J. Worell, Editor. 2001, Boston: Academic Press. pp. 481–492.

147. Swain, S., Covert intimacy: Closeness in men's friendships, in *Gender in intimate relationships: A microstructural approach,* B. R. P. Schwartz, Editor. 1989, Belmont, CA: Wadsworth. pp. 71–86.

148. Strayer, F., and J. Noel, The prosocial and antisocial functions of preschool aggression: An ethological study of triadic conflict among young children, in *Altruism and aggression: Biological and social origins,* C. Zahn-Waxler, E. M. Cummings, and R. J. Iannotti, Editors. 1986, New York: Cambridge University Press. pp. 107–131.

149. Quinn, P. C., J. Yahr, A. Kuhn, A. M. Slater, and O. Pascalis Representation of the gender of human faces by infants: A preference for female. *Perception,* 2002. 31(9): pp. 1109–1121.

150. Zosuls, K. M., et al., The acquisition of gender labels in infancy: Implications for gender-typed play. *Developmental Psychology,* 2009. 45(3): pp. 688–701.

151. Fagot, B. I., M. D. Leinbach, and C. O'Boyle, Gender labeling, gender stereotyping, and parenting behaviors. *Developmental Psychology,* 1992. 28(2): pp. 225–230.

152. Martin, C. L., D. N. Ruble, and J. Szkrybalo, Cognitive theories of early gender development. *Psychological Bulletin,* 2002. 128(6): pp. 903–933.

153. Kohlberg, L., and E. E. Maccoby, A cognitive-developmental analysis of children's sex-role concepts and attitudes, in *The development of sex differences,* E. E. Maccoby and R. G. D'Andrade, Editors. 1966, Stanford, CA: Stanford University Press. pp. 82–173.

154. Mischel, W. (1970). Sex typing and socialization. In P. H. Mussen (Ed.), Carmichael's manual of child psychology (Vol. 2, pp. 3–72). New York: Wiley.

155. Parke, R. D., *Fatherhood.* 1996, Cambridge, MA: Harvard University Press.

156. Cohen-Kettenis, P. T., A. Owen, V. G. Kaijser, S. J. Bradley, and K. J. Zucker Demographic characteristics, social competence, and behavior problems in children with gender identity disorder: A cross-national, cross-clinic comparative analysis. *Journal of Abnormal Child Psychology,* 2003. 31(1): pp. 41–53.

157. Cunningham, J. A., D. S. Strassberg, and B. Haan, Effects of intimacy and sex-role congruency of self-disclosure. *Journal of Social and Clinical Psychology,* 1986. 4(4): pp. 393–401.

158. Bianchi, F. T., et al., Partner selection among Latino immigrant men who have sex with men. *Archives of Sexual Behavior*, 2010. 39(6): pp. 1321–1330.

159. van der Meer, T., Gay bashing—a rite of passage? *Culture, Health and Sexuality*, 2003. 5(2): pp. 153–165.

160. Kite, M. E., and B. E. Whitley, Sex differences in attitudes toward homosexual persons, behaviors, and civil rights: A meta-analysis. *Personality and Social Psychology Bulletin*, 1996. 22(4): pp. 336–353.

161. Wallen, K., Sex and context: Hormones and primate sexual motivation. *Hormones and Behavior*, 2001. 40(2): pp. 339–357.

162. Cantarella, E., The androgynous and bisexuality in ancient legal codes. *Diogenes*, 2005. 52(4): pp. 5–14.

163. Friedman, R. C., *Bisexuality in the Ancient World:* By Eva Cantarella. Translated by Cormac Ó Cuilleanáin. New York/London: Yale University Press. *Psychoanalytic Quarterly*, 1995. 64: pp. 617–619.

164. Diamond, M., Homosexuality and bisexuality in different populations. *Archives of Sexual Behavior*, 1993. 22(4): pp. 291–310.

165. Kinsey, A. C., W. B. Pomeroy, and C. E. Martin, Sexual behavior in the human male. *Journal of Nervous and Mental Disease*, 1949. 109(3): p. 283.

166. MacCoun, R. J., Sexual orientation and military cohesion: A critical review of the evidence, in *Out in force: Sexual orientation and the military*, R. M. Carney, G. M. Herek, and J. B. Jobe, Editors. 1996, Chicago: University of Chicago Press. pp. 157–176.

CHAPTER FOUR

—◆—

Organizing the Military: Groups of Egalitarian Men

When two tribes of primeval men, living in the same country, came into competition, if the one tribe included (other circumstances being equal) a greater number of courageous, sympathetic, and faithful members, who were always ready to warn each other of danger, to aid and defend each other, this tribe would without doubt succeed best and conquer the other. (Darwin, 1871, p. 162)

Aggression is an intensely co-operative process—it is both the product and cause of strong effective ties between men. (Tiger, 1969, p. 247)

Human males present a paradox: They love to compete against one another—and to cooperate with one another. They do both far more than unrelated women do. They are far more cooperative than individuals in most other species, except maybe insects [1].

Male Groups

All-male groups exist in every human culture. Secret societies, college fraternities, entertainment clubs, bars, street gangs, the mafia, sports teams, gambling houses, government, businesses, religion, police forces, and the military classically have been all-male institutions [3]. Even in the simplest of hunter-gatherer societies, such as the Ache of Paraguay or the Hadza of Tanzania, it often is the unrelated men and older boys of the community who work together to hunt game or search for honey. If one man catches an animal, he shares it with other men, as well as with their families. A woman rarely shares food with unrelated women, channeling most of the plant foods and occasional small game to her own children, husband, and female relatives [4].

There are very few all-female institutions that involve genetically unrelated women. Brothels constitute a universal exception. However, in many brothels, either a man is in charge or the women have been coerced. Historically, most all-female institutions were created by men for men. Harems, polygynous households, and women's jobs during wartime were usually organized by men. Women traditionally have remained closer to their families and dependent children. While women in hunter-gatherer communities often search for fruits and tubers together with older children, they try to take along an adolescent male or older man too. Women are vulnerable to predation or kidnapping by a neighboring community, so they need protection [5]. Social scientists who study human sex differences believe that across cultures, unrelated men engage in group activities more than unrelated women do [6].

Why do unrelated males form groups? Working together of course can reduce one's workload and increase efficiency, especially if group members contribute different kinds of expertise. But groups require sharing resources and increase exposure to germs and conflicts between members. Women find these risks worth taking with family members, but they must be more careful with unrelated women.

I suggest that male groups are formed initially because male peers are so drawn to one another, and away from everyone else. They may fight; they usually compete; they prefer others who are physically and emotionally strong and self-confident, who follow the rules and demonstrate some skill. But simply enjoying one another's company comes first. Their mutual attraction is there early in life, once again suggesting a biological basis. It grows stronger as men enter adulthood. Adolescent boys, with their powerful sexual desires mostly directed toward girls, and strong competitive instincts, nonetheless spend a lot of time in one another's company. Even boys with behavioral problems, who cannot follow any adult authority's directions, group together, through graffiti writing, skateboarding, or gang fights.

After the initial attraction to one another comes the appeal of group life. Despite popular stereotypes about the antisocial, status-striving nature of boys and men, my observations indicate otherwise. I believe that if a boy or man could choose between being the lone superhero with no group or a supreme expert working with others united against a common enemy, most would choose the latter. Even Batman needs to work with the Gotham City police force. Even James Bond needs the British secret service. Current warlords have a large retinue of male supporters, or they wouldn't be where they are today.

This makes sense from an evolutionary perspective. Being an alpha male provides prestige, resources, and females, among other perks. If the alpha male's community gets overrun by another community, however, neither he nor anyone else survives. Better to surrender some individual status and subordinate personal aims to the greater good than to lose everything. Maximizing the probability of belonging to a victorious group requires not putting your own needs ahead of the group's goals. This basic assumption underlies the rules of competitive team sports, as well as successful businesses, governments, religions, and most any organization. No one wants a teammate who shows off his own prowess at the expense of the team's success. The skills that benefit the warrior easily transfer to any type of group.

Even Darwin [7], who emphasized individual one-on-one competition as the key factor in evolution, concluded that for human males, cooperation may trump competition when an enemy looms large:

> A community including a large number of well-endowed individuals increases in number and is victorious over other and less well-endowed communities; although each separate member may gain no advantage over the other members of the same community. (Darwin, 1871, p. 155)

Cooperation requires giving up personal rewards to allow the group to function well. This requires group members to help, not hinder, one another. This is such an important component of group functioning that even 6-month-old infants do not like hinderers. When these tiny humans see a living being trying to thwart another being's progress, they get angry. They refuse to touch the hinderer, often batting it on the head [8, 9]. They do this even though they have not been personally affected. Studies with adults show the same response. An adult will surrender money in order to punish another one who behaves badly toward a member of the community [10–12].

Group cooperation depends on this. Otherwise, why not take what you can get, and forget everyone else? The intuitive desire to punish noncooperators, along with the fear of being punished oneself, combine to push humans where no other species has gone—toward cooperative competition. This is particularly critical for those who are fighting the enemy. While girls and women have their own reasons for wanting peace, large-group cooperation with unrelated females seems less important.

What is critical, however, is that males seem more willing than females to punish a noncooperator. In the study in which adult men and women played against a cheater, males not only displayed less empathy than females did but actually showed pleasure when the cheater received a painful shock. Policing the community for hinderers, noncooperators, and cheaters may be particularly pleasurable for males.

The Development of Males' Preferences for Groups

Boys' preference for groups begins in infancy. When my students and I showed 6-month-old babies pictures of one cute moving animal puppet (a tiger or a leopard) next to three identical moving animal puppets, the male babies looked more at the group of puppets, whereas girls didn't look more one way or the other [13]. Baby boys also prefer looking at videos of groups of children playing together more than videos of single individuals; again, baby girls don't look more one way or the other [14]. Interestingly, testosterone seems to drive boys' attraction to groups. Three-month-old males with higher levels of testosterone look more at groups than infant males with lower levels of testosterone [15]. This provides additional evidence for the biological origins of boys' attraction to groups.

If groups are so important to males' social behavior, then young boys should do more than just look at groups; they should want to interact with them as well. To examine this, I paid a professional puppeteer to interact with individual 3- and 4-year-old boys and girls, either using one puppet or using a group of three puppets. Sure enough, boys smiled and looked more at the group of three puppets than at one puppet [16]. One little boy refused even to look at the single puppet. Instead, he untied his shoelace and retied it around his neck, slowly beginning to strangle himself. Fortunately, when the puppeteer brought out the group of puppets, the boy changed his mind and started talking to the puppets with evident enjoyment. Quite a few of the boys barely looked at the single puppet.

Girls of course loved interacting with the one puppet, with one girl gazing at the puppet 99% of the time.

Observations in many preschools show that between the ages of 3 and 5 years, boys spend more time near larger numbers of same-sex peers than girls do [17]. In addition, the more other boys are present, the more boys move farther away from teachers. The reverse happens for girls, who spend more time closer to the teacher when more girls are present.

Some social scientists believe that the equipment, fields, and coaches provided by adults encourage boys to play games and sports. They also believe that girls and women just haven't had time to play in the past, because they had to care for children [18]. If they only had the time, perhaps girls and women would play team sports as much as boys and men.

In order to test this possibility, I brought groups of six preschool- or kindergarten-age children from several schools in a wealthy American suburb to an empty classroom that contained only small animal puppets and small foam balls. All children were the same sex and told me they were friends with one another. My students and I told the children to do whatever they wanted as long as they didn't hurt each other [19]. No adult was present except for the video person, who could not interact with the children.

What happened? Almost all of the groups of 5- to 6-year-old boys spontaneously divided themselves into two opposing groups and played "war." They rarely touched the balls or puppets, although they sometimes grabbed a puppet by the tail as a weapon and used it to beat another boy. They spent most of their time fighting in pitched battles, one team against another, mostly in one-on-one competitions. Timeouts would be called during which new tactics were considered secretly by one team or the other, then the two teams would reunite on the battlefield. Not a single girl's group engaged in any type of competitive game or even in a prolonged activity that included the whole group. The girls told stories with the puppets, tossed one of the balls back and forth, and occasionally chased one another, but mostly talked.

The boys often were piled on top of one another, so it was impossible to know who was speaking. Nonetheless, here is a typical exchange, with the lines in chronological order:

Brother Todd. Save me! Brother Todd! Brother Todd! (screaming)
Matthew. Matthew. I'm on YOUR team.

No, you're not on Steve's team.

I'm on Steve's team.

Yes, I am on Steven's team.

We can get to play with balls.

Can I be on your team?

Oh yes, you are on our team.

Oh yes.

Similarly, in another classroom:

There's 3 against 3.

Who needs a snapping turtle? Andrew? Adam?

I do.

I'll help you Adam.

I'm on your team.

Me too.

There's 3 against 3.

All right.

Andrew and Adam and me. We're on the same team. We have to beat up
other people.

Yes

Yeah.

We don't beat up Adam. We don't beat up Andrew.

I'm on your team. I got him.

I got the ball.

Help! Help!

He's on our team.

No, he's on our team.

No, I'm not. I'm on your team.

No

Ah ha.

You're on that team.

These young boys had invented their very own team competitions. At that age, the schools did not provide sports. I didn't give them the right equipment. No field or coach was present. Yet, these boys got a lot of pleasure from competing in teams. They were rambunctious and enthusiastic, and they didn't want to leave when the time ended. In contrast, the girls played with the balls and puppets far more than the boys. But the girls didn't create teams or competitions, and they had far less fun [20].

In most cultures, boys' enjoyment of team competition explodes in middle childhood [21]. Why do boys and men like sports? One reasonable and common explanation is that team sports mimic warfare. Sports have all the elements that provide pleasure: play fighting, the presence of the enemy, one-on-one competition, and, critically, intergroup battles. Team sports allow players to display their own unique skills and ally with one another to defeat the other team. Boys who might have been competing to best one another easily become teammates when another team materializes. Even boys who dislike each other intensely will cheer each other on when an enemy or opposing team arrives. Boys seem to be spontaneously attracted to team sports. It's not that society does not facilitate male team sports—it does. But thousands of years before society poured resources into equipment and fields and coaches, boys and men were playing team sports [22, 23].

Boys and men not only like organized team sports but also enjoy informal pickup games. In the Western world, in many public parks, boys and men play competitive games. In contrast, girls and women talk to each other, look after children, or watch the boys and men. Compilations of the games of history consistently show that human males play competitive team sports across countries and centuries more than girls and women do [22, 23].

The ability to compete as a team is a remarkable feat. In the primate world, only chimpanzees have been observed to compete group against group, and the amount of cooperation is minimal. Everyone does more or less the same thing [24, 25]. While intergroup hostilities abound in canine and some primate species, intergroup competitions in which the losers die and surrender their territory may exist only for humans and chimpanzees.

Of course, the key part of groups is the relationship formed among their members. Male bonding is what makes boys' groups work. Early preferences for looking at groups or being close to lots of male peers are only the beginning. Male bonding blossoms when boys are cognitively and physically able to organize a group activity, which starts around 5 years of age. Cross-cultural observations clearly show that between the ages of 5 and 7 years, boys begin to form all-male groups [26–28]. This has been found in the most diverse cultures, including Australian, Aboriginal, Balinese, Ceylonese, Indian, Japanese, Kikuyu, Navajo, and Taiwanese boys; in boys from Korea and eastern India; and in the American Pawnees and the Ngonde of East Africa.

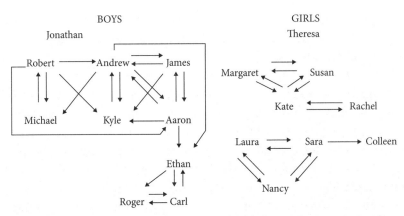

FIGURE 4-1. Patterns of same-sex best friend relationships in one class for boys and girls. ©1990 Sage Publications. Originally published in the *Journal of Early Adolescence.* 10: 472–495. doi: 10.1177/0272431690104004.

Similar observations have been made with the Taiwanese Hokkien, the Tzeltal of southern Mexico, the Khoikhoi of South Africa, the Woleasisans of Micronesia, the Gond of India, the Lepcha of the Himalayas, and the Iroquois of North America; in China, Israel, Germany, East Africa, and Samoa; the Mundugumor, the Bahtonga of South Africa, and the Native American tribes of the Iroquois and the Dakota [29–31]. While boys are spending time in large and lively groups around the world, girls in these societies are helping their mothers with family chores or spending time with a close friend.

In modern school environments, the same differences appear in the way boys and girls organize their friendships. To demonstrate this, I asked all the boys and girls in several Boston area classrooms to check off on a list the names of their best friends in the class [32]. I then connected the best friend ratings of all the boys and all the girls in the class to make a picture of the relationships. The difference in how boys and girls organize their friendships appears in figure 4-1 (Benenson, 1990, p. 482). In this classroom, boys formed one large group, with central and peripheral members. Further, the boys' friendships were mostly interconnected: If a boy was friends with a few other boys, then they were friends with one another too. Girls, on the other hand, formed either one-on-one relationships or small cliques. Further, the girls divided themselves up. This was true in almost every classroom I studied.

Not only do boys and girls initially organize their friendships differently, but their friendships change in different ways over the course of the year.

Boys tend to expand the size of their group of friends with time. In contrast, girls' small clique relationships are unstable and break down into simple one-on-one friendships [33].

While this might be news to some people, even preschool-age children intuitively understand this basic fact about boys' friendships. My colleagues and I showed young preschoolers cartoon drawings of a child playing either with one same-sex friend or with three same-sex friends. We then asked them to tell us in which situation the child was happier. The preschoolers uniformly judged that boys would be happier playing with three friends than with one friend. They also judged, though with less certainty, that girls would be happier playing with one friend. By elementary school and continuing through adulthood, children, adolescents, and adults all believe the same thing. In addition, when we asked them whether a boy's friends were friends with one another too, they responded yes. In contrast, when we asked them whether a girl's friends were friends with one another too, they said no. In other words, even young children have an intuitive understanding that boys tend to form large groups in which everyone interacts with everyone else.

At summer camp too, adolescent boys reported that they spent time with many other boys at a time, and that their friends were friends with one another. In contrast, over the course of the summer, girls' relationships became more and more divided, so that many girls ended up in friendships that were unconnected to other girls in the camp [34].

In Ritch Savin-Williams's [30, 31, 35] classic studies of summer camp, the counselors living in the male and female cabins recorded their observations of the interactions between their campers. Savin-Williams found that boys formed cohesive bands with the other boys who lived in the same cabin. Although boys could get together with other groups of boys when necessary, their identities remained tightly bound to their own cabins. In contrast,

"During 'freetime' the girls were seldom together as a group; rather, they preferred to associate with sisters or cousins, home-town friends, extra-cabin friends, or one of their close cabin buddies." (Savin-Williams, 1980, p. 360).

This is such a strong part of boys' psychology that many different organizations from British private schools to the military rely on its power to complete many tasks.

What happens when adolescent boys start becoming sexually attracted to girls? As romantic and sexual liaisons form, mixed-sex groups, as well as romantic couples, become more common. Nonetheless, researchers who have looked closely at adolescent friendships have found the same patterns as before: adolescent boys still hanging out in groups. Interestingly, mixed-sex groups in adolescents often form because girls are drawn into groups of boys, not vice versa [36].

Consider the following exercise conducted with young adults at a university. Ask a typical American man and woman to complete a sentence starting with the words "I am...". Men and women respond in different ways [37]. A man is more likely to say that he is part of a group, as in "I am a member of X fraternity." A woman, in contrast, is more likely to refer to her personal relationships, as in "I am so-and-so's daughter."

Groups also are more accessible to the minds of men than women. Male minds store memories about groups in a place where important information resides, and female minds don't. If men and women read a story about a group, such as a country, university, team, or club, men remember it better and recall it faster than women [37, 38]. Men also report that they are more willing than women to help their group [39]. However, if the word "group" is replaced by the word "individual," such as a friend, sibling, or teammate, then women remember better than men. No wonder, then, that a man forgets his wife's and children's ages and birthdays but remembers the dates of important battles as well as the outcomes of sports games (though statistics about individual team members who led to the group's victory or defeat also come to mind). Even when women belong to groups they value, such as an academic club or a sports team or a sorority, they do not care about their identity as a group member as much as men do [39]. Instead, it is the friendships with individuals in the group that women care about. Not that men don't value individual friendships too, but the group itself is more important to the identities of men than it is to women.

The Dynamics of Groups

Why are groups so attractive to boys and men? What is a group besides a bunch of individuals? Well, there is a lot more going on in a group than when there are only two or three individuals present. For one thing, groups are physically more stimulating. Even in infancy, male babies spend more time than female babies looking at images that move more [14]. Further, from the first day of life through at least middle adulthood, boys and men move more than girls and women do [40]. If you want to move around, it's easier to do so when there are lots of moving parts to move with you.

Second, groups also have a lot more relationships to follow. With every new member, there is an exponential increase in the number of relationships that are possible. No longer can individual A simply have separate relationships, with individuals B, C, D, and E, but in a group, A can also form a number of trios and foursomes, and so forth, and A must keep track of who fellow group members are particularly friendly with.

Third, a lot more information that is relevant to group functioning must be learned and continually updated. In the group, some individuals get along better than others; some are more skilled at particular tasks than others; some are better leaders than others. Depending on the activity at hand, the group must be flexible enough to allow an individual to play varying roles with different group members, so that individuals can do what they are best at and maximize the group's functioning, whether it is debating or throwing or competing against another group.

Finally, groups allow allies to strive together for a common goal. If they succeed, a lot of pride and loyalty follow. The quintessential all-American group in the civilian world is a sports team or a business. Early in life, boys on teams play all kinds of competitive sports—football, hockey, baseball, basketball, and soccer, among many others. Although girls in America do too, partly because the law requires that American schools provide equal access to sports, in other countries few female sports exist. Further, few American females spontaneously play team sports [2].

Later in adulthood, businesses contain many males who cooperate to make the business successful. While increasingly women are accepted into business, and in many countries it is against the law to exclude them (in some places quotas for women now exist), they do not interact with one another as easily as males do. Not only that, but males have set up their group businesses in ways that are comfortable for them. When it comes time for socializing with the group, women often feel out of place [41].

Part and parcel of a group is continually figuring out which individuals should play which roles with whom, and switching these as needs change, all the while teaming up with allies against the competition. A group is a fluid enterprise as needs and times and members change. Men relish this looseness. This is not a female's type of group. In strictly female groups, such as book groups or groups for survivors of sexual abuse, everyone is equal and roles never change. Women relish this stability.

Males seem predisposed to benefit from loose, dynamic groups in a way that females do not. One of the most frequent complaints about boys in school is that they don't try very hard. They're the last ones to do their homework; they don't pay attention in class; they don't have the same thing on their minds as the teacher does. Are boys really that lazy or unfocused?

I believe that the dynamics of boys' groups suggest something very different. After all, a boy who did not pull his own weight for his team or his group could easily be abandoned. Watch boys playing together, and you can see how hard they work, how closely they observe every play, and how simultaneously focused they are on winning the game. I wanted to know whether boys would keep up their concentration when working on something less inspiring than building a fort or playing a game, if it were done in a group.

So, my student and I asked male and female groups of 10-year-olds to come to a room at their schools either with one other same-sex friend or with a group of five same-sex friends. The children all agreed to be videotaped while solving a word game based on Scattergories. This is a type of game at which girls generally excel because of its reliance on verbal memory for words that begin with different letters [42].

To win a point, children had to come up with four words beginning with the same letter that fit a category, such as four things found in a kitchen that begin with the letter "s." Whichever pair and whichever group won the most points would receive a plaque with their names on it for their classroom.

Now, 10-year-old children generally cannot think of all four words by themselves that start with the same letter—they need help. We found that when girls worked in a group, they did no better than when they worked with only one other girl, even though there were three more girls present to come up with words. Boys, on the other hand, did much better in groups than when they worked with only one other boy [43].

Why were the boys so much more efficient when working together in larger groups? In their groups, the boys started by separating the letters, with each boy responsible for one problem. Although there was much laughter and jousting, most boys in the groups worked attentively. When a boy in a group got stuck and needed another word, he turned to his mates and yelled out his request for help, which was quickly responded to. Not so in the girls' groups. Girls working in groups spent a lot of time trying to figure out who in the group was a compatible partner. They focused their attention on this one girl, ignoring most of the rest. Because the lucky girls who found partners spent a lot of their time talking with their partners and ignoring everyone else, they didn't ask for help from any of the others. The girls managed to transform their group into several one-on-one pairs. When we measured how much time boys and girls actually spent on the task, the results of these differences became very clear. When working with only one other partner, girls worked harder than boys. But, when working in groups, boys worked harder than girls.

The magic of groups also works on adult males. For example, in a classic study, Piliavin and Martin [44] asked groups of four men or four women to discuss how best to resolve some moral issues: how to cope with a roommate who is using drugs, how to deal with a case of racial insensitivity, and what they thought about the case of a well-known criminal. Men's groups were clearly focused on the task. They spent most of their time asking for and requesting more information, and giving their opinions. In contrast, women's groups were more likely to behave politely to one another, tell one another that they agreed with their positions, laugh together, and recount unrelated stories. Women want to get to know their social partners: who they are, what they feel, what concerns they have [45–47]. This sex difference has been found repeatedly: Unrelated boys and men focus on a group task more than unrelated girls and women do [48].

By competing to have the most important information to provide, a man improves his whole group's performance. When its members provide their unique perspectives through disagreements and even open conflicts, the group receives a lot of helpful input. In contrast, by desiring to avoid conflicts, women often end up undermining the information available to the group.

In my interviews with boys in early and middle childhood, boys told me and my students that they prefer killing and capturing enemies to most other exciting masculine activities, such as putting out fires or going to the moon [49]. I once reported this to groups of young adult males, and they all agreed that killing is more exciting and pleasurable. When I asked them why, several volunteered that the excitement depends on the chase and successful capture of the enemy. Killing something lying quietly at one's feet is not fun. After some thought, these young men concluded that the best part of playing killing is when each man excels at his job as part of a team working to bring down the enemy. Ultimately, it is a group effort.

Subgroups and Hierarchies

A key attribute of any successful group is its flexibility. This is true for groups both in the military and in civilian life. Subgroups must be available to reinforce each other when necessary. Group members must reorganize rapidly, so that novel responses to unexpected conditions can be executed. One of the marks of an effective military commander is his ability to direct his troops in just this way. When necessary, troops are used to reinforce particularly weak positions, to apply specific expertise, or to reconnoiter separately.

Early in life, boys spontaneously respond to their local needs by forming loose, flexibly organized groups. Boys who are already functioning in a group are remarkably willing to integrate their group with other groups that they perceive as similar to their own, when this is useful for everyone.

A study in London, England, illustrates this clearly. Observers recorded the playground behaviors of 7- to 8-year-old children from a wide variety of ethnic and socioeconomic backgrounds [50]. Boys mostly interacted with a core group of friends. However, this core group also played with a second group of boys when it wanted to do something that required more boys. The resulting cluster of boys allowed larger-scale activities and sports to be accomplished. Not only that, but when even more players were required, the boys extended their interactions even further, so that the resulting group consisted of the core, their larger cluster, plus other boys with whom they normally played with even less often. In other words, by the beginning of middle childhood, boys naturally organize themselves in an increasingly inclusive fashion based on relative distance from a central group of boys. When an activity or task requires additional participants, the boys can call upon their larger network. A boy's largest network contained virtually all of his friends. We can picture the resulting organization in the following way in figure 4-2, which makes it clear just how flexibly boys can intuitively organize themselves.

What about the girls? Like boys, girls had a core group of friends with whom they spent most of their time. But unlike boys, girls did not add more members to this core. They almost never incorporated other groups of friends into joint activities but tended to remain in small, isolated, and separately interacting networks. Often, girls had best friends who were not

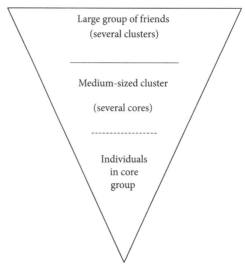

FIGURE 4-2. Organization of 7-Year-Old Boys' Interactions.

members of any of their social networks. The girl and her best friend simply spent time by themselves.

From childhood onward, males organize themselves into increasingly larger and more integrated networks. How effective is this? Here's a clue: The military employs the same horizontal structure evident in young boys' social networks. figure 4-3 shows how the US Army is organized. Amazingly, the US Army is organized the same way that 7-year-old boys are organized. While the army probably prides itself on having thought up such a clever arrangement, the boys thought of it first! Actually, this kind of organization has existed for millennia in various armies. Could boys have somehow learned about this? Well, since most boys couldn't describe exactly what they were doing, and certainly there is no evidence that they have much contact with military expertise in their early primary school years, this is very unlikely. Instead, boys and young men appear to have an innate, biological intuition about the best way to organize competitive groups. It is this intuition that gets translated into the most effective military structures that characterize both ancient and modern armies.

For a group to function properly and maintain its coherence over time, however, it must have a clear leadership structure. Horizontal groups in which everyone is equal cannot transform themselves or adapt to changes

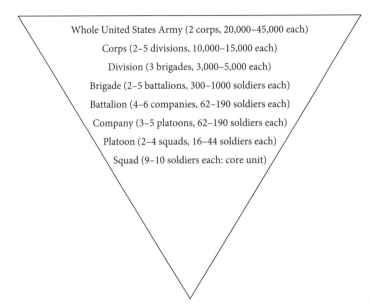

Whole United States Army (2 corps, 20,000–45,000 each)

Corps (2–5 divisions, 10,000–15,000 each)

Division (3 brigades, 3,000–5,000 each)

Brigade (2–5 battalions, 300–1000 soldiers each)

Battalion (4–6 companies, 62–190 soldiers each)

Company (3–5 platoons, 62–190 soldiers each)

Platoon (2–4 squads, 16–44 soldiers each)

Squad (9–10 soldiers each: core unit)

FIGURE 4-3. Organization of the US Army.

because all the members must agree on everything. In the few groups of girls and women I have observed, everyone sits in a circle, each one equal to the next—no subgroups, no division of labor, no leader, just one static entity focused on a particular topic.

Groups that need to respond efficiently to changing conditions require a leader and obedient followers. The leader must assign group members to appropriate and distinct roles, depending on the task at hand. The leader must select individuals to create subgroups. And all of these—the leader, the role assignments, and the subgroups—must be thrown out the window when the group confronts a different task: new leadership, new roles, new subgroups, new organization of the whole group.

The competitive instinct in males, however, provides a valuable avenue for leadership selection. Boys and men devote their precious time to figuring out who is best at the most varied and seemingly unimportant pursuits. Should a leader be required to accomplish that task, however, they all know immediately who the star is.

Not only do boys compete continually over everything, but they take turns trying on the role of leader. Boys' directives are harsh and leader-like compared with those of girls. In the following dialogue, some boys in early and middle childhood are practicing their leadership voices in Goodwin's participant-observation study of children in a Philadelphia neighborhood [51]:

> *Creating things with coat wire:*
> MALCOLM: *G*ive it to me man. Where's yours at. Throw that piece of shit *out*.
> CHOPPER: ((gives Malcolm his cut-off piece of hanger)) Now I got some of "em.
> TONY: Go downstairs. I don't care *what* you say you aren't—you ain't no
> good so go down*stairs*.
> (Goodwin, 1990, pp. 103–104)
> *Regarding a hanger which Ossie is cutting with pliers*
> MALCOLM: Put your foot on it Stupid. You afraid?
> *Regarding coat hangers*
> MALCOLM: Gimme the *th*ings *d*ummies. If you expect me to *b*end "em. Y'all
> act *d*umb.
> DOUGLAS: Get outa here *s*:ucker.
> CHOPPER: You sh:ut up you big lips.
> PETE: Dag. Stop boy. Should be mindin' your business.
> (Goodwin, 1990, pp. 84–85; : indicates sound is lengthened; bold italics
> indicates emphasis)

These boys are good friends. They wouldn't be after these interactions had they been girls.

Girls do not rehearse leadership skills with one another. They take great care not to overtly boss one another around. The exceptions are when they are engaging in imaginary play and pretending to be the mother or teacher, where the role (not the girl) demands leadership qualities. Then they can deny that they are bossing one another around. Instead, girls' speech contains many egalitarian words such as "let's" and questions rather than direct statements. Commands or insults are forbidden. Here are some girls who are collecting bottles in Goodwin's study:

> KERRY: Let's go. There may be some more on Sixty-Ninth Street.
> MARTHA: Come on. Let's turn back y'all so we can safe keep "em. Come one.
> Let's go get some.
> *Girls are looking for bottles.*
> MARTHA: Let's go around Subs and Suds.
> BEA: Let's ask her 'Do you have any bottles.'
> (Goodwin, 1990, p. 110)

The military is predicated on rank. Someone must lead the group, and the others must obey orders and follow. In the US Army, Air Force, and Marines, the highest-ranking individual is the general, followed by the lieutenant general, major general, brigadier general, colonel, lieutenant colonel, major, captain, first lieutenant, and second lieutenant. Clearly, rank has been well thought out. Even the smallest militia or informal group of guerrilla fighters, however, must have a commander. Groups that do not delegate the most skilled, experienced, socially astute individuals to those tasks they can best accomplish will lose to a more efficiently organized group. Thus, rank requires continual respect, challenge, and renegotiation. As the context changes, the composition of the group is modified, and individuals' relative positions must be realigned. Men excel at this, as do little boys. This suggests that boys have an innate desire to demonstrate their leadership abilities. They also are prepared, however, to defer to leaders with the right skills.

The classic study of the Eagles and the Rattlers at a summer camp in Oklahoma in the 1940s shows the relationship between a boy's particular skills, his leadership, and the functioning of the whole group [52]. At the beginning of the study, two groups of 11-year-old boys were brought to separate locations at the camp. One group named itself the Eagles, and the other group, the Rattlers. For the first week of camp, each group thought that they were alone. Individuals within each group competed and established a hierarchy based on personalities and expertise.

After a while, the researchers planted clues that another group was in the vicinity. Immediately, each group instigated preparations for competing against their adversary. To observe what happened, the counselors created formal competitions: baseball, tug-of-war, and tent pitching. The boys generated informal competitions, such as midnight cabin raids and flag burnings.

As the intergroup competitions began, each group flexibly adjusted its ranks to ensure that the experts led, so that their own group would be victorious. Regardless of who may have been respected most overall, when it came to playing baseball, the best baseball player directed the shots. Likewise, in a tug-of-war contest or during a midnight raid, those boys with the greatest skill in the particular pursuit led the way. You never know what skill might come in handy. For example, standing upright on a rolling board generates great adulation among the skateboarding set. I observed male adolescents when skateboarding and hip-hop first became popular. They each tried to outdo the other, and all of them respected the most skilled boy. Yes, boys and men relish internal competition and the status and roles it generates, but they flexibly allow another boy to hold higher status if that boy would improve the performance of their group vis-à-vis another group. The group takes precedence. If not, a less skilled boy would simply leave.

Continual competition across differing contexts requires different skill sets with lots of varying players. This translates into fluid hierarchies that reflect true expertise. Rank must be earned and maintained or it is lost. Constant competition maximizes group superiority as much as it exposes an individual's strengths and limits. For males, part of the nature of competition is that it is a never-ending process of selecting the most suitable man for the job. Occasionally, of course, tyrants who won't abdicate their leadership roles can ruin the whole enterprise, or the whole group is up to no good. But it is groups that make warfare possible.

Groups and Aggression

Boys and men compete and cooperate within their fluid groups. Simply learning that you are a member of one group, and not another, triggers an innate preference for your own group, and often a negative view of the other group. This happens even in 3-year-olds [53], and it happens across the world [54]. Everyone is both an individual and a member of all kinds of groups [55]. This is true for both men and women.

Complete strangers arbitrarily separated into two groups, on the most mundane basis, in full sight of one another, show this in-group preference. The person who demonstrated this best was Henri Tajfel [54], who assigned adults to one of two groups in completely arbitrary ways, such as which of two artists they liked better or whether they overestimated or underestimated the number of dots on a page. Then, Tajfel asked individuals to hand out money to all the other people. Amazingly, in these completely arbitrary groups of strangers, people gave more money to members of their own group than the other group. Introducing a competition accentuates this.

While men and women share this basic in-group bias, men have stronger views than women about the intrinsic inferiority of groups to which they do not belong [56, 57]. Sidanius and Pratto [56] report that across diverse cultures, and even in the most modern societies, men are more likely than women to agree with the following statements:

1. Some groups of people are simply inferior to other groups.

2. In getting what you want, it is sometimes necessary to use force against other groups.

3. It's OK if some groups have more of a chance in life than others.

4. To get ahead in life, it is sometimes necessary to step on other groups.

5. If certain groups stayed in their place, we would have fewer problems.

6. It's probably a good thing that certain groups are at the top and other groups are at the bottom.

This attitude is useful when entering a battle.

One final ingredient, though, is required to get from intergroup competition to war: large numbers. As a group gets bigger, its members are more likely to denigrate the other group, choose to compete, and launch aggressive attacks. This makes sense from the perspective of self-preservation.

As many people instinctively realize when stuck in a crowd, it is easy to lose your identity. The bigger the crowd, the lower your personal responsibility. Crowds activate the group brain within each person, and individual personality features disappear.

This can lead to groups wreaking havoc. Freud's book *Group Psychology and the Analysis of the Ego* [58] and an earlier book, Le Bon's *Psychologies des foules* or The Crowd [59], describe the inhibition of empathy, servility, conformity, fearlessness, and fear of exclusion that groups promote. These emotions can take over an individual's mind.

Size is critical. When two groups each composed of two, three, four, or five members faced off against one another, the level of confrontation became more aggressive as the numbers in competing groups increased [60]. The effect is stronger for men than for women. Some mechanism within the human male brain must look around, appraise the size of one's group, and decide that when there are more group members present, it is more likely that the group will prevail. Unfortunately, this brain appraisal doesn't always take into account the size of the potential enemy's group [61].

When large numbers of similar males in your group are nearby, enthusiasm over the desire to fight, to target the enemy, and to compete can overwhelm rational decision making. In real life, the probability of violence increases when a group is involved [62, 63]. One group of researchers even calculated that an individual was three times more likely to engage in violence as part of a gang versus on his own [64].

Boys' and men's groups are thus set up to propagate intergroup aggression. This is what can easily lead to war. All that's required is a cause. Studies of warfare show that the most common cause of war by far is a dispute over territory [65]. Why? Well, sometimes your group needs more territory, because you have run out of food or oil or diamonds. If another group has these resources on its territory, then the unfairness is difficult to swallow. Unfortunately, the other group feels the same way. Consequently, it is unacceptable for another group to hold territory that includes a mountaintop overlooking your group. You never know when they might run out of their own resources. You never know when they might decide that an expansion is in order. Finally, some territory seems to hold spiritual significance for some people. They believe that territory just belongs to them, and other claims have no merit.

War enriches and saves lives, of those in your own group. Thus, most people believe in war as a solution of last resort. They delegate young men to fight the wars, so that other group members can increase their chances of survival.

The Myth of Antisocial Males

One problem that can arise is that the ingredients of war, those behaviors that I believe have an innate basis because they appear in boys so early across diverse cultures, can backfire. They can be turned against one's own group. Boys, and in particular adolescent boys, are often sent to a clinic and diagnosed as "antisocial."

What clinicians mean by antisocial, of course, is that these boys and men are engaging in behaviors that are not beneficial within a peaceful, civilian society. Beating up others, destroying others' property, stealing, and killing are problems when they occur inside the community. They are not problems when they are directed against the enemy who is trying to obliterate your own group.

The antisocial label is particularly misleading when you consider that most of these behaviors are carried out by a group of like-minded individuals. "Antisocial" boys in these groups actually are highly social, even though their behavior is disruptive to the rest of the community. The more social they are, the more they wreak havoc. Larger groups are more violent.

In the United Kingdom, Anti-Social Behavior Orders can be issued to offenders who disrupt peaceful, civilian society. According to the Home Office of the United Kingdom [66]:

> Anti-social behaviour is virtually any intimidating or threatening activity that scares you or damages your quality of life.

Examples include:

- rowdy, noisy behaviour
- "yobbish" behaviour
- vandalism, graffiti and fly-posting
- dealing or buying drugs on the street
- fly-tipping rubbish
- aggressive begging
- street drinking
- setting off fireworks late at night

> Anti-social behaviour doesn't just make life unpleasant. It holds back the regeneration of disadvantaged areas and creates an environment where more serious crime can take hold.... It has a negative effect on many people's lives, and we are committed to tackling it.

Although this type of behavior is not even particularly aggressive, these kinds of thing are most often perpetrated by sociable groups of adolescent males. Having spent much time in the United Kingdom, I have found it quite unnerving when groups of males in restaurants, the underground metro, the bus, the streets, and so forth exhibit these behaviors. As non-violent as the United Kingdom is compared with the United States, it is not uncommon for loud, drunk groups of males to terrify their fellow citizens. Of course, when actual violence erupts, then arrests are made.

In the United States, of course, things are worse. Gang violence is rampant in some places. Gang violence is even more prevalent in South Africa.

In some countries, no government exists; every male seems to belong to a gang or group that can be quickly converted into an informal militia. The way the United States handles the same problem that the United Kingdom is trying to address is by diagnosing an individual (only adults can receive this diagnosis) with antisocial behavior disorder (ASBD). The *Diagnostic and Statistical Manual of Mental Disorders* [67] provides a definition of antisocial behavior disorder commonly found in men. "Examples include the behavior of professional thieves, racketeers, or dealers in illegal psychoactive substances" (DSM-IV-TR, p. 740). These are activities (some would call them jobs) that are best accomplished in groups.

In the United States, after childhood and before adulthood, individuals with severe behavioral problems are diagnosed simply as juvenile delinquents. The prevalence of these problems is far greater for males than for females, in the most extreme cases by a factor of 10 [63]. Juvenile delinquents generally congregate in gangs. Thrasher's [68] classic study of 1,313 Chicago gangs in the United States showed that only 6 of them were female. These gangs engaged in the behaviors described in the previous psychiatric diagnoses.

Although gangs can be fearsome units to people on the outside, they are organized in the same way as other male groups. Males in a gang value the same traits as all males—physical strength and emotional toughness, self-confidence, adherence to the rules of male peers, and expertise in a relevant domain. They may at times undermine the rules of civilian society, but they obey their own rules, and they exhibit behaviors necessary for a successful fighting force. Accounts of the few all-girl gangs that exist demonstrate that they are far less sociable and efficient than male gangs. Female gang members do not display the same camaraderie as male gang members. Anne Campbell [69] interviewed some of their members and concluded, "Almost every account stresses that membership of girls' gangs compared with boys' shows a higher turnover, a shorter life span, a failure of effective leadership and organization, and pervasively a sense of purposelessness" (Campbell, 1984, p. 32). Girls and young women fail to demonstrate good gang behavior [70].

Conclusion to Part I: The Unique Problems of Boys and Men

In these chapters, I have argued that human males spontaneously organize their social lives so that they are prepared to fight wars. I do not mean to say that all males want to go to war, or even that they are conscious of potentially wanting to do so. Many males will never fight a war. Further, the ingredients that facilitate successful warfare can be transferred to many other types of group activities.

I simply propose that these particular ingredients seem to fit very well the goal of warfare. Because these behavioral proclivities appear very early in life, across diverse cultures, and continue through adulthood, I believe they likely have an innate basis. Girls and women who live in the same societies do not share these particular traits. In other ways, the two sexes are very similar. Over thousands of years, these behaviors may have been selected because they led to greater victory against an enemy. Those who possessed these traits survived to pass on their genes to their sons; those without these traits did not.

Boys seem uniquely equipped with intuitive behavioral preferences that in the right circumstances allow them as young men to rapidly form an efficient fighting force with fellow male community members. These preferences start with young boys' enjoyment of play fighting, fascination with enemies, and desire to compete. These individual preferences draw young boys to other young boys who share the same basic tendencies. The most attractive male peers are those who are physically and emotionally tough and self-confident and who follow the rules and demonstrate valuable expertise. Together, these young boys organize themselves into a group.

From infancy onward, human males are attracted to groups. By 5 years of age, they consciously organize themselves into groups. As they grow older, they readily integrate their smaller groups into larger ones. The interconnectivity among boys both within their core groups and with neighboring groups facilitates creating ever larger groups. Individual boys and men work efficiently within a group, focusing on the task and taking advantage of the expertise that different group members provide. Thus, the large size of boys' groups of same-sex peers, the stimulation provided by so many potential and changing relationships, the role differentiation, interconnectivity, and task orientation motivate boys from early in life. This means that members with the most expertise and leadership abilities ideally can shift smoothly into different positions, and subgroups can materialize and vanish, depending on the task at hand. It also means that group members feel respected for their skills and, in turn, respect those in the group.

Once an individual identifies with a group, that group becomes preferred over other groups. If it grows large enough, the probability of aggression erupting increases. Males' easy denigration of other groups propels them further toward war. A shared preference for one country, one political party, one religion, one town, one team, or any other group, under the right conditions, joins male peers. Competition, particularly over territory, resources, or even ideologies, increases the probability that the spark can precipitate a conflagration. The enemy becomes defined.

The larger community of course determines whether war actually breaks out. It can encourage warfare by insisting that men wear identical face paint, a similar jacket and tie, the same camouflage, or simply matching stripes, stars, scars, numbers, or other markings. These superficial signs greatly heighten positive feelings toward other community members, increasing loyalty and solidarity [71]. Marching, singing, dancing, playing instruments, performing calisthenics, rowing, flying, speaking, sharing emotions, praying, drilling, or executing just about any bodily movement in unison further increases in-group feelings across the most diverse cultures [72, 73]. In contrast, physical and emotional closeness to maternal figures, wives, and children pulls boys and men away from one another and diminishes interest in warfare. When societal conditions are secure, men can invest in their families.

Warfare provides a context that combines better than most a man's predilections for play fighting, enemy targeting, and direct competition, along with his respect for physically tough and emotionally cool and confident fellow males who follow rules and demonstrate expertise—and work together well in a communal, hierarchical group ideally based on earned roles and rank. Fortunately, other contexts too provide these basic ingredients, such as companies, governments, and other institutions. Indeed, the metaphor of business as a form of warfare is very common.

As a result of these very basic tendencies, boys' and men's social lives are thoroughly intertwined. If you belong to a boys' group, your allies may not remember your birthday, but they know very well if you can run fast, hit well, respect rules, and make good decisions. They may be competitors, but when things get tough, they're also the ones who will protect you and root for you, and maybe even die for you.

Girls and women don't demonstrate these traits. Their favorite activities do not include play fighting, targeting the enemy, or competing against one another. They don't choose friends who are the physically and emotionally toughest and self-confident. Nor do they reify rules or revere expertise. Groups are simply many conglomerations of individuals. What, then, are female traits?

References

1. Wilson, E. O., *The social conquest of Earth*. 2012, New York: Norton.
2. Deaner, R. O., et al., A sex difference in the predisposition for physical competition: males play sports much more than females even in the contemporary US. PloS one, 2012. 7(11).
3. Tiger, L., *Men in groups*. 1969, New York: Random House..
4. Hawkes, K., The evolutionary basis of sex variations in the use of natural resources: Human examples. *Population and Environment*, 1996. 18(2): pp. 161–173.
5. Marlowe, F., *The Hadza: Hunter-gatherers of Tanzania*. 2010, Los Angeles: University of California Press.
6. Winstead, B., and J. Griffin, Friendship styles, in *Encyclopedia of women and gender*, J. Worell, Editor. 2001, Boston: Academic Press. pp. 481–492.
7. Darwin, C., *The descent of man and selection in relation to sex*. 1871, London: John Murray.
8. Bloom, P., The moral life of babies, *New York Times Magazine*. May 5, 2010
9. Hamlin, J. K., K. Wynn, and P. Bloom, Social evaluation by preverbal infants. *Nature*, 2007. 450(7169): pp. 557–559.
10. Fehr, E., and U. Fischbacher, The nature of human altruism. *Nature*, 2003. 425(6960): pp. 785–791.
11. Fehr, E., and U. Fischbacher, Third-party punishment and social norms. *Evolution and Human Behavior*, 2004. 25(2): pp. 63–87.
12. Marlowe, F. W., et al., The "spiteful" origins of human cooperation. *Proceedings of the Royal Society B: Biological Sciences*, 2011. 278(1715): pp. 2159.
13. Benenson, J. F., V. Duggan, and H. Markovits, Sex differences in infants' attraction to group versus individual stimuli. *Infant Behavior and Development*, 2004. 27(2): pp. 173–180.
14. Benenson, J. F., V. Duggan, and H. Markovits Explaining sex differences in infants' preferences for groups. *Infant Behavior and Development*, 2007. 30(4): pp. 587–595.
15. Alexander, G. M., T. Wilcox, and M. E. Farmer, Hormone-behavior associations in early infancy. *Hormones and Behavior*, 2009. 56(5): pp. 498–502.
16. Benenson, J. F., Greater preference among females than males for dyadic interaction in early childhood. *Child Development*, 1993. 64(2): pp. 544–555.
17. Fabes, R. A., C. L. Martin, and L. D. Hanish, Young children's play qualities in same, other, and mixed sex peer groups. *Child Development*, 2003. 74(3): pp. 921–932.
18. Belle, D., The impact of poverty on social networks and supports. *Marriage and Family Review*, 1983. 5(4): pp. 89–103
19. Benenson, J. F., N. H. Apostoleris, and J. Parnass, Age and sex differences in dyadic and group interaction. *Developmental Psychology*, 1997. 33(3): pp. 538–543.

20. Benenson, J. F., T. Morganstein, and R. Roy, Sex differences in children's investment in peers. *Human Nature*, 1998. 9(4): pp. 369–390.

21. Schneider, B. H., J. F. Benenson, M. Fulop and M. and M. Sandor, Cooperation and competition, in P. K. Smith and C. H. Hart (Editors), *The Wiley-Blackwell handbook of childhood social development.* 2010, New York: Wiley-Blackwell. pp. 472–490.

22. Craig, S., *Sports and games of the ancients.* 2002, Westport, CT: Greenwood.

23. Leibs, A., *Sports and games of the Renaissance.* Vol. 4. 2004, Westport, CT: Greenwood.

24. Mitani, J. C., D. P. Watts, and S. J. Amsler, Lethal intergroup aggression leads to territorial expansion in wild chimpanzees. *Current Biology*, 2010. 20(12): pp. R507–R508.

25. Boesch, C., Cooperative hunting roles among Tai chimpanzees. *Human Nature*, 2002. 13(1): pp. 27–46.

26. Freedman, D. G., *Human infancy: An evolutionary perspective.* New York. 1974, Hillsdale, NJ: Erlbaum.

27. Pitcher, E. G., and L. H. Schultz, *Boys and girls at play: The development of sex roles.* 1983, South Hadley, MA: Praeger.

28. Weisfeld, G., D. R. Omark, and C. Cronin, A longitudinal and cross-sectional study of dominance in boys, in *Dominance relations*, F. F. Strayer. D. R. Omark and D. G. Freedman, Editors. 1980, New York: Garland. pp. 205–216.

29. Fine, G. A., The natural history of preadolescent male friendship groups, in *Friendship and social relations in children*, H. C. Foot, A. J. Chapman, and J. R. Smith, Editors. 1980, Piscataway, NJ: Transaction. pp. 293–320.

30. Savin-Williams, R. C., Dominance hierarchies in groups of early adolescents. *Child Development*, 1979. 50(4): pp. 923–935.

31. Savin-Williams, R. C., Social interactions of adolescent females in natural groups, in *Friendship and social relations in children*, H. C. Foot, A. J. Chapman, and J. R. Smith, Editors. 1980, Piscataway, NJ: Transaction. pp. 343–364.

32. Benenson, J. F., Gender differences in social networks. *Journal of Early Adolescence*, 1990. 10(4): pp. 472–495.

33. Eder, D., and M. T. Hallinan, Sex differences in children's friendships. *American Sociological Review*, 1978. 43(2): pp. 237–250.

34. Parker, J. G., and J. Seal, Forming, losing, renewing, and replacing friendships: Applying temporal parameters to the assessment of children's friendship experiences. *Child Development*, 1996. 67(5): pp. 2248–2268.

35. Savin-Williams, R. C., Dominance hierarchies in groups of middle to late adolescent males. *Journal of Youth and Adolescence*, 1980. 9(1): pp. 75–85.

36. Douvan, E. A. M., and J. Adelson, *The adolescent experience.* 1966, New York: Wiley.

37. Gabriel, S., and W. L. Gardner, Are there "his" and "hers" types of interdependence? The implications of gender differences in collective versus

relational interdependence for affect, behavior, and cognition. *Journal of Personality and Social Psychology*, 1999. 77(3): pp. 642–655.

38. Markovits, H., J. Benenson, and S. White, Gender and priming differences in speed of processing of information relating to social structure. *Journal of Experimental Social Psychology*, 2006. 42(5): pp. 662–667.

39. Seeley, E. A., W. L. Gardner, G. Pennington, and S. Gabriel Circle of friends or members of a group? Sex differences in relational and collective attachment to groups. *Group Processes and Intergroup Relations*, 2003. 6(3): pp. 251–263.

40. Eaton, W. O., and L. R. Enns, Sex differences in human motor activity level. *Psychological Bulletin*, 1986. 100(1): pp. 19–28.

41. Kanter, R. M., *Men and women of the corporation*. 1977, New York: Basic Books

42. Kimura, D., *Sex and cognition*. 2000, Cambridge, MA: MIT Press.

43. Benenson, J. F., and A. Heath, Boys withdraw more in one-on-one interactions, whereas girls withdraw more in groups. *Developmental Psychology*, 2006. 42(2): pp. 272–282.

44. Piliavin, J. A., and R. R. Martin, The effects of the sex composition of groups on style of social interaction. *Sex Roles*, 1978. 4(2): pp. 281–296.

45. Bales, R. F., *Interaction process analysis: A method for the study of small groups*. 1950, Oxford: Addison-Wesley.

46. Borgatta, E. F., and R. F. Bales, The consistency of subject behavior and the reliability of scoring in interaction process analysis. *American Sociological Review*, 1953. 18(5): pp. 566–569.

47. Parsons, T., R. F. Bales, and E. A. Shils, *Working papers in the theory of action*. 1953, Westport, CT: Greenwood.

48. Aries, E., *Men and women in interaction: Reconsidering the differences*. 1996, New York: Oxford University Press.

49. Benenson, J. F., H. P. Carder, and S. J. Geib-Cole, The development of boys' preferential pleasure in physical aggression. *Aggressive Behavior*, 2008. 34(2): pp. 154–166.

50. Baines, E., and P. Blatchford, Sex differences in the structure and stability of children's playground social networks and their overlap with friendship relations. *British Journal of Developmental Psychology*, 2009. 27(3): pp. 743–760.

51. Goodwin, M. H., *He-said-she-said: Talk as social organization among black children*. 1990, Bloomington: Indiana University Press.

52. Sherif, M., Harvey, O. J., White, B. J., Hood, W. R., and Sherif, C. W. *Intergroup conflict and cooperation: The Robbers Cave experiment*. 1961, Norman, OK: University of Oklahoma.

53. Aboud, F. E., The formation of in-group favoritism and out-group prejudice in young children: Are they distinct attitudes? *Developmental Psychology*, 2003. 39(1): pp. 48–60.

54. Tajfel, H., *Human groups and social categories: Studies in social psychology*. 1981, New York: Cambridge University Press.

55. Ellemers, N., The group self. *Science*, 2012. 336(6083): pp. 848–852.
56. Sidanius, J., and F. Pratto, *Social dominance: An intergroup theory of social hierarchy and oppression*. 2001, New York: Cambridge University Press.
57. Van Vugt, M., D. De Cremer, and D. P. Janssen, Gender differences in cooperation and competition. *Psychological Science*, 2007. 18(1): pp. 19–23.
58. Freud, S., *Group psychology and the analysis of the ego*. 1921/1990, New York: Norton.
59. Le Bon, G., *The crowd*. 1895/1960, New York: Viking.
60. Schopler, J., et al., When groups are more competitive than individuals: The domain of the discontinuity effect. *Journal of Personality and Social Psychology*, 2001. 80(4): pp. 632–644.
61. Wrangham, R., Is military incompetence adaptive? *Evolution and Human Behavior*, 1999. 20(1): pp. 3–17.
62. Farrington, D. P., L. Berkowitz, and D. J. West, Differences between individual and group fights. *British Journal of Social Psychology*, 1982. 21(4): pp. 323–333.
63. Rutter, M., H. Giller, and A. Hagell, *Antisocial behavior by young people*. 1998, New York: Cambridge University Press.
64. Spergel, I. A., *Gang suppression and intervention: Problem and response: Research summary*. 1994, Washington, DC: US Department of Justice, Office of Justice Programs, Office of Juvenile Justice and Delinquency Prevention.
65. Frieden, J., D. Lake, and K. Schultz, *World politics*. 2010, New York: Norton.
66. UK. *What is ASB?* 2010; available from http://www.homeoffice.gov.uk/ukgwacnf.html?url=http://www.homeoffice.gov.uk/anti-social-behaviour/what-is-asb/index.html.
67. American Psychiatric Association, *Diagnostic and statistical manual of mental disorders*. 4th ed. Text Revision (TR). 2000, Arlington, VA: American Psychiatric Association.
68. Thrasher, F. M., and J. F. Shor, *The gang*. 1963, Chicago: University of Chicago Press.
69. Campbell, A., Girls' talk. *Criminal Justice and Behavior*, 1984. 11(2): pp. 139–156.
70. Campbell, A., *The girls in the gang*. 1992, Cambridge, MA: Blackwell.
71. Sosis, R., H. C. Kress, and J. S. Boster, Scars for war: Evaluating alternative signaling explanations for cross-cultural variance in ritual costs. *Evolution and Human Behavior*, 2007. 28(4): pp 234–247.
72. McNeill, W. H., *Keeping together in time: Dance and drill in human history*. 1997, Cambridge, MA: Harvard University Press.
73. Wiltermuth, S. S., and C. Heath, Synchrony and cooperation. *Psychological Science*, 2009. 20(1): pp. 1–5.

PART II

---◆---

Worriers

CHAPTER FIVE

—◆—

Protecting Herself: A Woman's Basic Instinct

SIGMUND FREUD TRIED TO EXPLAIN WOMEN'S DEVELOPMENT. He took his theory of male sexual development and reversed it [1, 2]. Although most of his patients were women, in the end Freud admitted he couldn't understand what women want [3].

Female anthropologists took another approach. They documented women's universally subordinate status and attributed it to women's role as caregivers [4].

The journalists Nicholas Kristof and Sherry WuDunn provide extreme examples of women's subordinate status today [5]. Traveling the world, they portray the dire fate of many girls and women. Compared with boys, from birth more girls are left to die (or aborted); fewer are treated for childhood illnesses; more are forced to work every waking hour to support their families; many are captured as child sex slaves and sold into early marriages or prostitution; and hundreds of thousands are murdered as adults for not behaving deferentially to their husbands or mothers-in-law, or not bearing children or sons. As Kristof and WuDunn emphasize, lower pay for equal work, lower-ranked corporate positions, and even the inability to vote or drive are small beans in comparison.

Why should being a caregiver give women lower status? Why haven't women gotten together and stopped their denigration and abuse?

The answer lies in women's focus: They must solve different problems than men. Women bear children. They must find some way to keep themselves and their children alive. They must ensure that their children live to reproduce. They must carefully select others who will provide critically important assistance. Even if a woman never has a child, she still sees the world through a different lens than a man.

My Body, Myself: The Greater Importance of a Woman

Men will put their lives on the line alongside unrelated men to defeat the enemy. Women can't afford to do the same. It's not that some women don't volunteer for the military, but this happens rarely.

I suggest that women's genes have programmed them to keep themselves, their children, and their closest relatives alive and healthy. Men love risks. Women avoid them whenever possible. The reason is simple.

An individual woman's survival and general good health are much more important than a man's. A man's basic contribution to procreation requires a few minutes of activity. Further, if he is not available, another man can easily substitute. Not so for a woman. A woman's body is responsible for successfully carrying the fetus to term, ensuring that it stays healthy. She then has to successfully give birth to her child, which is quite risky in humans. After birth, she has to feed her baby, which in most periods of history has meant producing enough milk to keep the baby alive and well nourished for a couple of years. After that, women also are primarily responsible for maintaining the health and security of their children for many more years, before their children are old enough to survive on their own. Even after their children give birth themselves, they often help out with their grandchildren.

Staying alive and healthy therefore is absolutely critical. Women must keep this problem, and its solutions, in their sights at all times throughout their lives, until they become very old. One mistake, and their health, and the health of all of their living and future children, is compromised. It's an enormous burden.

Boys and men needn't worry on a second-by-second basis. If a man manages to impregnate one or more women who will carefully take care of the resulting children, his genes will survive—even if he doesn't. He's free to fight, to go exploring, or take whatever risks might lead to finding more women to have sex with.

Women's and men's internal biology directly reflects this difference, but not as Freud described it [1]. A man's body contains a sperm-manufacturing plant that begins production at puberty and never stops until he dies. In fact, should a man crush one of his testicles, he can still produce sperm with the other one. He needn't even be alive. Shortly after a man dies, his sperm can be successfully retrieved. Sperm are relatively insignificant, and easy to make and implant. A woman's body has a lot more to do than a man's, and is correspondingly much more fragile. Right from the start, women put a lot more into reproduction than men. Female ova are much bigger and more difficult to produce than sperm. In fact, a girl's body arrives at birth with a limited number of ova. These can be permanently damaged at any point and can never be replaced. Her internal and external reproductive organs mature following a much more complex and fragile trajectory than that of a boy. Her fallopian tubes and womb must avoid being twisted or perforated. By puberty, a woman's hormones must begin cycling monthly in the right rhythm. Every month, female hormones must be released at the correct time, for the proper interval, at the right dosage in order for a woman to conceive. Puberty for girls involves enormous changes, including developing breasts that will become intermittent milk-producing glands and monthly menstruation, which in many traditional cultures frightens the toughest of men [6]. Boys at puberty do not suddenly grow two new appendages for everyone to notice; they do not experience weekly mood changes that repeat monthly for about 35 years. Even in simple societies with no birth control, a woman cycles between the stages of pregnancy, lactation, a few months of menstruation, miscarriages, pregnancy, lactation, and so forth. Constant change is inescapable. Life by definition is a roller coaster until menopause brings some stability, if a woman is lucky.

Compared with a man, a woman cannot produce as many children. Further, if she gives birth when she didn't want to, has a child with many problems, or finds herself in a difficult situation that's not conducive to having children, she cannot just walk away and hit the restart button. She's stuck, for life.

In addition, the sheer complexity of women's reproductive biology multiplies the effects of illness or poor health. Too much weight loss or gain, ingestion of toxic chemicals, overexertion, or high stress can all produce amenorrhea, or menstrual irregularities, and prevent a woman from conceiving [7]. Ill health itself prevents conception.

After conception, the hormonal environment must be maintained at acceptable levels, the fallopian tubes must remain unblocked, and the uterus, placenta, and umbilical cord remain healthy. Food eaten by the mother becomes the fetus's meal too. A mother's illnesses or ingestion of poisonous substances can harm the developing fetus. Delivering a baby is also potentially dangerous, for both the baby and the mother. Complications during delivery from vaginal obstructions or maternal illness can produce miscarriages or stillborn babies. Women die in childbirth, even with modern technology, with up to 1 out of 10,000 women currently dying due to pregnancy-related causes in the United States [8]. In developing countries, as many as 1 out of 15 mothers die this way, with 500,000 deaths each year [9, 10].

A mother's ill health can also result in premature or low-birth-weight infants whose chances of surviving as healthy babies are relatively poorer. After delivery, for a woman to feed her child, her breasts must begin to produce milk. It doesn't matter if her breasts ache, swell up, or develop abscesses. Her baby must drink. Then, for a mother to produce a second child, she must search for food and mash it so it is suitable for her first child. Then, her breasts must slowly cease to produce milk so she will return to ovulating, allowing the whole process to begin all over again.

A mother's illness or severe accident during gestation will often kill or damage a fetus. Her illness or death during lactation, the early years of the child's life, or even when the child is older in many cultures often means the death of her child. Even in modern cultures, a mother's death decreases the child's opportunity to thrive. It takes an unusual father or substitute mother to replace a child's mother completely.

It is worth repeating just how critical a mother's survival has always been. Theoretically, the baby of a dead mother might be cared for by another woman. But this would have involved someone giving her own supply of milk destined for her own biological child to another child, which was never very likely [11]. Even a woman's sister wouldn't want to divert milk destined for own children to her niece or nephew. It takes a lot of calories to produce breast milk. It saps a mother's energy. Why would a mother endanger her own children? Historically, most unweaned children without living mothers died. Even weaned children without a living mother were more likely to die [12, 13]. This does not even consider the critical support and care that a mother provides to her older children as they grow up and must learn how to survive on their own and make social connections so they too will be able to reproduce. If they don't, then a mother hasn't done her job.

Genes care most about the survival of children, so they will have a new body in which to reside. When a woman becomes ill or dies young, it is not only her own personal survival that is at risk but that of all of her living children and her potential children. If this happens, then the woman's genes disappear.

This is much less so for men. Women who did not worry about their health and survival produced fewer children. A woman could not have sex with an attractive man, go off to help conquer a kingdom or build a corporation, and return to see her child for the first time, well taken care of by her attentive mate. Her genes simply would not be passed on. No one else is available to gestate, breastfeed, and raise a woman's children. Thus, women who produced and successfully cared for children were those who were intuitively very careful about their own health and survival and maintaining proximity to their children. These basic intuitions influence a woman's thoughts and behaviors. With few exceptions, even those women who choose not to have children nonetheless have genes that prepare them to have children.

Consider figure 5-1 [14], which shows the probability that people had of surviving to any given age over much of human history. For most of this time, more than 40% of all children did not survive past the first couple of years of life, and half died before they turned 15 [1a]. In fact, for most of human history, the average life expectancy was about 25 years. It is only very recently that this has changed, although even now in underdeveloped countries, as many as 10% of infants die before their first birthday.

Although modern life has greatly improved health and longevity, the genes' instructions that underpin our basic reactions were generated much earlier. Further, babies and young children are still more vulnerable to death, even today. Because women bear sole responsibility for the survival of children, particularly until the children are weaned, they indeed have a great deal to worry about. When a mother with many resources raising seemingly perfect children becomes obsessed with seemingly trivial issues such how strict to be, what type of schedule is best, who has the most friends, what are the best colors for clothes, and so forth, it can seem ridiculous. I believe, however, that women are guided by genes to worry, even when there is nothing serious to worry about. It does not feel comfortable to admit that everything is okay, unless a major disaster has just been averted. The push to worry is strong and persistent. Anxiety is part of being a woman.

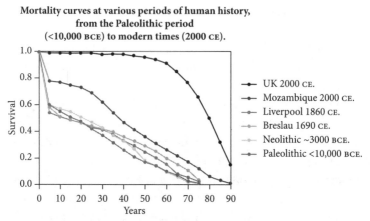

Mortality curves at various periods of human history, from the Paleolithic period (<10,000 BCE) to modern times (2000 CE).

UK 2000 CE.
Mozambique 2000 CE.
Liverpool 1860 CE.
Breslau 1690 CE.
Neolithic ~3000 BCE.
Paleolithic <10,000 BCE.

Casanova J, Abel L J Exp Med 2005;202:197-201

FIGURE 5-1. Figure 1. Mortality curves at various periods of human history, from the Palaeolithic period (<10,000 BCE) to modern times (2000 CE). Contemporary data for the UK and Mozambique are available from the WHO site (www.who.int/topics/global_burden_of_disease). Older data were obtained from the book by John Cairns (2). Life tables for the Palaeolithic and Neolithic periods are based on skeleton examinations, assuming that 60% of newborn infants survived to the age of five, because few very young skeletons were found in the burial grounds. The gradual adjustment of the immune system by natural selection did not increase life expectancy until the end of the 19th century, due to the coevolution of microorganisms and the emergence of new infectious threats. Thus, the increase in life expectancy in the 20th century does not reflect the sudden and global natural selection of high-quality immune genes. The area between the four ancient curves and the curve for the UK in 2000 corresponds to 65% of individuals currently alive. Most of these individuals have retained specific immunodeficiencies masked by medical progress.

Reprinted with permission ©2005 Rockefeller University Press. Originally published in the *Journal of Experimental Medicine*. 202:197–201. doi: 10.1084/jem.20050854.

What are the specific worries of a woman? Women think about themselves on a second-by-second basis: "Why do my eyes look funny today?" "How come I don't feel well?" "Am I sick?" "Why did I cancel my doctor's appointment?" "Why am I always last?" "Why am I always so tired?" "How come she smiled at me in such a crooked way?" "Who does she think she is, doing that without asking me first?" "Why does he look at me like I'm an idiot?" A woman appears to keep a running dialogue with herself about her own state. Men don't seem to do this. Many researchers believe that the self-focus of women can have dire consequences, accentuating or even causing mood disorders such as depression or anxiety [15, 16]. While this running dialogue may appear to be counterproductive, it likely reflects a woman's basic biological interest in keeping herself alive and healthy. It is likely that anxiety precedes as well as follows these thoughts.

In particular, women are far more worried than men about their bodies [17, 18]. For example, when more than 10,000 Finnish women and men of all ages were asked how satisfied they were with their bodies, the results were striking: Women were much less satisfied than men with every single aspect of their bodies [19].

Women of course worry about their bodies for more than one reason. One is health; another is attractiveness to men. No one questions that women use their bodies to compete for men, and the resources that come along with a man. Many men are more than willing to share their resources with a physically beautiful woman [20]. Thus, women are very attentive to their body's attractiveness to men. They use chemicals to make their skin and hair look better; they wear jewelry and costly clothes; they are willing to use surgery to look better. A woman's desire to be attractive to men, however, relates to her health: A man's wealth can improve a woman's health [21]. How she protects her health is what's most important. A woman's best friend is fear.

Women's Fear

Fear is a girl's suit of armor. Girls exhibit more fear than boys from birth. In a newborn nursery, when another infant starts crying, a newborn girl is much more likely than a boy to start crying too. Interestingly, this works only for real crying but not for other loud noises [22, 23]. Some people think that infant girls simply have more empathy. That is one possibility. I think it's more probable that these baby girls interpret crying as an alarm signal. When an alarm sounds, girls are more anxious to get away.

In fact, in the first few months of life, mothers report that their female infants show fear much earlier than their male infants [24]. Could it be that female babies are just less positive? Quite the contrary. Female babies generally smile more and make more babbling sounds than male babies [25]. Despite this, when babies see strange objects or unfamiliar adults, girls smile less and make fewer sounds than boys. Clearly, female babies are already more wary of unfamiliar things than male babies, who enjoy new and strange things.

This pattern continues with increasing age. By the time daughters are 1 year old, mothers rate them as being shyer than sons [26]. By 13 months, female infants in an unfamiliar room will remain closer to their mothers than boys will [27]. Likewise, in a strange laboratory, female toddlers show more fear than male toddlers [28]. Further, by 14 months, females become more distressed than males when they see an adult in pain [29]. Clinicians also report that young girls are more afraid of things than young boys [30]. Unless they live in an environment that's so dangerous that everybody is terrified, girls express more fear than boys do at all ages [31, 32]. In childhood, girls are twice as likely as boys to be diagnosed with anxiety disorders [33].

This begins so early that it seems very likely that it is innate. If you need to stay alive to make sure that your children do, one of the consequences is staying attuned at all times to potential danger. You can't afford to slip up. Little girls are already helping to keep their genes alive.

So it is not a surprise that those young girls who spend more of their time caring for dolls and playing house have the highest levels of fear and anxiety [34]. They should. In many cultures, it is not just play. Young girls in early childhood begin caring for children and helping their mothers with household duties [35]. While mothers almost never abandon their children [36], it is hard for a mother to keep track of older children and also care for a baby. A careful little girl can be a wonderful child minder [37]. She allows her mother to take better care of all of her children by sharing the workload.

Why just girls? Mothers report that they ask their sons to help too, but it doesn't work as well [35]. Even when a little boy might be willing to help, who's more likely to accidently drop the baby? Not surprisingly, girls are the favored choice of mothers everywhere. Studies of mothers in many different agricultural societies show that although mothers do ask both their daughters and their sons to help care for babies, the sons are far less reliable. Girls simply pay more attention, while boys play with one another.

Here is an example of the care a young girl takes with her baby sister in a village in the Philippines:

> Yuriko (Tairan girl, age 6) carries her sister on her back and walks around a banyan tree where a group of girls are playing. Although the baby is quiet, Yuriko lightly pats the baby's behind to pacify her. The girls by the tree are all looking at a book, but Yuriko merely looks in their direction

and continues to walk around. The baby coughs a little, and Yuriko says, "Don't cry," and hops up and down in order to calm the infant. She walks back with rapid steps. As she walks up the road past the store, Yuriko hums to herself and taps the baby's behind again. On the way she meets Kazufumi (boy, age 5), who is also carrying a baby on his back. His baby is crying. "Attend to the child," she shouts as he passes by. Kazufumi walks on, without looking back (Maretzki and Maretzki, field observations, 1955). (Whiting & Edwards, 1988, pp. 164–165)

Contrast the care and attention bestowed by Yuriko with that of Romulo, a 7-year-old boy from the same village:

Romulu (boy, age 7) stands with Jimmy, the baby. He carries him to the middle of the yard. He stands Jimmy up by holding one of his hands and saying, "Stand. Balance yourself." Jimmy stands for a moment then squats. Romulu again helps Jimmy stand, holding his hands and saying "Stand, stand! You stand!" Romulu slowly lets go of Jimmy's hand and backs off laughing as Jimmy stands alone staring at him. Romulu says, "Stand and do not open your eyes wide." (Whiting & Edwards, 1988, p. 180)

The tone is totally different.

For 30 years, I have conducted observations and experiments with children. My students and I always observe the same sex difference. Regardless of what we are doing, girls are more wary of us than are boys. Even though I was once a girl too, as were many of my students, girls hesitate more than boys to approach us, to join our studies, and to interact with us. They need to be sure that we won't hurt them.

Fear ensures that a girl or woman will pay close attention to her own and her children's health and safety. Women exhibit more and stronger fears than men do about all kinds of things: social fears, fear of large spaces, fear of injury and death, and fear of harmless animals [38]. Furthermore, women pick up on others' fears. Around the world, women identify fear expressed by others faster than they recognize any other emotion [39, 40]. If the fear is expressed by her child, a mother can respond as quickly as possible. If a woman observes fear in another person, she can escape quickly. This can be frustrating to men, who are prepared to coolly hang around to find out whether the danger is real or not. Of course, some of these men will die while checking out the situation. No problem, their wives will take care of their children.

The physiology of fear is well known [41]. It takes less than a second for adrenaline to begin pumping in response to a fearful situation. In contrast, it takes hours for the response to diminish. When someone's life is threatened, it can take years for fear to disappear. This is the case with post-traumatic stress disorder (PTSD). Despite highly publicized reports of PTSD in men returning from battle, PTSD is more than twice as common in women as in men [42, 43]. The same traumatic event, whether it's a car accident or physical abuse or a battle, causes more extreme stress in women than in men and takes longer to disappear. Thus, the physiological and subjective consequences of trauma, whether minor or catastrophic, are greater for women. Negative life events, even minor ones, are more traumatic for females than for males of all ages. This is true from childhood through adulthood and has been reported in more than 100 studies with tens of thousands of people for both minor and major stressors [44]. At the extreme, a woman's emotions are strongest when her life is in danger. I suggest that this allows her to never forget that she almost died early, so that she will avoid that situation for the remainder of her life.

Women more generally exhibit all forms of emotion faster and with greater intensity than men, except possibly for anger [45]. This again makes sense from a biological perspective. Strong emotions focus attention on one's immediate environment and in the short run may allow a woman to keep herself and her children alive.

Extreme danger of course merits extreme forms of emotion. One of the largest sex differences in emotions is in rates of anxiety and depression. As soon as puberty starts, anxiety and depression increase twice as much for girls as for boys [46–49]. No one has ever been able to find any convincing reasons for this. Why should girls become more anxious? I suggest that when girls become capable of bearing children, they need to be even more careful. Anxiety and depression keep one close to home and children, focused on details, expecting and preparing for disaster. In fact, girls and women become more anxious and depressed not only during puberty but also during other periods of strong hormonal changes, such as the time just preceding menstruation and shortly after giving birth. What better time to be slower, more alert, and, especially, more cautious than when one may be conceiving or caring for a baby?

Anxiety produces feelings of fear, worry, and dread. Women have much higher rates of specific forms of anxiety, or phobias, than men. Most of these forms of anxiety seem particularly useless in modern societies. Why should women develop these phobias? Again, I would suggest that many of these phobias would have been highly protective in the more dangerous environments that humans have mostly lived in. As just one example, women are more likely to have agoraphobia, or fear of crowded spaces. This would have kept them away from dangerous places full of predators and potentially aggressive males. As another example, women develop social phobias more often than men. Why should this happen? For the same reason: Other people can pose a threat to a woman and her child, and keeping away from them is safer.

Fear and anxiety can protect women and their children from danger. Too much, however, can keep women from functioning properly. The World Health Organization (WHO) reports that rates of anxiety disorders and depression are more than twice as high for women as for men across diverse cultures [16, 50, 51]. However, despite this, most women do not develop disabling phobias, chronic anxiety, or depression. Thus women's biology keeps them in a state of high alert, but mostly not to the point where it becomes counterproductive.

Further support for the notion that fear and anxiety and even depression may be helpful to a woman comes from age changes in these emotions. While fear and anxiety are clearly protective when children are around, they are no longer of any real use afterward. In most times and places in the world, women have had their first baby by 25 years of age. Most women who develop serious anxiety do so by exactly this age. Furthermore, anxiety and depression become much less severe as women pass their reproductive years, just when these emotions are no longer needed [52]. If a woman lives long enough, the end of her reproductive years therefore brings some serenity. Across widely diverse cultures, the ratio of positive to negative emotions increases with age at least until age 80 [52].

Simply being more anxious and fearful is not as effective as having something specific to be anxious and fearful about, however. People die of a variety of causes. Accidents are the most avoidable. Some, such as disease and illness, could not be controlled until fairly recently in human history. Physical aggression and social conflicts, too, are potentially avoidable. All are threatening to women and their children. Women worry about all of them.

Accidents

A woman simply cannot jeopardize her health by having an accident. Some accidents simply can't be avoided, but many can. Avoiding dangerous situations is the best way to prevent an accident. From a woman's perspective, men do a lot of stupid things that lead to accidents. Women avoid those situations. Reaching to pet a poisonous snake, managing to be bitten a second time by a different poisonous snake, climbing on a rooftop to chase a lost object, eating food off the floor, jumping out of a tree—the list could go on forever. Most women would never do these things. A vivid illustration of this occurred at a conference at Harvard University on the role of evolutionary biology in enjoyment of video games, which was attended by roughly equal numbers of men and women. One panelist asked the conference attendees to raise their hand if they had ever climbed onto the roof of a house. About 60 of the approximately 100 people present raised their hands. Then, the panelist asked only the women who had done this to keep their hands up. Two hands remained raised.

This sex difference, of course, is not a secret. Insurance companies know this well. A man is more than twice as likely as a woman to have a car accident and almost three times more likely to have two car accidents [53]. Even when they are not driving, men are just more careless; twice as many men are killed simply crossing the street in the United States [54] and other countries [55, 56]. You don't need to be very perceptive to figure out who would be more likely to take the following risks: volunteer for medical research, expose themselves to potentially toxic chemicals, engage in unsafe sexual practices, swim far away from shore, explore an unknown locale, or chase a bear out of a campground [57]. Girls and women just don't engage in such stupid behavior—stupid, that is, if one is really concerned about staying alive.

Somehow, even very young girls' intuitions tell them that walking along a cliff, playing with a sharp object, teasing a wild animal, or getting too close to a fire can potentially harm their bodies and must be carefully avoided. One area of northwestern China tabulated hospitalizations due to unintentional accidents among children younger than 14 months. Even as infants, the number of girls who were involved in accidents was less than one-third the number of boys [58]. Even infant girls know how to avoid precarious situations.

As children grow older, girls continue to steer clear of risky situations. In 150 studies of risk-taking in 3-year-olds through adults, girls and women took fewer risks than boys and men at every age [59]. Whether the activity involves playing in the street, riding an animal, climbing a steep hill, guessing an answer to a test, gambling, or driving fast, to name a few, girls and women simply take fewer risks. The researchers who looked at all these studies further concluded that girls and women didn't take risks, even when it might have been a good idea, for example, to take a chance on an intellectual idea. In marked contrast, boys and men took risks, even when it was clear that it was a very bad idea. Throughout their lives, girls and women take better care than men to avoid accidents, whereas boys and men sometimes almost seem to seek them out.

Interestingly, it's not only girls themselves who worry more. Both mothers and fathers perceive their infant daughters as more vulnerable than their sons. Golombok and Fivush in their textbook on gender [60] reported that "female infants are perceived as softer and more vulnerable than male infants..., and this despite the biological evidence that females are physically hardier than males from conception through old age" (Golombok & Fivush, 1994, p. 22). It's worth repeating this last part. In actual fact, girls and women are healthier and less prone to disease and illness than men.

Why, then, do parents think they're not? Even new parents intuitively must know that girls must be healthier than boys to successfully solve the problems in life that are women's specialty. Parents may know at some level that a baby girl contains all the ova she ever will have for producing children. They may realize subconsciously that her anatomy is more complicated and fragile. Or they may understand that a girl will spend a much greater portion of her life bearing the responsibility for keeping their genes alive and passing them on to the next generation. A girl who is sick will have a difficult time producing and raising a child. An unhealthy boy still can reproduce.

Illness and Disease

Women worry a lot about illness and disease. It is worth putting this into a modern perspective. As anybody who has visited a retirement community can immediately see, women in developed countries live much longer than men. In fact, on average women live about 7 years longer [61, 62]. Even at birth, female fetuses have a higher survival rate than male fetuses [63]. More to the point, at any given age, modern women die much less often from disease and illness than males. If anyone should worry about disease and illness, it should be men. Yet men are too worried about who will win the next football game to be very concerned about getting sick. It is women who worry about health. They even worry about men's health [64]. Most of all, they worry about their children's health.

Once again, this is not really a secret. Look at women's magazines. After the articles about attracting a wealthy man, there are articles about how to stay healthy and which diseases are most worrisome. Modern technology has produced an endless supply of new and unusual health worries. For example, every modern woman I know lives in fear of developing ovarian cancer. This is a perfect disease to worry about because it has no clear symptoms, other than some stomach pain. Who hasn't had stomach pain? At the first sign of anything not quite right, modern women become convinced that they have ovarian cancer. The only foolproof test requires surgery to inspect the ovaries. Despite the fact that very few women actually die of ovarian cancer, a great many end up requesting diagnostic tests, which themselves are potentially dangerous.

One of the clearest signs of women's worrying is their use of health care. Where health care is available, women use it much more often than men do. A good example of this comes from a detailed study of health care use in the Canadian province of Manitoba. Because Canada provides a single-payer health plan, health care is provided to any individual legally living in Canada, and every visit is recorded [65]. What these records show is very revealing. Excluding visits due to pregnancy and childbirth, during their reproductive years, women visit the doctor much more often than men. Females and males use health care services fairly equally, however, before puberty and after about 50 years of age.

The same thing was found in a recent yearlong study in Ohio. Of all visits to doctors' offices, 64% of the patients were women [66]. These women reported being in poorer health and having a greater history of anxiety and depression than the men. Not only that, but women were much more likely than men to visit the doctor when there was nothing wrong with them. Further, when they were at the doctor, women asked more questions, wanted more preventive screening, and requested more counseling. Finally, despite the fact that more men were suffering from chronic diseases, more women left the doctor's office with a drug prescription.

Across a number of countries, women report they are sicker and more disabled than men. They request more medical help from doctors at every age. The only exception is that men are more likely to show up in the emergency room, usually because whatever is wrong is seriously wrong, like being bitten by a snake or falling off a roof, or failing to take seriously symptoms of a potentially fatal condition [67].

This begins early. Even in childhood, around the world, girls are more afraid than boys of death and dying. Girls are more afraid of being sick too. When Canadian 10- and 15-year-olds were asked how worried they were about their health as indicated by agreeing with statements such as "When I notice that my heart is beating fast, I worry that there might be something wrong with me," the girls were much more afraid than the boys [68].

The positive aspects of worrying about health are evident, even in modern societies. For example, women are more concerned than men about preventive health measures. This difference is particularly strong in younger women [69], but it persists at all ages [67, 70, 71]. Women are also more likely than men to follow a doctor's advice about diet or exercise [72]. Likewise, at least in the United States, where obtaining health care can be a problem, women spend more time than men thinking about health care coverage [73]. Further, more American women than men have supplemental medical insurance plans and consider them to be important [74]. The preoccupation of women with health care is true across the world. A particularly curious manifestation of this happens in some poor, polygynous societies. When a man brings a younger co-wife into a household, usually, and understandably, the younger and older co-wives end up in conflict. One of the only ways that a bond between them can be formed is if the younger woman agrees to provide medical care for the older one as she ages [75]. The younger wife becomes the older one's health insurance policy. In turn, the older wife tolerates her younger interloper.

In the distant past, people died overwhelmingly from infectious diseases [14]. They had no scientific understanding of how these diseases were transmitted. Over thousands of years, women developed instincts to spot illness and disease faster. Early detection is a good strategy. It might allow avoidance or faster remedies that could save their own, or a family member's, life. This begins in childhood and occurs across the world.

Despite living longer and being mostly protected from the kinds of diseases that affect women all over the developing world [5], even today women in modern societies remain much more worried about illness and disease than men. Women do this because their genes have programmed them to worry about illness and disease. Those who worried more got sick less, and they passed their worry genes onto their daughters.

Of course, there are other ways to die early too. Not getting along with others in the community is a big one, especially for women who become caregivers. Social conflict can lead to murder. More commonly, it can lead to social exclusion. A woman who has to raise multiple children needs the assistance of others. She simply cannot afford not to get along with others.

Femininity is often defined using the Bem Sex-Role Inventory [76]. Accordingly, being feminine means being affectionate and compassionate, not using harsh language, being sensitive, soft-spoken, sympathetic, and shy, to name a few critical characteristics. Femininity according to Bem's scale is much admired in women around the world. I would argue that femininity means avoiding social conflicts. By being nice, a woman can achieve greater protection for herself and her children. All she must do is follow a few rules: Avoid physical aggression, be on the lookout for more subtle forms of conflict, and, should conflict threaten, try to smooth it out as soon as possible.

Social Conflict

No Physical Aggression

If a woman punches someone in the face, the victim is unlikely to just stand there. Retaliation is likely—and dangerous. Anne Campbell [77] brilliantly described this in an article titled "Staying Alive," her explanation of what women need to do to ensure that their genes are passed on to the next generation. For a woman, physical fighting makes no biological sense. Even if a woman wins a fight, she might be damaged enough to reduce her chances of producing and caring for her children.

While men easily lose their tempers and enter into fights, the opposite is true for women. This is not to suggest that women do not get angry and upset. Around the world, women get at least as angry as men [78]. But expressing anger can be dangerous. A woman could easily be beaten up or killed, or her children could be threatened. So women must struggle hard to control their feelings.

Exploding in anger, whether verbal or physical, means failure for a woman. Biologically, it should. She has invited retaliation, which could be deadly. As Anne Campbell [79], who has studied women's anger more thoroughly than anyone, puts it:

> When the lid blows off a woman's anger, there is a tremendous fury waiting to boil over. Perhaps that should not be surprising, given the years of slow simmering that have gone before.... Women explode as a means of release, and it can take the form of anything from throwing pans or kettles to kicking or biting.... A woman fights to show that self-control has lost

the battle with anger. For her, physical aggression is about losing, not winning. (Campbell, 1993, p. 50)

It is thus no accident that direct physical and even direct verbal aggression are extremely rare in females. Even when women do get into fights, they are much more restrained than men [77]. This is such a basic difference that it is easily seen even in very young children. Male toddlers hit, punch, bite, pull, push, kick, and trip others much more than female toddlers do [80]. This difference continues throughout life [81–83]. By adolescence and young adulthood, in the most extreme case, more than 90% of all murders are committed by males, in every country that has ever been studied [84].

For a girl or woman to become angry and physically aggressive, she needs to have a powerful reason. For example, women who have children that they cannot support sometimes engage in fighting. This might allow them to compete for the attention of a man who might provide food and other resources. Fighting might allow a desperate woman to steal someone's food. Even so, girls and women almost never engage in the more dangerous forms of physical aggression [80, 85].

In her review of 317 societies around the world, Burbank [86] concluded that by and large, when women behave aggressively they do so for good reasons. The fidelity of a woman's husband; the condition and quality of her crops, implements, and fields; the health and well-being of her children; the abundance of her food; and the manner in which others treat her are all factors with great potential relevance for the quality of her life.... [However,] female aggression involves little injury, even when it is physical. (Burbank, 1987, p. 95)

Economically poor women in modern societies fight for similar causes. They especially fight over men and the money the men can provide [85].

When women do fight, they fight other women twice as often as they fight men [86]. Fighting a man is really dangerous, because men are bigger and stronger and could inflict more severe injuries.

One of the most frequent situations in which women physically fight each other is in the extreme case of polygynous societies where co-wives share a husband. Here women are stuck competing for their husband's attention in order to get food and resources for themselves and their children. Any additional co-wife threatens to reduce the amount of a common husband's resources that a woman and her children will receive. This threatens the survival and well-being of an older wife and her children. Not surprisingly, women in this situation have been universally found to be the most aggressive and the most physically violent toward one another [75, 86].

Even when a woman attacks a co-wife, however, she usually does so indirectly. A woman will first attack her co-wife's property, destroying her cooking pots damaging her house or uprooting her garden. This is preferably done when the co-wife is absent, in order to minimize retaliation.

Only if it is absolutely necessary will a woman use direct physical violence against her co-wife. In these instances, the goal is simply to reduce a rival's attractiveness to their joint husband. Beating a co-wife, wrestling with her, pouring pepper into her eyes, scratching her face, pulling her hair, or poisoning her children can be effective [86]. A battered face or a poisoned child makes a rival co-wife less attractive. Nonetheless, these are risky maneuvers, to be avoided as much as possible.

Women avoid physical aggression, except sometimes with family members. Families serve to ensure that women can keep their children alive and well. Thus, according to the "valuable relationships hypothesis" [87], when something is off between a woman and a member of her family, sometimes extreme means must be employed.

In modern societies where women have some degree of legal protection against retaliatory violence, wives may occasionally punch out their husbands as much as or more than vice versa [88]. Should a physical fight erupt, husbands of course still inflict more damage on their wives than vice versa, so this is not a wise strategy on a woman's part. Most husbands still are bigger and stronger than their wives. But a misbehaving husband presents a serious problem for a woman who depends on him to keep her and her children alive.

Likewise, sometimes a woman hits her children as well. As paradoxical as this seems, a woman must care for her children to the best of her ability. Sometimes, she has little ability. Other times, her children do not cooperate. Surprisingly, more than 90% of children in America are physically punished sometimes, and mothers inflict this punishment as much as or more than their husbands do. The same occurs in Europe [89, 90]. Some studies even find that mothers physically abuse their children more than fathers do. This happens much more often when the mothers have little money and no support from husbands or other family members. It happens much less often after children turn 13 years and become adolescents who could retaliate and inflict injury on their mothers [91]. Physical punishment of children varies from society to society around the world and seems to depend on the society's norms [92]. When it happens, though, mothers are the perpetrators as least as much as fathers. Little children cannot hit back. They do not endanger a mother's well-being. Very rarely does a mother endanger her child's well-being either.

Most women avoid physical conflicts whenever possible. They also avoid nonphysical conflicts. How? Women are highly vigilant. They keep their eyes and ears alert to any sign of potential conflict that could bring danger to themselves or their children. Should a conflict appear on the horizon, women try hard to mitigate its impact through cordial behavior, even with their worst enemies.

Getting along with others is essential for a woman to procure the resources and status that will keep her and her children alive and well, and ideally thriving. Engaging in peaceful interactions with others therefore greatly helps to prevent dying early [93]. Thus, it is an essential strategy for women. A woman must concentrate on identifying, then avoiding or smoothing over any conflicts that might arise.

Keep Your Eye on Others
One way to do this is to be highly vigilant. Women keep an eye on others more than men do. They figure out faster and more accurately what others' intentions are. They do so even without language.

One of the first times that you notice this is when women meet. Put two women together, and they spend a lot of time looking into one another's eyes. Put two males together, and they often will assume parallel positions, as if riding side by side in a car. They often completely avoid eye contact [94].

A woman learns a lot about another person's emotions or intentions from gazing into her, or his, eyes. As Confucius proclaimed, "Look into a person's pupils, he cannot hide himself" (Grumet, 1983, p. 119) [95]. Not only that, but when two people gaze into each other's eyes, it increases the intensity of the interaction [96]. This can accentuate both negative and positive messages. A woman can figure out whether the person directly in front of her harbors any harmful intentions. Further, when mutual eye contact is accompanied by pleasant facial expressions, the person conveys interest, caring, affection, and honesty [95]. A woman can be reassured that no imminent danger lurks.

Indeed, if the other woman does not look you in the eye, something might be amiss. In a recent study, researchers videotaped interviews with a female adult about questionable behavior (such as not finishing her work). Half the time, the interviewee looked straight into the camera. The other half, she looked to the side of the camera. Six- and 9-year-old children and young adults watched the video clips and then judged how truthful the adult was. At all ages, everyone thought the interviewee was more likely to be lying when she was not looking directly into the camera. Girls and women believed she was lying when she didn't look them in the eye even more than boys and men did [97].

That eye contact is a critical strategy for women that likely has an innate basis comes from studies with babies. Newborn girls make more eye contact than boys [98]. Furthermore, 1-year-old babies exposed to lower levels of testosterone prenatally make more eye contact [99]. Because girls are exposed to much less testosterone than boys, they make much more eye contact. This continues throughout life. Study after study shows that girls and women make more eye contact more than males do at all ages [96, 100].

Boys and men, on the other hand, find mutual eye contact disturbing. This has been found with men who are negotiating [101] and even with young boys looking at a puppet [102]. Men find it difficult to think clearly when someone is looking them in the eye [101]. This is not to say that men are unable to pick up messages from eye contact. For example, several male veterinarians I have met have asserted that they can tell whether one of their canine patients plans to bite by looking at the dog directly in the eye. Rather, males are just less interested than females in the intentions of their immediate social partners. Boys and men don't care as much whether someone plans to aggress against them. Some boys and men have even told me they welcome it. A punch in the face allows a retaliatory punch, which in the right circumstances can feel good. So while eye contact might allow a man to pick up some additional information, it is not that important. Furthermore, mutual eye contact raises the intensity of an interaction. Thus, in the wrong circumstances, many males just avoid it.

Pay Attention to Nonverbal Cues

If someone plans on doing you harm, usually they don't announce it with words. Much research has been devoted to figuring out whether nefarious intentions can nevertheless be discerned without words. The answer is clear: They can [103].

What is most interesting is that women are far better at this than men. To prove this, researchers asked people to watch different scenes: for example, a horror movie, a comedy, or specific scenes like a terrible automobile accident or the death of a dog. A second layer then is added by asking lots of observers to judge the emotions of the people watching the scenes. The observers sometimes can see just the audience's facial expressions; sometimes they can see the audience's body language; and sometimes they can hear the audience's intonations (but not the words) when they describe the scenes.

The observers then have to guess what kind of scene the audience was watching. Close to 90% of these studies have shown that women are more accurate than men [40, 104, 105]. In fact, these kinds of studies have been conducted in diverse regions of the world, including Japan, Sumatra, Vietnam, Poland, and Hungary, all with the same results [103]. Women are more accurate than men at decoding nonverbal emotional cues, and it does not matter whether the nonverbal cues are visual or auditory, or come from the face, body, or voice [106].

Now, the ability to decode nonverbal emotional meaning is highly useful in many contexts. For example, reading nonverbal cues of children who can't speak is particularly useful for mothers. This would certainly allow a mother to help her child survive. But these studies don't involve children.

A woman's ability to figure out an adult's emotions helps her to detect potentially hostile intentions. The faster she can do this, the faster she can escape if need be. A hostile person may try to disguise their intentions; they may not tell you right out that they intend to do you harm. Surprise certainly would give them the upper hand. In this case, nonverbal signals are the only clues that exist. Not only that, but nonverbal signals likely convey intentions more quickly than a verbal explanation. If you see another person shaking with fear, waiting for the person to tell you exactly what she or he is afraid of wastes precious time. Because fear signals potential danger, women should be particularly sensitive to nonverbal use. Indeed, women's advantage over men in decoding nonverbal cues is greatest with fear [40]. The same logic should also apply to expressions of anger by individuals, although this is more difficult to study. Anger signals potential threat. Therefore, women should be particularly attuned to nonverbal cues of anger, since this would allow them to escape attack more rapidly. This has not yet been proved, but I expect it will be found to be true.

Again, girls' advantage begins early. Infant girls notice a change in emotional expression more quickly than boys do. Girls continue to be faster than boys at identifying changes in emotional expression throughout childhood. Not only that, but in adolescence, girls' relative advantage becomes even stronger [107, 108]. Intriguingly, recent neurological research shows that women's brains appear to be hardwired to make decisions using emotional information more rapidly than men's brains [108]. Because women are superior to men at picking up on another's emotional intentions more quickly and more accurately from infancy onward, this ability is likely to be innate. The question is why. I suggest that it gives a woman an advantage in avoiding early death by allowing her to escape a dangerous individual or situation as fast as possible. There are other, slower means to avoiding conflict too.

Gather Personal Information Before Forming a Friendship

One of these entails collecting a lot of information about another person. Words can also be valuable tools in this case, as they allow a woman to obtain concrete information about many areas of a potential friend's life. This ensures that the friend is trustworthy and won't inflict harm. There are two primary types of information that a woman must collect before she becomes friends with another woman: (1) basic demographic information (name, rank, age) and (2) information about personal vulnerabilities and relationships.

The first type of information is the same type any concerned mother would collect about a friend if her child wanted to sleep over at the friend's house: the name of the friend, where she resides (rank), her age, the names of her family members, the names of her closest relationships, and any significant major life events and vulnerabilities that she has. From early childhood into adulthood, girls and women are very efficient in gathering this type of personal information [109]. This kind of information is not important to a man. A man does not care particularly where another man comes from, what his name is, or what his intentions are, as long as he has the skills that are required for the task at hand.

The second type of information concerns emotional details about the personal problems and significant relationships of the potential friend. Intimate, graphic, emotionally laden details are necessary to convey honestly the vulnerabilities and the strength of the relationships with others who can deal with these vulnerabilities [110]. Because each friend is assessing the other, both individuals are required to divulge this information equally. This type of information does not interest boys or men.

As examples, women discuss in great detail the problematic aspects of their relationships, both with other women, and with romantic partners, and children. They share their problems. They display their vulnerabilities and through doing so demonstrate their unconditional emotional support for one another [110–113].

Critically, what is not shared helps define what it is that girls and women are sharing. Girls and women do not share common activities, which is what men share with their friends [110, 114]. They do not share solutions to real-world problems, feelings of accomplishment and successes, or descriptions of positive relationships with third parties, such as other females or male partners. They also do not address conflicts with one another. Boys and men, in contrast, are more likely to share these things because they share common work and leisure activities. The single largest difference between the same-sex friendships of women versus men is that women verbally discuss vulnerabilities in themselves and their relationship partners, whereas men focus more on shared activities [110, 111, 113, 115]. This sex difference is present early in childhood, and it becomes enormous in adolescence and adulthood [116]. This basic difference has been found around the world in places such as the Netherlands, Turkey, Morocco, southern Europe, and Asia [117]. The need for intimacy between human females thus appears to have an innate basis. It seems that collecting this information is mandatory for the formation of a friendship between females.

I believe that by mutually sharing one another's problems and relationship difficulties, as well as basic demographic information, female friends build trust. Who but a true friend would disclose vulnerabilities? Who but a true friend would tell you who else they trust and who they distrust? Certainly, two enemies would not divulge their weakest positions to one another. Furthermore, should a conflict erupt between two female friends, each has powerful information that can be used against the other. Each knows where the other's family lives and their names. Each knows which girlfriends the other likes and dislikes. Each knows the weaknesses of the other's relationship with her boyfriend or husband. This information serves as a major deterrent to mutual destruction.

Put another way, divulging personal vulnerabilities provides an insurance policy against potential future attacks. For girls or women to remain friends, they must be able to reassure each other that they have no intention of usurping the other's status, stealing her food, or taking off with her male romantic partner. Females reveal their vulnerability as a sign of their honest intentions not to compete, not to try to harm the other by taking something from her.

How many professional women have I met who have been highly successful, but still manage to devote most of their time with one another to disclosing their personal vulnerabilities, such as a flaw in their appearance, a conflict with a third party, a mishap at work, or a long-ago romantic disappointment? Should a woman truly be a failure or major negative events actually have transpired, well then women have a lot to say. Talking from such a position of weakness provides no threat whatsoever.

Some women even specialize in accumulating friends with vulnerabilities. It might seem terribly bad fortune that these women have a close friend dying of cancer, another friend whose husband has just left her, a third friend whose child suffers from neurological damage, and a fourth friend who cannot afford to pay her bills. Upon closer inspection, however, it is apparent that these women are selectively choosing others who are particularly vulnerable. Someone who is vulnerable will not go after what you have because she is too weak. Avoiding a potential competitor who could attempt to interfere with your success is serious business for a woman.

In fact, women of all ages are well aware that their friends will not be happy should they advertise, or even mention, their personal successes. To show this, my students and I asked girls and women how they thought their friends would feel if the girls and women suddenly became successful [118, 119]. Unlike boys and men, girls and women replied that they thought their closest friends would think poorly of them if they became more successful than their friends. They also added that any greater achievement by one friend might destroy the friendship. Even businesswomen know that they must present themselves as "dead even" to their female coworkers or else risk the end of the friendship [120]. No woman wants a coworker with higher status, and hence more resources for herself and her children, as a friend. Further, a girl or woman with higher status has the power to hurt her friend.

Thus, to reduce any threats to one another, girls and women focus on mutual vulnerabilities. Clinicians call this co-rumination, and it is a specialty of girls and women. Boys and men don't do this. Unfortunately, co-rumination can lead both partners to become increasingly anxious, stressed, and depressed [121, 122]. Nonetheless, most females engage in this process regularly. Forget any positive events; do not mention that almost everything is going right at the moment; find that one event that has a negative undertone and play it for all it's worth. This forms the glue of females' relationships. It takes two highly confident women to avoid this kind of mutually supportive and ultimately destructive interaction. I believe it happens so often because it serves to reassure each participant that the other one does not wish to compete and is not powerful enough to inflict harm.

What happens, then, if all these precautions fail, and a conflict erupts anyway? What happens if a woman decides not to share her basic demographic information and personal vulnerabilities and relationship status with another woman? What if a woman decides that another woman is not to be trusted? What if a stranger suddenly appears and a woman doesn't know anything about her? Unlike males, girls and women rarely express negative feelings directly. Instead, they have two basic tools to deflect current or potential conflict: smiling and politeness.

Smile No Matter What

When two familiar women pass in the street, they must smile. If not, the one not smiled at begins to ruminate. "Why didn't she smile at me?" "Did I do something wrong?" "Is my dress on backward?" "Who does she think she is, anyway?" "I remember another time she did something unpleasant." "My other friend, Jane, thinks she's not very nice, and after all maybe she's right. This proves it." And so it goes.

I have heard this refrain many times over the years. When I ask a man what he thinks if someone he knows passes by and doesn't smile at him, the man tells me he doesn't think anything. It never enters his mind.

The first rule of conflict management for a female, whether she is friends with another female or just simply knows her, is to smile. When a possible conflict is brewing—smile even harder. Across diverse cultures, girls and women smile more than boys and men [123]. Importantly, females are even more likely than males to smile when there is a conflict with the other person. They are also much more likely than males to smile when meeting a stranger. Most critically, women smile most of all during their reproductive years. After that, by middle adulthood, women no longer smile so much more than men. The sex difference diminishes and is smallest in old age. After a woman has produced her children, and they have grown, she can relax—without having to smile so much.

Although researchers argue about the meaning of smiling, one function on which everyone agrees is that it reduces social tension. For example, in a clever study, researchers surreptitiously recorded the smiling behavior of people at bowling alleys. They wondered whether people would be more likely to smile after they had scored a spare or strike (which would indicate happiness presumably), or when they interacted with others (which would indicate smoothing social interactions). In fact, bowlers smiled more often when interacting with others than after getting a high score [124]. Thus, it appears that the primary function of smiles is to communicate friendliness to others. Smiling smooths interactions between individuals, just as it does in other primates.

Smiling constitutes such an important tool for reducing social conflict that not being allowed to smile makes women terribly anxious. To demonstrate this, Marianne LaFrance [125] asked undergraduate students in Boston to read a story in which the following occurred: First, a person approached and recounted a recent accomplishment: "I'm so happy! After years of trying, I was finally able to complete the Boston Marathon." Second, students were asked to imagine that they had said "Congratulations!" Half of the students then were told to imagine that they smiled when congratulating the runner. The other half were told to imagine that they did not smile but maintained a neutral expression. Finally, the students were asked how they felt. Everyone reported feeling more uncomfortable when they did not smile. They also felt that the runner would think that they were less friendly and less caring. The women, however, felt much worse than the men.

The smile is such a powerful tool that even imagining being without it provokes great anxiety in women. How unpleasant for a woman to be confronted by a perfect stranger who brags about her accomplishments. How useful a social smile would be to defuse the negative emotions arising in herself and to pretend that she cared about this stranger's competitive behavior.

Girls smile more than boys from birth onward [25, 126]. Girls and women smile more than boys and men across the most diverse cultures [123]. Because even newborn girls smile more than boys, it is likely that genes have prepared females to smile more. This should help females to reduce conflicts whomever they should meet. Even after a conflict has broken out, a smile most likely helps, automatically, to douse the flames, to decrease the chances of danger. Likewise, even when the other person is a perfect stranger, a smile conveys an ardent desire to avoid conflict.

Always Be Polite

Politeness operates similarly to smiling. When conflict arises or an unknown social partner arrives, politeness is another important tool. Politeness etiquette exists for many contexts that include just about every conceivable meeting between humans. It is not just women who behave politely when tension rises.

However, women seem to specialize in rules of etiquette for the home and the local community. Many books of etiquette are in fact targeted toward girls and women. Current books aimed at girls and women include titles such as *Debrett's Etiquette for Girls; A Little Book of Manners: Courtesy and Kindness for Young Ladies' Dear Miss Perfect: A Beast's Guide to Proper Behavior; A Smart Girl's Guide to Manners;* and of course, the perennial favorites like Emily Post and Dear Abby.

Classic etiquette books are designed to avoid, or more practically to alleviate, social tension. These often suggest rules of behavior that can appear archaic, or even ridiculous. Certainly in these more modern times, politeness, whether nonverbal or verbal, often invites ridicule. It is easy to make fun of social conventions and miss their contribution to smoothing social interactions. Given the social nature of human societies, however, combined with the conflicts that naturally occur between individuals who spend a lot of time together, politeness begins to make more sense.

The introduction to Emily Post's [127] classic book on social etiquette begins with the bold assertion that manners caused apes to evolve into human beings. Scolding those who belittle politeness, she writes, "People who ridicule etiquette as a mass of trivial and arbitrary conventions, 'extremely troublesome to those who practice them and insupportable to everybody else,' seem to forget the long, slow progress of social intercourse in the upward climb of man from the primeval state" (Post, 1922, p. 3). A number of primatologists agree. For example, it is difficult for an ape to wait politely while another ape begins his or her meal. The waiting ape generally attempts to grab the food, shattering one of the first rules of politeness taught to children.

But not so fast. If the dominant ape is eating first, then the more subordinate ape demonstrates exquisite manners. Learning to consciously restrain one's behavior in order to follow social conventions is something that even apes do sometimes. They just don't do it all the time, or perhaps possess the conscious knowledge that they will be beaten on the spot if they don't wait their proper turn. Humans therefore follow more refined and internalized rules of politeness. Of course, it is possible that manners helped prod our prehuman ancestors to override their first impulses and execute greater planning skills, thereby producing the current version of human beings. Politeness, as even subordinate apes know well, reduces social tension and diminishes the chances of being hurt. It is no accident, therefore, that women have greater levels of nonverbal and verbal politeness than men.

Different human cultures have thrown up a huge variety of social rules. As an example, here is some advice given by Post to women:

> How many have noticed that Southern women always bow with the grace of a flower bending in the breeze and a smile like sudden sunshine? The unlovely woman bows as though her head were on a hinge and her smile sucked through a lemon.... Nothing is so easy for any woman to acquire as a charming bow. It is such a short and fleeting duty. Not a bit of trouble really; just to incline your head and spontaneously smile as though you thought "Why *there* is Mrs. Smith! How glad I am to see her!".... Even to a stranger who does her a favor, a woman of charm always smiles as she says "Thank you!" (Post, 1922/2010, p. 21)

Of course, many rules pertain to gentlemen as well, and some apply to both sexes. For example, under a section titled "Gentlemen and Bundles," Post describes clearly the following rules:

> Nearly all books on etiquette insist that a "gentleman must offer to carry a lady's bundles." Bundles do not suggest a lady in the first place, and as for gentlemen and bundles!- they don't go together at all. Very neat packages that could never without injury to their pride be designated as "bundles" are different. Such, for instance, might be a square, smoothly wrapped box of cigars, candy, or books.... And yet, many an unknowing woman... has asked a relative, a neighbor, or an admirer, to carry something suggestive of a pillow, done up in crinkled paper and odd lengths of joined string. Then she wonders afterwards in unenlightened surprise why her cousin, her neighbor, or her admirer, who is one of the smartest men in town, never comes to see her anymore! (Post, 1922/2010, p. 22)

However strange these might be, from very early in life, girls learn to follow the specific social rules for their home and community more strictly than boys. A perfect illustration comes from studies using the "disappointment paradigm" [128, 129]. In these studies, children are asked to help with two tasks. They are told that they will receive a separate gift for helping with each one. Before starting, the children are given 10 toys. Each child then tells the researcher which toys she likes best and which ones she likes least in order. One toy is always broken, and naturally this is liked least by all children.

After the children finish the first task, they are given one of their favorite toys. But when they finish the second task, the children are given the broken toy. What happens next? The girls smile much more than the boys. The boys look really unhappy, and sometimes even make snide comments. Importantly, this was not because the girls liked the broken toy. To prove this, in another study, some of the girls were given the broken toy in wrapping paper. They unwrapped it later when they were alone. Videotapes of their expressions show that these girls were not happy: They smiled less and exhibited more negative expressions than girls who unwrapped the broken toy while the experimenter stood there. Girls are simply more polite than boys.

Politeness involves words too. To be polite when engaged in conversation, you need to follow several rules. First, you must listen carefully to what the other person is saying and wait until they are finished before speaking yourself. Second, you have to affirm and be positive about what the other person is saying. Third, if necessary, you must present possibly contradictory ideas in a soft way. For example, if you think that you have a better idea, you might say, "Maybe this is right." Or if you want the other person to do something they don't want to do, you might say, "Shouldn't we do this?" Fourth, it is helpful to include lots of expressions such as "thank you" and "sorry" to show how much you value the other person's efforts. Fifth, competitive language must be avoided. It is not polite to issue orders, make threats, boast about how good you are, or criticize the other person.

Girls are much more verbally polite than boys. Numerous studies have shown that girls and women use polite speech much more than boys and men [130–133]. This difference has been found as soon as children begin to speak to one another [134–136]. It has been found in many diverse countries and cultures [137], including Korea [138], Japan [139], Mayan Indians [140], in Vanuatu, an island in the Southwest Pacific ocean [141], and in a variety of ethnic and socioeconomic groups in the United States [142]. Once again, the early beginnings of girls' greater politeness combined with women's greater politeness across many cultures suggest that it has an innate basis. I believe that part of what motivates girls and women to be more polite is that politeness helps avert conflict. Whether a conflict already has begun to brew, or a stranger with unknown intentions appears, politeness reduces the chances of danger. It decreases the probability that a woman will find herself at odds with someone who is right in front of her and could potentially do her harm.

Politeness is not trivial. Girls and women invest time and energy in being polite. As an illustration, researchers asked female and male Canadian undergraduate students to keep a diary for 12 days [143]. The students' task was to record in real time when they apologized to someone. They also recorded when something they did required an apology, and when something someone else did required an apology. Unsurprisingly, the researchers found that the women apologized more than men. Interestingly, the women also reported having committed more acts that required apologies than the men did. Thus, the women were more concerned about their own behavior and its effects on others. This was not the end of the story, however. The women also reported that others committed more offenses against them. Men didn't find others' behavior so offensive. Perhaps women just behave more offensively, or interact with others who are more offensive. This does not seem likely, however. What seems more probable is that women are more sensitive than men to any type of offensive behavior—their own or another's. Why? I believe any sign of offensive behavior signals potential danger. A woman doesn't want to instigate a fight, and she surely doesn't want to be the victim.

Women have an arsenal of preventive behaviors designed to reduce overt conflict with other women. What happens if these fail, for example, if mutual eye contact turns up disturbing information? If the other person's nonverbal behavior hints at malicious intent? If intimate information is withheld, what to do? An anxious girl or woman can always smile and behave politely. But this might not suffice.

Avoiding direct physical or even verbal aggression might help to keep women safe, but it is, at the same time, a major disadvantage. If a woman will not attack or even verbally retaliate when someone hurts her, then what stops another person from taking her resources, stealing her husband, or excluding her from the community? Furthermore, how does a woman manage to advance her position in the community? A woman who must ensure her own and her children's survival and well-being, and if possible enhance her family's status so they all can thrive, cannot be defenseless.

A "feminine" woman must protect her own and her children's lives. How does she accomplish this when she is expected to be so nice? In economically poor societies, resources are scarce. In other communities, husbands are scarce. In still others, grandmothers don't live long enough to help a woman raise her children. Even in the richest societies of today, there is a limited supply of high-paying jobs, highly paid husbands, top doctors, places in elite children's schools. Girls and women live in the same world as boys and men—a social world with limited resources and property, with competitors and allies. Conflicts over scarce resources inevitably arise. Other women want the same things for themselves, their children, and their extended families.

Femininity aside, a woman has to compete. Because women have been victims and subordinate to men for so long, women's strategies simply have been overlooked. Men, who typically hold more power, pay less attention to those who are subordinate [144]. Meanwhile, women, who are generally subordinate members of society, keep a low profile so they won't be hurt by those in power. A woman's primary competitors are unrelated women, because these are the people who share the same goals. Women must compete against other women.

References

1. Freud, S., Some psychical consequences of the anatomical distinction between the sexes, in *The standard edition of the complete psychological works of Sigmund Freud*, Vol. 19, J. Strachey, Editor. London: Hogarth Press. 1925, pp. 241–258.
1a. Volk, A. A. and J. A. Atkinson, Infant and child death in the human environment of evolutionary adaptation. *Evolution and Human Behavior*, 2013. 34(3): pp. 182192.
2. Freud, S., Female sexuality, in *The standard edition of the complete psychological works of Sigmund Freud*, Vol. 21 J. Strachey, Editor. London: Hogarth Press. 1931, New York: Norton. pp.221–243.
3. Freud, S., *Femininity. The standard edition of the complete psychological works of Sigmund Freud*, J. Strachey, Editor. London: Hogarth Press. Vol. 22 1933. pp. 112135
4. Rosaldo, M. Z., L. Lamphere, and J. Bamberger, *Woman, culture, and society.* 1974, Stanford, CA: Stanford University Press.
5. Kristof, N., and S. WuDunn, *Half the sky: How to change the world.* 2010, London: Virago.
6. Abu-Lughod, L., *Sentiments, honor and poetry in a Bedouin society.* 1986, Berkeley: University of California Press.
7. Master-Hunter, T., and D. L. Heiman, Amenorrhea: Evaluation and treatment. *Am Fam Physician*, 2006. 73(8): pp. 1374–1382.
8. Berg, C. J., H. K. Atrash, L. M. Koonin and M. Tucker Pregnancy-related mortality in the United States, 1987–1990. *Obstetrics and Gynecology*, 1996. 88(2): pp. 161–167.

9. Duley, L., Maternal mortality associated with hypertensive disorders of pregnancy in Africa, Asia, Latin America and the Caribbean. *BJOG: An International Journal of Obstetrics and Gynaecology*, 1992. 99(7): pp. 547–553.

10. Rosenfield, A., Maternal mortality in developing countries. *JAMA: The Journal of the American Medical Association*, 1989. 262(3): pp. 376–379.

11. Hrdy, S. B., Mother nature: A history of mothers, infants, and natural selection. New York: Pantheon. 1999.

12. Hill, K., and A. M. Hurtado, *Ache life history: The ecology and demography of a foraging people*. 1996, New York: Aldine de Gruyter.

13. Voland, E., Differential infant and child mortality in evolutionary perspective: Data from late 17th to 19th century Ostfriesland (Germany), in *Human reproductive behaviour: A Darwinian perspective*, L. Betzig, M. B. Mulder, and P. Turke, Editors. 1988, Cambridge: Cambridge University Press. pp. 253–261.

14. Casanova, J. L., and L. Abel, Inborn errors of immunity to infection. *Journal of Experimental Medicine*, 2005. 202(2): pp. 197–201.

15. Nolen-Hoeksema, S., The role of rumination in depressive disorders and mixed anxiety/depressive symptoms. *Journal of Abnormal Psychology*, 2000. 109(3): pp. 504–511.

16. Nolen-Hoeksema, S., Gender differences in depression. *Current Directions in Psychological Science*, 2001. 10(5): pp. 173–176.

17. Davison, T. E., and M. P. McCabe, Relationships between men's and women's body image and their psychological, social, and sexual functioning. *Sex Roles*, 2005. 52(7): pp. 463–475.

18. Tiggemann, M., Body image across the adult life span: Stability and change. *Body Image*, 2004. 1(1): pp. 29–41.

19. Ålgars, M., The adult body: How age, gender, and body mass index are related to body image. *Journal of Aging and Health*, 2009. 21(8): pp. 1112–1132.

20. Buss, D. M., Sex differences in human mate preferences: Evolutionary hypotheses tested in 37 cultures. *Behavioral and Brain Sciences*, 1989. 12(1): pp. 1–49.

21. Marmot, M. G., et al., Health inequalities among British civil servants: The Whitehall II Study. *Lancet*, 1991. 337(8754): pp. 1387–1393.

22. Simner, M. L., Newborn's response to the cry of another infant. *Developmental Psychology*, 1971. 5(1): pp. 136–150.

23. Sagi, A., and M. L. Hoffman, Empathic distress in the newborn. *Developmental Psychology*, 1976. 12(2): pp. 175–176.

24. Nagy, E., et al., Different emergence of fear expressions in infant boys and girls. *Infant Behavior and Development*, 2001. 24(2): pp. 189–194.

25. Freedman, D. G., *Human infancy: An evolutionary perspective*. New York. 1974, Wiley.

26. Schmitz, S., et al., Temperament and problem behaviour during early childhood. *International Journal of Behavioral Development*, 1999. 23(2): pp. 333–355.

27. Goldberg, S., and M. Lewis, Play behavior in the year-old infant: Early sex differences. *Child Development*, 1969. 40(1): pp. 21–31.

28. Robinson, J. L., J. Kagan, J. S. Reznick, R. Corley The heritability of inhibited and uninhibited behavior: A twin study. *Developmental Psychology*, 1992. 28(6): pp. 1030–1037.

29. Zahn-Waxler, C., J. A. L. Robinson, and R. N. Emde, The development of empathy in twins. *Developmental Psychology*, 1992. 28(6): pp. 1038–1047.

30. Bowlby, J., *Attachment and loss: Volume 1: Attachment*. 1969, London: Hogarth Press and the Institute of Psycho-Analysis.

31. King, N. J., et al., Fears of children and adolescents: A cross-sectional Australian Study using the Revised-Fear Survey Schedule for Children. *Journal of Child Psychology and Psychiatry*, 1989. 30(5): pp. 775–784.

32. Ollendick, T. H., B. Ying, N. J. King, Q. Dong, and A. Akande Fears in American, Australian, Chinese, and Nigerian children and adolescents: A cross-cultural study. *Journal of Child Psychology and Psychiatry*, 1996. 37(2): pp. 213–220.

33. Lewinsohn, P. M., I. H. Gotlib, M. Lewinsohn, J. R. Seeley, and N. B. Allen Gender differences in anxiety disorders and anxiety symptoms in adolescents. *Journal of Abnormal Psychology*, 1998. 107(1): pp. 109–117.

34. Muris, P., C. Meesters, and M. Knoops, The relation between gender role orientation and fear and anxiety in nonclinic-referred children. *Journal of Clinical Child and Adolescent Psychology*, 2005. 34(2): pp. 326–332.

35. Whiting, B. B., and C. P. Edwards *Children of different worlds: The formation of social behavior*. 1988, Cambridge, MA: Harvard University Press.

36. Brown, D. E., *Human universals*. 1991, Philadelphia: Temple University Press.

37. Kramer, K. L., Children's help and the pace of reproduction: Cooperative breeding in humans. *Evolutionary Anthropology: Issues, News, and Reviews*, 2005. 14(6): pp. 224–237.

38. Arrindell, W. A., A. M. Kolk, M. J. Pickersgill, and W. J. J. M. Hagemen Biological sex, sex role orientation, masculine sex role stress, dissimulation and self-reported fears. *Advances in Behaviour Research and Therapy*, 1993. 15(2): pp. 103–146.

39. Brody, L. R., and J. A. Hall, *Gender and emotion*. 1993, New York: Guilford.

40. Hall, J. A., J. D. Carter, and T. G. Horgan, Gender differences in nonverbal communication of emotion, in *Gender and emotion: Social psychological perspectives*, A. H. Fischer, Editor. 2000, Cambridge: Cambridge University Press. pp. 97–117.

41. Gray, J. A., *The psychology of fear and stress*. Vol. 5. 1987, New York: Cambridge University Press.

42. Breslau, N., G. C. Davis, P. Andreski, E. L. Peterson, and L. R. Schultz Sex differences in posttraumatic stress disorder. *Archives of General Psychiatry*, 1997. 54(11): p. 1044.

43. Tolin, D. F., and E. B. Foa, Sex differences in trauma and posttraumatic stress disorder: A quantitative review of 25 years of research. *Psychological Bulletin*, 2006. 132(6): pp. 959–992.
44. Davis, M. C., K. A. Matthews, and E. W. Twamley, Is life more difficult on Mars or Venus? A meta-analytic review of sex differences in major and minor life events. *Annals of Behavioral Medicine*, 1999. 21(1): pp. 83–97.
45. Fischer, A. H., and A. S. R. Manstead, The relation between gender and emotion in different cultures, in *Gender and emotion: Social psychological perspectives*, A. H. Fischer, Editor. 2000, New York: Cambridge University Press. pp. 71–94.
46. Leach, L. S., H. Christensen, A. J. Mackinnon, T. D. Windsor, and P. Butterworth Gender differences in depression and anxiety across the adult lifespan: The role of psychosocial mediators. *Social Psychiatry and Psychiatric Epidemiology*, 2008. 43(12): pp. 983–998.
47. Nolen-Hoeksema, S., Epidemiology and theories of gender differences in unipolar depression, in *Gender and psychopathology*, M. V. Seesman, Editor. 1995, Washington, DC: American Psychiatric Publishing. pp. 63–87.
48. Nolen-Hoeksema, S., and J. S. Girgus, Explanatory style and achievement, depression, and gender differences in childhood and early adolescence, in *Explanatory style*, G. M. Buchanan and M. E. P. Selligman, Editors. 1995, Hillsdale, NJ: Erlbaum. pp. 57–70.
49. Nolen-Hoeksema, S., and J. S. Girgus, The emergence of gender differences in depression during adolescence. *Psychological Bulletin*, 1994. 115(3): pp. 424–443.
50. Gater, R., et al., Sex differences in the prevalence and detection of depressive and anxiety disorders in general health care settings: Report from the World Health Organization Collaborative Study on Psychological Problems in General Health Care. *Archives of General Psychiatry*, 1998. 55(5): pp. 405–413.
51. Pigott, T. A., and L. T. Lac, Gender differences in anxiety disorders, in *Biological psychiatry*, H. D'Haenen, J. A. den Boer, & P. Willner, Editors. 2003, New York: Wiley. pp. 1025–1038.
52. Isaacowitz, D. M., S. T. Charles, and L. L. Carstensen, Emotion and cognition, in *The handbook of aging and cognition*, F. Craik and T. A. Salthouse, Editors. 2000, Mahwah, NJ: Erlbaum, pp. 593–631.
53. Turner, C., and R. McClure, Age and gender differences in risk-taking behaviour as an explanation for high incidence of motor vehicle crashes as a driver in young males. *Injury Control and Safety Promotion*, 2003. 10(3): pp. 123–130.
54. Peng, R. Y., and F. S. Bongard, Pedestrian versus motor vehicle accidents: An analysis of 5,000 patients. *Journal of the American College of Surgeons*, 1999. 189(4): pp. 343–348.
55. Híjar, M. C., E. Vazquez-Vela, and C. Arreola-Risa Analysis of fatal pedestrian injuries in Mexico City, 1994–1997. *Injury*, 2001. 32(4): pp. 279–284.

56. Montazeri, A., Road-traffic-related mortality in Iran: A descriptive study. *Public Health*, 2004. 118(2): pp. 110–113.

57. Wang, X. T., D. J. Kruger, and A. Wilke, Life history variables and risk-taking propensity. *Evolution and Human Behavior*, 2009. 30(2): pp. 77–84.

58. Jiang, X., et al., An analysis of 6215 hospitalized unintentional injuries among children aged 0–14 in northwest China. *Accident Analysis and Prevention*, 2010. 42(1): pp. 320–326.

59. Byrnes, J. P., D. C. Miller, and W. D. Schafer, Gender differences in risk taking: A meta-analysis. *Psychological Bulletin*, 1999. 125(3): pp. 367–383.

60. Golombok, S., and R. Fivush, *Gender development*. 1994, New York: Cambridge University Press.

61. Giampaoli, S., Epidemiology of major age-related diseases in women compared to men. *Aging* (Milan, Italy), 2000. 12(2): pp. 93–105.

62. Mathers, C. D., R. Sadana, J. A. Salomon, C. J. L. Murray, and A. D. Lopez Healthy life expectancy in 191 countries, 1999. *Lancet*, 2001. 357(9269): pp. 1685–1691.

63. Wells, J. C. K., Natural selection and sex differences in morbidity and mortality in early life. *Journal of Theoretical Biology*, 2000. 202(1): pp. 65–76.

64. Seymour-Smith, S., M. Wetherell, and A. Phoenix, "My wife ordered me to come!: A discursive analysis of doctors' and nurses' accounts of men's use of general practitioners. *Journal of Health Psychology*, 2002. 7(3): pp. 253–267.

65. Mustard, C. A., P. Kaufert, A. Kozyrskyj, and T. Mayer Sex differences in the use of health care services. *New England Journal of Medicine*, 1998. 338(23): pp. 1678–1683.

66. Tabenkin, H., M. A. Goodwin, S. J. Zyzanski, K. C. Stange and J. H. Medalie Gender differences in time spent during direct observation of doctor-patient encounters. *Journal of Women's Health*, 2004. 13(3): pp. 341–349.

67. Redondo-Sendino, Á., P. Guallar-Castillón, J. R. Banegas and F. Rodríguez-Artalejo Gender differences in the utilization of health-care services among the older adult population of Spain. *BMC Public Health*, 2006. 6(1): p. 155.

68. Walsh, T. M., S. H. Stewart, E. McLaughlin, and N. Comeau Gender differences in Childhood Anxiety Sensitivity Index (CASI) dimensions. *Journal of Anxiety Disorders*, 2004. 18(5): pp. 695–706.

69. Viera, A., J. Thorpe, and J. Garrett, Effects of sex, age, and visits on receipt of preventive healthcare services: A secondary analysis of national data. *BMC Health Services Research*, 2006. 6(1): p. 15.

70. Nathanson, C. A., Illness and the feminine role: A theoretical review. *Social Science and Medicine* (1967), 1975. 9(2): pp. 57–62.

71. Verbrugge, L. M., Gender and health: An update on hypotheses and evidence. *Journal of Health and Social Behavior*, 1985. 26(3): pp. 156–182.

72. Goldman, M. B., and M. Hatch, *Women and health.* 2000, San Diego: Academic Press.
73. Schur, C. L., Berk, M. L., Wilensky, G. R., and Gagnon, J. B., Paying for health care in retirement: Workers' knowledge of benefits and expenses. *Health Affairs*, 2004. W4-385-W4-395. doi: 10.1377/hlthaff.w4.385
74. Hira, T. K., and C. Loibl, Understanding the impact of employer provided financial education on workplace satisfaction. *Journal of Consumer Affairs*, 2005. 39(1): pp. 173–194.
75. Jankowiak, W., M. Sudakov, and B. C. Wilreker, Co-wife conflict and co-operation. *Ethnology*, 2005. 44(1): pp. 81–98.
76. Bem, S. L., The measurement of psychological androgyny. *Journal of Consulting and Clinical Psychology*, 1974. 42(2): pp. 155–162.
77. Campbell, A., Staying alive: Evolution, culture, and women's intrasexual aggression. *Behavioral and Brain Sciences*, 1999. 22(2): pp. 203–252.
78. Kring, A. M., Gender and anger, in *Gender and emotion: Social psychological perspectives*, A. H. Fischer, Editor. 2000, New York: Cambridge University Press. pp. 211–231.
79. Campbell, A., *Out of control: Men, women and aggression.* 1993, New York: Pandora.
80. Baillargeon, R. H., et al., Gender differences in physical aggression: A prospective population-based survey of children before and after 2 years of age. *Developmental Psychology*, 2007. 43(1): pp. 13–26.
81. Archer, J., Sex differences in aggression in real-world setting: A meta-analytic review. *Review of General Psychology*, 2004. 8(4): pp. 291–322.
82. Archer, J., Does sexual selection explain human sex differences in aggression. *Behavioral and Brain Sciences*, 2009. 32(3–4): pp. 249–266.
83. Maccoby, E. E., and C. N. Jacklin, *The psychology of sex differences.* 1974, Stanford, CA: Stanford University Press.
84. Daly, M., and M. Wilson, An evolutionary psychological perspective on homicide, in *Homicide: A sourcebook of social research*, M. D. Smith and M. A. Zahn, Editors. 1999, Thousand Oaks, CA: Sage. pp. 58–71.
85. Campbell, A., Female competition: Causes, constraints, content, and contexts. *The Journal of Sex Research*, 2004. 41(1): pp. 16–26.
86. Burbank, V. K., Female aggression in cross-cultural perspective. *Behavior Science Research*, 1987. 21(1–4): pp. 70–100.
87. de Waal, F. B. M., The integration of dominance and social bonding in primates. *Quarterly Review of Biology*, 1986. 61(4): pp. 459–479.
88. Archer, J., Cross-cultural differences in physical aggression between partners: A social-role analysis. *Personality and Social Psychology Review*, 2006. 10(2): pp. 133–153.
89. Straus, M. A., and R. J. Gelles, Societal change and change in family violence from 1975 to 1985 as revealed by two national surveys. *Journal of Marriage and the Family*, 1986. 48(3): pp. 465–479.

90. Johansson, S., Neglect, abuse, and avoidable death: Parental investment and the mortality of infants and children in the European tradition, in *Child abuse and neglect: Biosocial dimensions*, R. J. Gelles and J. B. Lancaster, Editors. 1987, Piscataway, NJ: Transaction Press. pp. 57–96.

91. Straus, M. A., and J. H. Stewart, Corporal punishment by American parents: National data on prevalence, chronicity, severity, and duration, in relation to child and family characteristics. *Clinical Child and Family Psychology Review*, 1999. 2(2): pp. 55–70.

92. Hewlett, B. S., and M. E. Lamb, *Hunter-gatherer childhoods: Evolutionary, developmental, and cultural perspectives*. 2005, New Brunswick, NJ: Aldine Transaction.

93. House, J. S., K. R. Landis, and D. Umberson, Social relationships and health. *Science*, 1988. 241(4865): pp. 540–545.

94. Tannen, D., *You just don't understand: Women and men in conversation*. 2001, New York: Harper Paperbacks.

95. Grumet, G. W., Eye contact: The core of interpersonal relatedness. *Psychiatry*, 1983. 46(2): pp. 172–180.

96. Kleinke, C. L., Gaze and eye contact: A research review. *Psychological Bulletin*, 1986. 100(1): pp. 78–100.

97. Einav, S., and B. M. Hood, Tell-tale eyes: Children's attribution of gaze aversion as a lying cue. *Developmental Psychology*, 2008. 44(6): pp. 1655–1667.

98. Hittelman, J. H., and R. Dickes, Sex differences in neonatal eye contact time. *Merrill-Palmer Quarterly: Journal of Developmental Psychology*, 1979. 25(3): pp. 171–184.

99. Lutchmaya, S., S. Baron-Cohen, and P. Raggatt, Foetal testosterone and eye contact in 12-month-old human infants. *Infant Behavior and Development*, 2002. 25(3): pp. 327–335.

100. Levine, M. H., and B. Sutton-Smith, Effects of age, sex, and task on visual behavior during dyadic interaction. *Developmental Psychology*, 1973. 9(3): pp. 400–405.

101. Swaab, R. I., and D. F. Swaab, Sex differences in the effects of visual contact and eye contact in negotiations. *Journal of Experimental Social Psychology*, 2009. 45(1): pp. 129–136.

102. Benenson, J. F., Greater preference among females than males for dyadic interaction in early childhood. *Child Development*, 1993. 64(2): pp. 544–555.

103. Biehl, M., et al., Matsumoto and Ekman's Japanese and Caucasian Facial Expressions of Emotion (JACFEE): Reliability data and cross-national differences. *Journal of Nonverbal Behavior*, 1997. 21(1): pp. 3–21.

104. Zuckerman, M., D. T. Larrance, J. A. Hall, R. S. DeFrank, and R. Rosenthal Posed and spontaneous communication of emotion via facial and vocal cues. *Journal of Personality*, 1979. 47(4): pp. 712–733.

105. Rosenthal, R., J. A. Hall, and M. R. DiMatteo *Sensitivity to nonverbal communication: The PONS test.* 1979, Baltimore: Johns Hopkins University Press.

106. Hall, J. A., *Nonverbal sex differences: Communication accuracy and expressive style.* 1984, Baltimore: Johns Hopkins University Press.

107. McClure, E. B., A meta-analytic review of sex differences in facial expression processing and their development in infants, children, and adolescents. *Psychological Bulletin,* 2000. 126(3): pp. 424–453.

108. McClure, E. B., et al., A developmental examination of gender differences in brain engagement during evaluation of threat. *Biological Psychiatry,* 2004. 55(11): pp. 1047–1055.

109. Markovits, H., J. Benenson, and E. Dolenszky, Evidence that children and adolescents have internal models of peer interactions that are gender differentiated. *Child Development,* 2001. 72(3): pp. 879–886.

110. Winstead, B., and J. Griffin, Friendship styles, in *Encyclopedia of women and gender,* J. Worell, Editor. 2001, Boston: Academic Press. pp. 481–492.

111. Coates, J., *Women talk: Conversation between women friends.* 1996, Oxford: Wiley-Blackwell.

112. O'Connor, P., *Friendships between women: A critical review.* 1992, New York: Guilford.

113. Wright, P. H., Toward an expanded orientation to the study of sex differences in friendship, in *Sex differences and similarities in communication: Critical essays and empirical investigations of sex and gender in interaction,* D. J. Canary and K. Dindia, Editors. 1998, Mahwah, NJ: Erlbaum. pp. 41–63.

114. Swain, S., Covert intimacy: Closeness in men's friendships, in *Gender in intimate relationships: A microstructural approach,* B. R. P. Schwartz, Editor. 1989, Belmont, CA: Wadsworth. pp. 71–86.

115. Blieszner, R., and R. G. Adams, *Adult friendship.* 1992, Thousand Oaks, CA: Sage.

116. Buhrmester, D. and K. Prager, Patterns and functions of self-disclosure during childhood and adolescence, in *Disclosure processes in children and adolescents,* K. Rotenberg, Editor. 1995, Cambridge: Cambridge University Press. pp. 10–56.

117. Verkuyten, M., Culture and gender differences in the perception of friendship by adolescents. *International Journal of Psychology,* 1996. 31(5): pp. 207–217.

118. Benenson, J. F., and D. Benarroch, Gender differences in responses to friends' hypothetical greater success. *Journal of Early Adolescence,* 1998. 18(2): pp. 192–208.

119. Benenson, J. F., and J. Schinazi, Sex differences in reactions to outperforming same-sex friends. *British Journal of Developmental Psychology,* 2004. 22(3): pp. 317–333.

120. Heim, P., S. Murphy, and S. K. Golant, *In the company of women: Turning workplace conflict into powerful alliances.* 2001, Los Angeles: Tarcher/Putnam.

121. Byrd-Craven, J., D. C. Geary, A. J. Rose, and D. Ponzi Co-ruminating increases stress hormone levels in women. *Hormones and Behavior,* 2008. 53(3): pp. 489–492.

122. Rose, A. J., W. Carlson, and E. M. Waller, Prospective associations of co-rumination with friendship and emotional adjustment: Considering the socioemotional trade-offs of co-rumination. *Developmental Psychology,* 2007. 43(4): pp. 1019–1031.

123. LaFrance, M., M. A. Hecht, and E. L. Paluck, The contingent smile: A meta-analysis of sex differences in smiling. *Psychological Bulletin,* 2003. 129(2): pp. 305–334.

124. Kraut, R. E., and R. E. Johnston, Social and emotional messages of smiling: An ethological approach. *Journal of Personality and Social Psychology,* 1979. 37(9): pp. 1539–1553.

125. LaFrance, M., Pressure to be positive: The effect of sex and power on reactions to not smiling. Revue Internationale de Psychologie sociale (*International Review of Social Psychology*), 1997. 10(2): pp. 95–108.

126. Korner, A. F., Neonatal startles, smiles, erections, and reflex sucks as related to state, sex, and individuality. *Child Development,* 1969. 40(4) pp. 1039–1053.

127. Post, E., *Etiquette.* 1922, New York: Funk and Wagnalls

128. Cole, P. M., Children's spontaneous control of facial expression. *Child Development,* 1986. 57(6): pp. 1309–1321.

129. Saarni, C., An observational study of children's attempts to monitor their expressive behavior. *Child Development,* 1984. 55(4): pp. 1504–1513.

130. Brown, P., and S. C. Levinson, *Politeness: Some universals in language usage.* Vol. 4. 1987, New York: Cambridge University Press.

131. Lakoff, R. T., *Language and woman's place.* 1975, New York: Harper & Row.

132. Leaper, C., and M. M. Ayres, A meta-analytic review of gender variations in adults' language use: Talkativeness, affiliative speech, and assertive speech. *Personality and Social Psychology Review,* 2007. 11(4): pp. 328–363.

133. Maltz, D. N., R. A. Borker, and J. A. Gumperz, A cultural approach to male-female mis-communication, in *Language and social identity,* L. Monaghan, J. E. Goodman, and J. M. Robinson, Editors. 1982, Marblehead, MA: Wiley. pp. 195–216.

134. Haslett, B. J., Communicative functions and strategies in children's conversations. *Human Communication Research,* 1983. 9(2): pp. 114–129.

135. Jacklin, C. N., and E. E. Maccoby, Social behavior at thirty-three months in same-sex and mixed-sex dyads. *Child Development,* 1978. 49(3): pp. 557–569.

136. Sheldon, A., Pickle fights: Gendered talk in preschool disputes. *Gender and Conversational Interaction,* 1993. 13(1): pp. 83–109.

137. Falbo, T., and L. A. Peplau, Power strategies in intimate relationships. *Journal of Personality and Social Psychology*, 1980. 38(4): pp. 618–628.

138. Holtgraves, T., and J. N. Yang, Interpersonal underpinnings of request strategies: General principles and differences due to culture and gender. *Journal of Personality and Social Psychology*, 1992. 62(2): pp. 246–256.

139. Smith, J. S., Women in charge: Politeness and directives in the speech of Japanese women. *Language in Society*, 1992. 21(1): pp. 59–82.

140. Brown, P., Gender, politeness, and confrontation in Tenejapa. *Gender and Conversational Interaction*, 1993. 13(1): pp. 144–162.

141. Meyerhoff, M., Sorry in the Pacific: Defining communities, defining practices. *Language in Society*, 1999. 28(2): pp. 225–238.

142. Leaper, C., H. R. Tenenbaum, and T. G. Shaffer, Communication patterns of African American girls from low-income, urban backgrounds. *Child Development*, 1999. 70(6): pp. 1489–1503.

143. Schumann, K., and M. Ross, Why women apologize more than men. *Psychological Science*, 2010. 21(11): pp. 1649–1655.

144. Galinsky, A. D., J. C. Magee, M. C. Inesi, and D. H. Gruenfeld Power and perspectives not taken. *Psychological Science*, 2006. 17(12): pp. 1068–1074.

CHAPTER SIX

◆

Female Friends: Smile—Then Eliminate the Competition

WOMEN COMPETE AGAINST UNRELATED WOMEN. IT MAKES little sense for a woman to compete against a man. Both familial and unrelated men are bigger, stronger, and louder and have different interests. As a toddler, a girl knows that another girl is less likely than a boy to beat her up [1]. Across cultures, women are more likely to be beaten up by a man than by another woman [3–7]. Except where there literally are no females around, girls grow up with other girls and women. By adulthood, even in the smallest hunter-gatherer societies, between their family ties and female work activities, women spend a lot of time around other women [8, 9]. Often these women are related to one another, but as a community grows larger, it includes an increasing number of women who are unrelated.

Competition between unrelated females is hard to spot. It's not just that women don't beat each other up. Women go to great lengths to be nice. Most girls and women walk into a situation and expect other girls and women to be nice. They leave, genuinely bewildered, when someone isn't nice. The next time they find themselves in a similar situation, they again expect everyone to be nice. They return again, befuddled and disappointed.

Compared with unrelated males, unrelated females look at each other and smile more. Their greater politeness includes paying more attention to a speaker's words, acknowledging them, and figuring out from nonverbal gestures what was actually meant. Girls and women want to know where each lives, who their families are, who they do and don't like, and what each worries about most. They learn a lot more than a man ever does about one another's likes and dislikes, particularly with regard to other individuals, including kin, friends, and unpleasant persons. What a peaceful refuge they can provide from life's hardships [10–13].

Why Compete?

These wonderful feminine attributes can be misleading, however. Although women can sometimes create a safe haven [14], they can't do this all the time. They have to navigate an uncertain world with difficult choices. What would happen to a woman who did not care whether she got plenty of food and a secure shelter? What would happen if she were not interested in whether a potential husband would be helpful or not? What would become of her if she showed no attraction to status or money? What would become of her children if she did not ensure that they got the best education and made the most of their talents? The answer is that she and her children would lose out. Other women who do care would get the best husbands, more resources, greater status, and better educations for their children. Ultimately, a woman who does not compete, and compete hard when necessary, will be more likely to die early and be less able to successfully raise her children. And that would be the end of her noncompetitive genes.

In this way, women are no different than female primates of many species. As Sarah Hrdy [15] long ago pointed out: "Competition among females is one of the major determinants of primate social organization, and it has contributed to the organisms women are today" [15]. Tim Clutton-Brock's years of research [16, 17] demonstrate that many mammalian females compete over what they need to ensure the well-being of themselves and their offspring. As just one example, females of many species often compete over the best territory. A bad neighborhood could spell genetic doom if it is too near predators or strange males of the species; if it lacks nutritious food such as fruiting trees, termites, or worms; or if it is too exposed to the elements. A good home is an enormous advantage.

In most primate species, females also compete for status. High status gives a female many advantages. For starters, higher status gives females access to better material goods, such as territory, which means greater safety, more food, and better protection from the elements. For another, once high status is attained (as long as it remains unchallenged), life is much less stressful [18]. Lower stress translates into greater immunity, which often means a longer life [19]. Across a variety of primate species, high-status primate mothers and their babies suffer from fewer illnesses and live longer [20]. High-status mothers are less stressed because their environment is safer from predators and strange males and provides more nutritious food. They live longer. They have more offspring. Their offspring then help them and their other offspring, especially when a conflict erupts.

High-status female primates also have more allies because unrelated females need favors from them [21]. Just like any other popular individual, a high-status female has things that others need [2]. If another female requires a better territory, more food, or assistance fighting a competitor or predator, a high-status female can lend a helping hand, or mouth or foot. The high-status female then can call in the favor at a later date.

A high-status primate mother also attracts the best babysitters [22]. Babysitters make life so much easier for a mother. Across primate species, prepubertal, nulliparous (an adult female who has not yet produced children), and pregnant females like to babysit the children of the highest-status females. Babysitting of course helps a mother-to-be practice caring for infants and small children. Babysitting a high-status female's children does more than that: It helps a mother-to-be to stay alive. That's because a high-status mother will protect her babysitter should the babysitter become embroiled in a conflict. No high-status mother would risk losing an excellent babysitter. A good babysitter is invaluable in giving a mother a break from child care responsibilities and allowing her to get some work done, like finding food. Not only that, but a babysitter allows her to socialize with allies and potential future mates.

Low-status primate mothers can't find babysitters. If they do, their babysitters don't do a very good job. Sometimes the babysitters carry off, injure, lose, or even kill their charges. This almost never happens to the baby of a high-status mother. That's because only a high-status mother provides excellent benefits in exchange for good child care.

Not only that, but high-status females can make life difficult for lower-status females. In many species, a high-status female can make a low-status female work so hard that her physical and psychological health suffer. Being malnourished or stressed can make it hard to conceive and can increase the rate of miscarriages, cause stillbirths, reduce the size of newborns, cause them to be born prematurely, and increase the rate of infants' illnesses or neurological impairments [23]. At the extreme end, in some species, high-status females can actually prevent other females from reproducing altogether [23]. They do this by stressing lower-status females so badly that they cease ovulating. Failing that, a high-status mother might kill another mother's baby or even physically expel the woman entirely from the social group. If she can't find another group, the expelled one might die. A high-status mother then has more of everything for her own children.

Competition among human females is so little understood that no one knows for certain exactly what they compete about. But the importance of competition to women can be clearly seen by what happens to those who lose out. The clearest example is the fate of low-status mothers and their children. Children of low-status mothers are more likely to be born prematurely, underweight, and with a range of physical and neurological problems [24, 25]. Their physical environment is worse [26]. Their air and water are more polluted. They live closer to garbage and toxic chemicals. Their homes are more dangerous, crowded, and noisy. They eat less well, have more parasites in their bodies, and suffer from more infectious diseases.

Their social environment is worse, too [26]. Crime is more common. Their parents are more likely to be violent. Their mothers are more likely to be young, depressed, and unresponsive to them. They are less likely to have fathers, or helpful fathers, in the home. They move more often. Their neighborhoods are more likely to contain peers with many problems. Their mothers don't supervise them as much. Their education is of poor quality, or in some even existent, especially for girls in poor parts of the world [27]. Increasingly, researchers believe that by early childhood, the brains of lower-status children do not function as well as they could [28, 29]. The genes that a girl should have to help protect her future children may not be able to function as well either. What woman would not compete as hard as she could to avoid these kinds of consequences for herself and her children?

One common way for human females to attain status is to marry a high-status man. Even in the most egalitarian of human societies, the very smallest hunter-gatherer communities, women want to marry men with the highest status. These men are the best hunters in the community [30, 31]. Even though male hunters share their food with the whole community, a man's family gets a larger share [32].

In larger hunter-gatherer communities, successful men can hide extra food without anyone noticing [9]. They are no longer so egalitarian. Extra resources mean less chance of dying early. Women want to marry men with extra resources, and they must compete to do so.

The quality of a mate is important to females in most species. A potential mother wants to mate with a male who has "good" genes. How can she know which male is best? The male who looks healthiest, strongest, makes good decisions, and generally has what it takes to thrive in her particular environment is a good bet. These good genes will help a female's offspring survive, even if the male does not provide any child care at all.

Sometimes an ovulating female may need to compete against other females to attract a male with good genes quickly. Her window of opportunity to become pregnant is brief. She cannot waste time waiting for his sexual attention but will try to quickly initiate sex. Many human females choose this path from time to time [33].

What is most important about human males is that some, although not all, actually contribute a lot more than just their genes. As in other monogamous species, females benefit greatly from choosing a male who will invest in her children [16, 17, 34].

But for human females who want a mate for the long term, competition is even more severe. If males with "good" genes who are unfaithful and males with "bad" genes are eliminated, the stock of excellent candidates is pretty small. Women must compete hard to attract a man with "good" genes who will invest in her children. In order to do this, they must figure out what men find attractive, then emphasize these parts of themselves. As in most species, what males find most attractive are characteristics that indicate that the female will be a good mother and produce and raise healthy children. For example, in chimpanzees, an old, gray-haired female who already has raised lots of children is the most attractive of all to males. By definition, she is a great mother [35].

A human male looking for a stable relationship cannot afford to wait to see how good a female is at producing and raising children. A woman's childbearing years are limited, and marriage lasts a while, so a man has to guess. He generally guesses that a young and energetic woman will be the best mother. She has more time to produce children and more energy to raise them. If he guesses wrong, and the woman can't have children, he might divorce or kill her [27]. So to marry a high-quality man, a woman must make herself look young and display her energy. Applying makeup, dressing in youthful clothes, and being in good shape helps. Food, shelter, lack of stress, allies, babysitters, status, and mates are all worth competing for. Supplies are limited. If a woman wants to prevent an early death, keep her children alive, and help them thrive, she must compete. But, in comparison to men, she cannot risk retaliation. Being attacked in any way might put her health and that of her children at serious risk. She must be extremely cautious.

How does a woman compete while minimizing the risk of retaliation? I suggest that women use a few simple strategies. Strategy 1 is that a woman does not ever let anyone else know that she is competing with them. This is an ideal strategy, since if she can disguise her intentions, the risk of retaliation is reduced. She preaches the mantra of equality for all, and sincerely believes it. This sincerity allows her to be maximally convincing to other women. Unaware of her own competitive instincts, she tries to get as much as she can for herself, while insisting that everyone else share equally.

If strategy 1 is not working out well enough, then a woman may switch to strategy 2, which requires employing social exclusion. She must ally with other females to run their target out of town. That way, they retain more resources, status, allies, babysitters, and high-quality mates for themselves. The virtue of social exclusion is that it allows overt competition but reduces the risk of retalitation because the target is outnumbered.

Should strategy 2 fail, the final fallback is strategy 3, which is reserved for emergencies. It entails a direct hit on a competitor, a physical or verbal assault. If a woman must use strategy 3, she has failed. She is no longer nice; she is mean [36]. No one likes mean girls or women [37]. She will be abandoned by former allies. Not only that, but she risks retaliation from her target. She endangers herself and her children's immediate survival.

Strategy 1: Compete Discreetly

In a woman's mind, she never competes. Rather, in fairness to all, she insists that every woman is equal. Accordingly, almost all social scientists and evolutionary biologists describe women as the noncompetitive and egalitarian sex [38, 39]. Most people believe this simply because males compete over everything at least in public [40]. Card games, horse races, football statistics, and running times, to name a few of males' passions, are not of interest to women. They can't waste time on frivolous pursuits. Women focus on whether they and their children are surviving and thriving. They must compete to do so, but because women always must be very careful to avoid retaliation, they must do so in private. Strategy 1 is a low-cost approach that is effective because it is so misleading.

While insisting—and believing—that she and other women do not compete, a woman then does her best to advance her own and her children's interests. If she manages to get more resources, a more worthy mate, a safer house, or a better school for her children without anyone else realizing it until it is too late, she succeeds. Her competitors are left bewildered that she got ahead of them. She was *so nice.*

This only works if a woman can convince others that she is not compet-ing. This works best when she herself is not aware that she competes [41]. Nonetheless, the outcomes of women's competitions count more than those between men. Should a woman lose, she and her children will inevitably suffer. Should a man lose, it doesn't make as much difference to the future of his genes because a woman is looking after them.

Strategy 1 greatly reduces a woman's chances of anything terribly harm-ful happening to her. Compared with men, women do not compete overtly. Rarely is a woman going to be hit over the head and have her food or her husband stolen. Rather, the food or husband will be stolen while she isn't home or while she is talking to the neighbor next door. Women are nice. They all maintain they would never compete with someone else.

At the same time, each woman must pay the closest attention to any subtle sign of competition emitted by another woman. They must read between the lines. Because women don't compete for fun, and they don't compete in public, women aren't used to seeing female-female competi-tion. Men cannot understand why women pay attention to such subtle signs. If another man is trying to compete, he generally does it in pub-lic. He openly bests his competitor, then helps himself to his competitor's food—or his wife.

Yet women are competing continually for the highest stakes. The evi-dence shows that from toddlerhood through adulthood, human females act as if they are not competing, try their best to catch any female who is getting ahead of them, then discreetly go for what they want.

In one of my first studies, I asked preadolescent children in Boston to describe each one of their same-sex classmates. Almost every girl spontane-ously judged the other girls in her class in terms of their "niceness" [37]. It was *the* most important quality in a female classmate. A few girls were very nice, some were really mean, and others were so-so. Boys were less inter-ested in others' niceness; they focused on the skills of their male classmates.

Niceness appears to mean more than simply smiling and being polite. From a girl's perspective, a nice girl is someone who does not compete with you. Researchers interviewing hundreds of women have reached the same conclusion: Nice women don't try to outdo their female peers [42, 43]. Of course, no woman really believes this enough to trust other women without constant reassurance. Women keep their eyes and ears glued to the nonverbal gestures and verbal intentions of other women. One competitive sign and it's over. The other female will never be trusted again. Despite the fact that a woman is unaware of her own competitive instincts [42, 44, 45], she remains constantly, if intuitively, on guard for the possibility that another woman is trying to better her, her children, her husband, or her whole family [42].

If a woman has successfully competed, she must still do her best to avoid retaliation. She does this by continuing to believe that she does not compete. Thus, should it become apparent that a girl or woman has gotten hold of a choice toy, received a better school mark, obtained nicer clothes, accrued more friends, married a richer man, bought in a bigger house, made more money, landed a more prestigious job, or accomplished anything more than her female peers, she states flatly that it's not her own doing. She truly believes that it's luck or divine intervention. It's not her fault or her responsibility. Girls and women are much more likely than boys and men to attribute their successes to luck [46]. Blaming luck diverts attention from a woman's own competitive efforts and avoids potential retaliation. From early in life, girls and women don't take credit for what they have achieved.

Should a woman achieve success, she may never mention it [42, 44]. As I described in chapter 5, there is a strong female taboo against discussing personal success. Instead of speaking of their many achievements, successful women focus on something that is not going well, some weakness that is of concern. There is always something that is not right.

A woman who states that she attained exactly the goal she was striving for is taking a big risk. Other women would feel extremely envious [42]. Envious females might attempt to ruin a woman's success by socially excluding her (see strategy 2). Better to maintain that all women are equal and that lucky outcomes are outside one's control. Best never to mention personal success at all. Only when a girl or woman feels she is failing can she speak freely [42, 43]. Other females truly are sympathetic. They can afford to be because they are ahead. That doesn't mean they won't try to help her sort out her feelings and improve her game plan. A true friend would, but only if the failing female doesn't eventually outperform her friend.

A woman's honest belief that she never competes with other females is what allows her to do just that. Nothing works better than self-deception at permitting one to gain the upper hand in interpersonal conflicts of interest without potential retaliation [41]. By being unaware of her own competitive instincts, a woman can go about her business of pursuing her goals, so that she and her children can survive and thrive. How else to ensure that she gets the best resources, territory, allies, babysitters, mates, and status? If she didn't compete to get what she can, her female peers certainly would. She and her children would then suffer. She would be letting her genes down.

Of course, a nice woman must smile and behave politely at all times. She must empathize with other women's problems and the reasons for their fears, sadness, and anger. She must share her own fears, sadness, and anger, which come from very similar experiences. She must exchange all sorts of demographic information about the important people in each other's lives. She must show that she invests time and energy in understanding another woman and expects the other woman to do the same. As described in chapter 5, that is how she gets along with other women.

Her genuine empathy for another woman's concerns, however, cannot interfere with her trying to take that woman's job or husband. Should she pass up an opportunity to do what seems beneficial for herself and her family, she loses very important resources, relationships, or status. Of course, the victim can't easily understand this, nor should she. By the time the victim realizes what has happened, it's usually too late. The victim then will review the situation, repeatedly, with other women, in the hope that she doesn't fall for this again. Just because a woman is victimized by another woman, however, does not mean that in the future she won't do the same herself. When she has the opportunity to advance her position in life, she too will take it. She too needs to ensure her own and her children's survival and ability to thrive. This happens even in the most primitive of hunter-gatherer societies [4].

Based on interviews with hundreds of women, several researchers independently have reached the same conclusion [42, 44, 45]. Women honestly do not believe they compete with one another. Women absolutely will not tolerate any other woman who competes with them.

As one example, Laura Tracy interviewed women of all ages [44] and concluded, "Good girls don't compete with each other. They wait to be asked, try not to harm each other, and give up what they want for the good of someone else.... the women I interviewed told me they did not compete with other women" (Tracy, 1991, pp. 6–7). Here is a description of one of Tracy's interviewees:

> Anne, twenty-two, feels selfish most of the time. Nearly six feet tall, with long brown hair and large hazel eyes, Anne is an arresting figure. Her body language, however, denies both her beauty and her outstanding achievements in school.
>
> Sitting with her shoulders carefully bent forward, her hands neatly crossed in her lap, and her legs wound around each other, Anne physically underlines her belief: "I don't want anything so much that I would compete with another woman to get it."
>
> Anne's body language expresses fear. Wanting makes her feel frightened, and her fear affects her self-esteem. Although she earned excellent grades in college, she feels: "Anyone could have done as well. I work so hard because I know I'm really not very smart...."
>
> Anne thinks, as do many women, that if she competes with other women she will be abandoned. Her fears of loneliness and isolation, of being thought by other women to be self-absorbed and selfish, overwhelm her. (Tracy, 1991, p. 5)

Anne feels that if she does too well, other women, including her own friends, will turn on her. Dozens of studies confirm what clinical interviews repeatedly find. Beginning as early as they learn to speak, girls behave as if all of them are totally equal. They know that no one will like them if they attempt to sound superior. Their words show this clearly. Females speak to one another as equals, at all times, from early childhood into old age, across diverse cultures [47–51]. They use the words "we" and "us" more often than males do [47, 52]. Should a preschool girl wish to do something that no one else thought of, she cannot even say something as trivial as "I just had a great idea. I am going to play in the kitchen. You come with me." She knows that would turn her female peers against her. Instead, she might inquire politely: "Do you want to play in the kitchen?" She might make a tentative suggestion that includes everyone, such as "Let's go play in the kitchen." Women do the same [13, 47–49].

Unlike boys, girls almost never boast, command one another, tell jokes at one another's expense, try to top one another's stories, call each other names, or in any way show off, and they sure don't let any other girl do this either. No girl is superior to any other girl [47, 53]. Should a girl appear superior, even accidentally, she faces social exclusion.

Here is the example again from chapter 2 in which middle-class White 3- and 4-year-old girls are in the nursery school kitchen [52]. They all want to have the pickle. If you read their words, however, you wouldn't know it. You have to look at the description of what they are doing.

> SUE: And strawberries for dinner, right?
>
> MARY: And the- this for dinner. (*Mary puts the pickle in a pot on the stove*)
>
> SUE: And the pickle. Do you like pickle? (*Sue takes the pickle out of the pot*)
>
> MARY: And this (*the hamburger*) is for dinner. (*Mary pulls the hamburger and pickle out of Sue's hand and puts them back in pot*)
>
> SUE: No, they aren't for dinner, no, Lisa wants pickles. (*Sue tries to grab the hamburger and pickle back from Mary but she holds on and puts them back in the pot*)....
>
> SUE: No, Lisa wants pickle. (*Sue tries to grab the pickle again*)
>
> MARY: She gots (*unintelligible*)....
>
> SUE: You want pickle, Lisa?
>
> LISA: Mmmhm. (*Mary brings the pickle over to Lisa at the table*)
>
> SUE: Lisa says she wants pickle.
>
> (Sheldon, 1990, p. 17)

In Goodwin's yearlong study of African American children and adolescents in a working-class Philadelphia neighborhood, the same rule is followed [54]. No girl can compete. All girls are equal, and none is superior. The only exceptions are if one girl is much older than the others, or if a girl gets to play the mother or teacher while they are engaging in pretend play. Every girl of course wants to play the mother or teacher. The others repeatedly remind her, however, that she isn't any better than anyone else; she is just pretending, for a short time, to be better.

It became apparent one day to some of the girls in Goodwin's study that one of their own was acting superior. It was an accident, of course. Goodwin described what happened. Several of the girls who played together in the neighborhood were between 10 and 12 years of age. All the 12-year-old girls' clothes came from older female relatives or from thrift shops. One 10-year-old girl, named Annette, however, had a mother who bought her new clothes. Over the course of several months, because of her nicer clothes, three 12-year-old girls ganged up on Annette. The older girls decided to never talk to Annette again and to not let anyone else talk to her either, for months. Their treatment of Annette was so bad that Annette's mother almost sold their home and moved away. It was heartbreaking for Annette.

Girls and women therefore must somehow advance their own interests and still maintain good relations with those in the vicinity. Otherwise, the others might go after them. Girls and women well know the risks of being seen as overtly competitive. My students and I asked almost 200 adolescent and adult participants to imagine they had done really well either academically or socially [55]. When we asked them how they would feel, every one of them told us they would feel very happy. Then we asked them how their closest same-sex friends would feel. Our female participants, both girls and young women, reported that their friends might not like them anymore. They checked the following items more than males did: My friend would feel "betrayed by me," "disappointed in me," "angry with me," and "jealous of me." They said their friends would feel much better if they all had done equally well. If they had outperformed their friends, they felt their friendships were in jeopardy. In contrast, boys and men felt their closest friends might be jealous but they would respect them and want them as friends. Jealousy between women is more common than between men in the most simple hunter-gatherer bands [3].

How do girls act when one girl becomes superior to another? To find out, my students and I created a small competition [56]. We asked groups of either four girls or four boys, who were either 5 or 9 years old, to come to a room at their school. We then asked each group to choose a leader who would tell the others what to do. We left the room and left a video camera behind.

Neutral observers later rated the videotaped negotiations in each group. The girls wanted to be the leader as much as the boys did. So what did the girls do? The girls looked a lot less comfortable than the boys did. The observers made notes: The girls were crossing their arms, frowning, looking around anxiously, and refusing to make eye contact. Furthermore, results showed that the longer the negotiations went on, the less comfortable the individual girls looked. Not so for the boys, who often relished competing to be the leader. The girls couldn't stand that one of their own would be superior.

Would this be true when only two girls competed to win a simple contest? To check this out, we asked pairs of girls or boys the same age as in the leadership study to work side by side on either piecing together a puzzle, matching sounds by remembering their locations, or a motor task that required removing spots from a toy moving ladybug [56]. The member of the pair who got the most puzzle pieces together, or matched the most sounds, or removed the most spots before the time was up would receive a "winner" certificate.

A barrier separated the two children while they worked. When the time was up, the barrier was lifted. Then the experimenter carefully counted the pieces, matches, or spots for each child, announced the winner, wrote the winner's name slowly on a certificate, and, with great fanfare, presented the prize.

Videotapes later showed what happened. Girls and boys worked equally hard and did equally well at their tasks. As before, however, observers' ratings showed that the girls looked a lot less comfortable than the boys, especially after the winner received the prize. In fact, the winner looked anxious, while the loser looked mad. The winning boy, in contrast, appeared to be pleased with himself.

One girl cannot be seen to be superior to another, not in plain sight at least. Because of this, girls have problems playing competitive games. This helps explain why Janet Lever [57] in her observations of 9- to 11-year-old children found that girls almost never play them. If they did play games, they did not play boys' kinds of games. Boys' games require directly interfering with someone else's progress, such as hitting an individual with the ball before he reaches the base or pushing him out of the way. When girls played competitive games, they chose jump rope or hopscotch, where competition is indirect. Even so, if any girl tried too hard or bragged about doing well, the game ended.

Not surprisingly, girls' games didn't last long. During the year, not a single girls' game lasted the full 25 minutes allotted to outdoor play. Most of the boys' games did, every single day. Not only that, but when a conflict broke out between the girls, even if the game hadn't even started yet, the girls just abandoned the game. According to Lever, girls "complained that their friends could not resolve the basic issues of choosing up sides, deciding who is to be captain, which team will start, and sometimes not even what game to play" (Lever, 1976, p. 483). When the game actually did get played, the winner was forbidden to say she won. She acted like she forgot. Meanwhile, the winning boys bragged for as many days as possible. Others have reported similar findings across the world [58].

Strategy 1 functions in the workplace too. Whether in psychology labs or in actual business operations, no woman can be seen to be visibly competing with or superior to any other. Women especially do not like female bosses, who are by definition successful in competition and can act like they're superior [59–61]. Social scientists attribute this difficulty women have with female leaders to the 'double bind' tension [that] emerges because leadership roles involve agential or task-related attributes while 'the female role' is stereotypically associated with interpersonal and cooperative traits that are *incompatible* with leadership' (Schieman & McMullen, 2008, p. 288) [6]. So what is a female boss to do?

Female and male leaders are similar in most respects, with one huge exception. In more than 90% of studies, female bosses behave in a more egalitarian and less autocratic fashion than male bosses. Women with authority act like they and their subordinates are equals. Unfortunately for women, this is not good enough. Studies show that both men and women would rather have a male boss, and women feel even more strongly about this than men do. In fact, a large survey showed that female bosses are more likely than male bosses to make women physically sick as well as emotionally distressed [5] (unless of course female bosses hire sicker or more distressed subordinates in the first place).

Maybe it's just female bosses who are the problem. Pat Heim and her colleagues [62] decided to find out what happens between female coworkers. They constructed a questionnaire titled "Have You Ever Been the Object of a Destructive Conflict? It posed the following questions:

1. Have I ever felt undermined by another female at work?
2. Have I ever felt unjustly snubbed by a female co-worker?
3. Have I ever heard secondhand that a female co-worker is upset about something I said or did?
4. Have I ever performed most of the work on a project and had a female co-worker take the credit?
5. Have I ever shared a secret in confidence with a female co-worker and found that she had leaked it to others?
6. Have I ever had untruths spread about me and been the victim of malicious gossip?
7. Have I ever been told "It's nothing!" when I asked a co-worker with an icy demeanor if something was bothering her?

8. Has any woman tried to diminish my power by making herself look better at my expense?
9. Has a co-worker gone to my supervisor with a complaint about me without discussing it with me first?
10. Has a female co-worker ever "forgotten" to tell me about a meeting, phone call, or message that was very important to me?

Heim and her colleagues continue:

If you answered "Yes" to at least one of the above questions, then it's likely you have at some point in your life been on the receiving end of another woman's particular wrath. Whether or not you were consciously aware of the special challenges that can arise when working with women, you knew enough to pick up this book. Perhaps you were the subject of nasty backbiting and gossip, or maybe you noticed that a female subordinate consistently refused to follow your orders and never completed assignments on time. Perhaps you realized that you just can't stand your female supervisor who constantly puts you down and makes you feel insignificant. Possibly you've been suffering in silence, believing that no one else has had to put up with this kind of pain or fearing that others will label you "difficult" if you complain.

You're not Alone

A recent study of one thousand women conducted by the American Management Association found that 95 percent of the research sample felt other women had undermined them at some time in their careers." (Heim et al., 2001, pp. 8–9)

According to Heim and her colleagues, the only coworkers who were acceptable were those who were "dead even." That is, they weren't obviously trying to compete. Needless to say, not many women were willing to remain "dead even" when they had the opportunity to advance.

What a shock to face a smiling, polite woman with whom you have shared the same work experiences, the same victories, defeats, and stressors, and exchanged personal vulnerabilities and details about the limits of all the important people in your lives, who just behaved in a cruel and blatantly

competitive fashion. Not only that, but she won't even admit she is competing with you. Men don't face this. They are always competing, and they have
no problem in admitting it.

Underneath their "nice" facade, women are always competing. In continuing her interviews, Laura Tracy [44] found that although her female
interviewees reported that they themselves never competed against another
woman, they also recounted that other women were always competing with
them. Many were their (former) friends. Not only that, but these other
women competed with Tracy's female interviewees over everything: jobs,
work assignments, friendships with bosses, boyfriends and husbands,
clothes, jewelry, the size of their homes, their cooking skills, the closeness
of their friends, the prestige of their family members, the competence of
their children. There was no end to the number of things over which these
women reported facing competition.

From toddlerhood through old age, human females compete over toys,
proximity to the teacher, friends, marks on school exams, body size, grace,
facial attractiveness, performance at work, prestigious jobs, high-status
romantic partners, and so on [42, 44, 45, 62]. And so they should. Otherwise,
their own and their children's survival and well-being would not be maxi-
mized. Just because in a girl or woman's mind, she is unaware that she competes does not mean that she doesn't. It would be self-destructive if she
didn't try to get what she needs to do well in life.

Because girls follow this strategy so early in life, across diverse cultures,
in so many areas, it seems likely that genes have arranged for women not to
be aware of competing with other women. That way, they can ensure that
no other female tries to outdo them [38, 39, 63], and they can compete with
less danger of retaliation. If they compete (without knowing it), they can get
what they want safely, as long as other women remain uncertain about what
has happened.

Sometimes this strategy doesn't work out well as well as it should, however. Someone succeeds at being superior in a way that sounds an alarm.
A posse gathers. It's time to continue on to strategy 2, elimination of the
perpetrator.

Strategy 2: Socially Exclude

Strategy 2 comes into play when one female stands out. She may stand
out because she obviously tries to outdo everyone else. She may stand out

because she is new, extremely talented, or simply has the resources or relationships that others want. She may even stand out simply because she is an easy target and has nothing going for her. She has no allies. It would cost little to be rid of her, leaving more for everyone else. In any of these circumstances, it might be worth using a more direct competitive strategy. However, any form of individual, direct competition leaves open the possibility of retaliation and potential harm. One way of minimizing this is for several girls or women to gang up on a single target. This way, there is little chance of any one of the group suffering harm. Social exclusion accomplishes just that.

To implement strategy 2, several steps are required. The first step is identification of the target. In most instances, there is only one at a time. The second step is that several female peers gather to make a plan. As long as there are several peers and only one target, there is no risk of retaliation. The target is outnumbered.

The final step is that the target must be made to disappear, temporarily or permanently. She has violated the rule of not overtly trying to get ahead of anyone else, of not standing out. By definition, then, she is mean. She may already have succeeded in getting hold of a critical resource or person or rung on the ladder of status. Even if she hasn't yet succeeded, she looks likely to. In some cases, even an unlikely competitor might be targeted simply because it doesn't cost much and having one fewer competitor is beneficial to all. Irrespective of the exact motive, elimination of a competitor for resources, relationships, and status will promote the survival and well-being of all the remaining females and their children.

I believe that barring imminent death of herself or her child, nothing strikes more fear into the heart of a girl or woman than the thought that she will be excluded. In one recent study, my students and I asked women and men simply to read about being socially excluded by a friend. Women's heart rates increased much more than men's heart rates did [64]. In contrast, women's and men's heart rates increased equally when they imagined being physically assaulted by a friend.

Why shouldn't men be just as afraid of social exclusion? Certainly, men are just as hurt as women should they be socially excluded. But they aren't. Social exclusion is primarily a female strategy. Women use it more because it is more beneficial to women [65]: Women do not need to form large groups and women cannot afford to engage in direct competition. Social exclusion allows women to reduce their number of competitors, safely.

Social exclusion results in the elimination of another woman. But women do not have that much to gain from other unrelated women. They actually have a lot to lose. If fewer unrelated women are around, then more food, territory, allies, babysitters, friends, mates, and high-status positions are available to a woman and her children. Not only that, but because most marriages are between one woman and one man, it takes only one extra woman to ruin a marriage or at least reduce the available resources. Getting rid of this extra woman could make the difference between being married, having extra resources, and providing a father for her children and being a poor, single mother. There is no obvious downside to eliminating a female from the community. Less really is more.

In contrast, a man generally does not want to completely eliminate a fellow community member. Most men could be an asset in an intergroup conflict. Should the enemy attack, the larger the home fighting force, the greater are the chances of victory. Better to fight over status, but keep anyone who could possibly contribute around. Tough men are needed, especially if they are tougher than the other men. Social exclusion is a last resort for men.

Female chimpanzees provide a helpful illustration of how this operates. Chimpanzees live in communities, with each female generally residing with her offspring in her own territory within the larger community. A female's territory can have a strong effect on her own and her offspring's survival. Territory farther from the boundary of the community is safer from attacks by groups of killer male neighbors. Territory with fruiting trees provides a lot more nutritious food. Females with the best property bear the most and the healthiest offspring [66]. At adolescence, however, a postpubertal female usually migrates and joins a new community.

Just how do resident chimpanzee females feel, then, when a young newcomer female arrives from a neighboring community and attempts to settle down in a piece of their territory to raise her children? Not good. Allowing a newcomer into their community would harm their own and their children's chances to survive and thrive. Resident females therefore occasionally form coalitions and attack the newcomer [67]. A newcomer's best hope is often to stick close to a male who might protect her from the resident females [68]. In several instances, the two highest-status females with the choicest property have even murdered the infant of a newcomer female [67, 69]. Attacks such as these may succeed in expelling the newcomer from the community [70].

How does social exclusion occur in humans? The process is quite simple [71, 72]. A girl or woman alerts her female peers to the presence of a female competitor who is outstanding in some manner, or maybe is an easy target. The first responder spreads the word through gossip or written notes. This typically happens initially in the target's absence, reducing the risk of retaliation and potential bodily harm.

Should the target be present, the first responder identifies her discreetly, using nonverbal gestures that other females can easily decode (and that potentially protective males miss completely). For example, the first responder can roll her eyes in disgust or flip her hair angrily in the direction of the target [73]. If the first responder and her female peers smile and otherwise behave politely, the target may not immediately realize what is happening. That safeguards members of the female coalition, who can leave the scene before the target catches on.

Next, the members of the coalition must meet to discuss their tactics. Direct threats can backfire. The target might retaliate. She will find out about the gossip. Smiling and politeness mixed up with subtle threats may disorient her, but only temporarily. As soon as she figures out what's really going on, what's to stop her from taking countermeasures? Eliminating her from the community by social exclusion provides a safer, and ultimately more beneficial, solution. Social exclusion is an important strategy for eliminating competitors, one at a time, without risk of retaliation. Girls practice it from early childhood [74, 75]. It has been used by females across diverse cultures in middle childhood and adolescence [76] and adulthood [71].

Norma Feshbach [77] designed one of the earliest studies to look at girls' tendency to exclude another girl. An experimenter brought two 6-year-olds, either girls or boys, to a room and told them they were to be part of a special club. The children then received special badges and special toys to play with. They had positions of status. One week later, the same two children returned to the room and were given the same badges and toys, but this time, a third child of the same sex was brought to the room after the pair had been playing for a while. The three children were left alone to play, with a camera recording what happened next.

When observers looked at the recordings, they found that pairs of girls were more likely than pairs of boys to exclude the newcomer. The girls initially avoided her, refused to talk to her, and would not play with her. Boys responded more quickly with positive overtures to the newcomer.

Feshbach then repeated her study with eighth-grade adolescents. This time, she asked the pairs to discuss some common social problems involving parents and children [78]. Later on, an unfamiliar seventh grader was brought in to discuss some additional problems.

Recordings of what happened showed that girls took more than three times as long as boys to speak to the newcomer. Girls also ignored the newcomer's suggestions more often. In 4 of the 15 girls' groups, the girls never spoke a single word to the newcomer. This happened only once with the boys. At the end of the study, the original pairs judged how nice the newcomer was. Girls thought that the newcomer was much less nice than the boys did.

In real life, how do girls plan social exclusion? John Gottman and his colleague's [79] audiotapes of children's natural conversations lay out the details. For example, Gottman recounts the following discussion between two 8-year-old girls, Erica and Mikaila, as they were discussing their target, Katie, who is guilty of many things:

E: Um, um Katie does lots of weird things. Like everytime she, we make a mistake, she says, "Well, *sorry*" [*sarcastic*].

M: I know.

E: And stuff like that.

M: She's mean. She beat me up once [*laughs*]. I could hardly breathe she hit me in the stomach so hard.

E: She acts like...

M: She's the boss.

E: "Now you do this." [Here we see fantasy as Katie is mimicked.]

M: "And I'll..."

E: "And Erica, you do this. And you substitute for the people that aren't here, Erica."

M: "And you do this, Mikaila. And you shouldn't do that, you shouldn't, you have to talk like this. You understand? Here, I'm the teacher here."

E: I know. She always acts like she's the boss.

M: So that's why we hid behind the sofa so she couldn't boss us around.

Later they continue:

M: She's mean.

E: No, she's mean.

M: Well, she is.

E: I know.

M: She says that she hates sugar and she eats it all the time. That's why she's so fat.

E: [*Laughter.*]

Later:

E: You know Elissa fed the spider two, two flies?

M: Yeah. Katie let one out.

E: She just went dunch and it went, and it buzzed out, you know?

M: Yeah, she just…

E: And she said…

M: …she started…

E: …"Katie, you left out one of the flies." And then she said, "Well, sooooory." Like she always does.….

M: Yeah, and she always cries about little things. Right, Erica?

E: Right, Mikaila?

M: *Laughter.*

E: Katie at my birthday, Katie doesn't write very good.

M: I know.

E: She wrote this, um, thing to me and I couldn't read it so I gave it back to her and said I couldn't read it and she said, "Well, I can read yours" and she went off and cried just because I said I couldn't read her writing.

M: Yeah. She whines a lot.

E: And just because we won't eat with her because I wanna eat with you…

M: Yeah, she starts crying.

E: "Cause she doesn't have anybody to eat with.

M: It's…

E: But there's thousands of people in the room to eat with.

M: Well she, she can eat with Charlotte but she just doesn't.(Gottman & Mettetal, 1986, pp. 204–206)

In Gottman and Mettetal's words [80], "This conversation lasted about 45 minutes, and most of it consisted of negative-evaluation gossip and building solidarity. It was done lightheartedly and with ease.…." (Gottman, 1986, p. 166). Even in early childhood, Gottman noted, "gossip usually occurs (1) primarily in dyads that contain a girl and (2) in the context of building solidarity using a summary description that I call 'we against others'" (Gottman, 1986, p. 166). Gottman does not use the expression "social exclusion," but Katie is already out the door.

Women do the same thing. In one study, a pair of young women or men were invited to a university laboratory and told they could talk for 5 minutes while they waited for the experimenter [81]. Female and male pairs talked for the same amount of time, but the women made more than twice as many negative comments about a third person as the men did. Further, when one woman made a negative comment about someone else, her female partner was very likely to encourage her to keep going. Not so for men. Here is a brief example:

> JOY: Amazingly, though, what's-her-name didn't say anything today.
> KARA: Oh yes!
> JOY: The brassy one.
> KARA: The big woman [laughs]
> JOY: [laughs]
> KARA: Ver-, the very obnoxious woman. Yes.
> (Leaper & Holliday, 1995, p. 244)

Someone is trying to show off. The coalition must stop her.

Rachel Simmons [82] set out to investigate competition and aggression among American high school girls. She interviewed 10- to 14-year-old American girls from a variety of ethnic and economic backgrounds about their experiences. What she found was social exclusion. In the following, she relates a story about Jenny:

Jenny is a newcomer to a very small town's middle school in Wyoming. According to the tale told by Rachel Simmons,

> Brianna and Mackenzie were the queen bees, and they presided over the seventh grade. Brianna was the prettiest, Mackenzie the best at sports. Their favorite hobby was having a boyfriend. Jenny wasn't really interested in a boyfriend, but she still like hanging out with the guys. Mostly she liked to play soccer and basketball with them after school. She liked to wear jeans and T-shirts instead of make-up and miniskirts.
>
> She had barely introduced herself when Brianna and Mackenzie gave her a code name and started calling her Harriet the Hairy Whore. They told everyone Jenny was hooking up with the boys in the woods behind

the soccer field. Jenny knew that being called a slut was the worst thing in the world, no matter where you lived. No one was even kissing yet. It was the lowest of the low.

Brianna and Mackenzie started a club called Hate Harriet the Hore Incorporated. They got every girl to join except two who didn't care. All the members had to walk by Jenny in the hallway and say "Hhiiiiiii…" They made a long sighing noise to make sure she knew they were sounding out the initials of the club: HHHI. Usually two or more girls would say it and then look at each other and laugh. Sometimes they couldn't even say the whole thing, they were laughing so hard.…

It seemed like Mackenzie and Brianna had suddenly made it their goal in life to ruin her. Nothing like this had ever happened before. In San Diego, she had three best friends. She had always been good at everything but not because it was easy. She strove for success in everything she did. In her head she heard her father's voice: "If you try hard enough, you can do anything." This was her first failure.

It was her fault.

She knew she'd never touched a boy, but maybe there was something really wrong with her. There were two other new girls in seventh grade, and they were doing just fine. They worked hard to fit in, and they did. They bought the same clothes and listened to the same music as everyone else.…

Jenny began to weep quietly in her room not long after she realized there would be no end to her torture. She managed to wait until her homework was done, and then she cried, silent always, her sobs muffled by her pillow. There was no *way* she'd tell her mother, and certainly not her father. She felt nauseous just thinking about telling her parents she was such a reject.

Every day was an endless battle. She was exhausted trying not to cry, stiffening her body against the hallway attacks, sitting through lunch after lunch alone. There was no one else to be friends with in the grade because everyone, the few that there were, was against her.…

One night Jenny's sadness left no room for her fear, and she picked up the phone. Jenny called Brianna, Mackenzie, and a few other girls. She asked each of them, "Why do you hate me?" They denied everything. "But why are you doing the Hate Harriet the Hore club?" she pleaded.

Their voices were light and sweet. "We don't have a Hate Harriet the Hore club!" each one assured her, as though they were telling her the earth was round. They were so nice to Jenny that for a second she didn't believe it was really them. Then she could almost feel her heart surging up through her chest. The next morning, she actually looked forward to getting out of bed. It would be different now.

Then she got to school.

"Hhhiiiiiiii...!" *Slam.*

Jenny blinked back tears and locked her jaw. She hated herself for being surprised. She should have known. The strange thing about it was, even though she was used to it, this time her heart felt like it was breaking open. Brianna and Mackenzie had seemed so genuine on the phone. And Jenny, stupid, stupid Jenny, she muttered to herself, and imagined herself at their lunch table in the back of the cafeteria. "Stupid, stupid, stupid," she repeated through gritted teeth, raising her books as a shield as a shield as she made her way into homeroom.

One day, months later, searching through desks after seeing the girls pass it around in homeroom, Jenny found the petition. "I Mackenzie T, promise to Hate Harriet the Hore forever," it said. Every single girl in the class had signed it, and it was appended with a long list of reasons why everyone should hate her. Jenny's eyes bore into the paper until the words blurred. She suddenly felt dizzy. The weight of her anguish was too heavy. She couldn't take it anymore. Jenny felt like her world was crumbling. (Simmons, 2002, pp. 26–29)

This is not an untypical story. A new girl, high-performing and self-confident, moves to a small school. She is a competitor. She must be excluded. Then, she is out of the running. The social ostracism was conducted so quietly that no adult in the school even knew.

Similar scenarios happen all over the world. In interviews conducted in Adelaide, Australia, middle-class girls in Catholic schools reported many instances of temporary and permanent exclusion of former friends, new girls, vulnerable girls with few friends or little self-confidence, or geeky girls [83]. No one was immune. At one of the Australian schools, two or three cases occurred per year in which the exclusion was so severe that a girl had to transfer to another school. Unfortunately, nothing is worse than entering a new school. These transfer girls often found themselves excluded again.

Phoebe Prince is one extreme example. She had moved from Ireland to a small town in western Massachusetts. She fell in love with one of the high-status boys who reciprocated her feelings, for a while. Not surprisingly, the resident girls were enraged. They bonded together. They made their plans. They even enlisted the help of a few boys. Phoebe was excluded from all activities, and even directly harassed, with the protection of the boys. The parents of the adolescents and school personnel did nothing, and eventually, Phoebe committed suicide. The publicity led to an outpouring of reports of similar reactions to girls and young women who are newcomers to a school or neighborhood [84].

Women seem to know intuitively how hard it is to join a new female group. Several studies show that they dislike moving more than men do. This is true even when these women are not leaving their families behind, and even when they are advancing their own careers [85–87].

One large American study looked at what happened to people who had moved within the past 5 years [88]. Many more women than men suffered serious depression. Further, the harder a woman tried to make new friends, the more serious the depression she developed. Only women who already had friends in their new neighborhoods escaped feeling badly.

It is possible to look at social exclusion experimentally. Girls begin to use social exclusion at least as soon as they start playing with each other. In one study, my students and I asked three same-sex 4-year-old classmates to come to a room to play [89]. We took turns giving the trio three puppets, two puppets, or just one wonderful big puppet and videotaped what happened. As anticipated, this became a problem. How does a 4-year-old get the one puppet? In the many trios of boys, it was a no-brainer. Each boy wildly chased whoever had the puppet, screaming about fairness and taking turns, all the while trying to grab the puppet, as the puppet owner raced round and round in circles.

Not the girls. When one girl had the puppet, the other two girls got together and excluded her. A typical situation went like this: The other girls, bereft of the puppet, began paying increasing attention to one another and ignoring the girl with the puppet. Then, social exclusion commenced. This was done in amazingly creative ways. For example, one pair of girls put their heads inside the box where the puppet had been and whispered to each other. Another two girls hid behind a piano and wouldn't come out. In a third instance, they hid under a chair together. Often, they didn't even stop when the girl with the puppet offered to give it to them. She could have the puppet, but she would never be part of their community again. Others have reported the same behaviors in preschool classrooms [75].

By middle childhood, social exclusion becomes more conscious [74]. Because girls compete in private, however, observing it is tricky. To see it in action, my students and I created a situation in which the girls would not be blamed if they socially excluded someone. We asked groups of five 10-year-olds from schools in Plymouth, England, if they would produce a short play [90]. The 10-year-old actresses and actors had 25 minutes to write the play, assign the roles, and rehearse their 5-minute play. To encourage them to take their plays seriously, we created a prize. We told each group that adult judges would pick the winning play, and each member of the winning group would receive 20 pounds (about $35), a lot of money for a child.

Every group worked hard. No adults were present. Final productions were videotaped and later judged, with the prize distributed to the winning group.

What did the groups think of? The seven boys' plays consisted primarily of skits based either on a popular television show or on football (soccer) matches between two well-known teams. Only one was a novel drama, about a family dealing with a corrupt businessman. All of the boys took part equally in these plays. No one was singled out.

In contrast, six of the seven girls' plays involved social exclusion of a target girl. In the most egregious case, a truly overweight girl with stringy hair played the part of a new girl who had just moved from France to the other girls' class. Three of her "classmates" took turns pushing and shouting insults at her. At the pinnacle of the play, these three "classmates" circled her for a full minute screaming synchronously in raucous voices "Loser! Loser! Loser!" She then ran out of the room, actually crying. The fifth girl, playing the role of the teacher, then physically captured and hauled her back. The "teacher" displayed overt frustration but secret pleasure at the behavior of her students. Had we been watching, we would have halted this play.

In another of the girls' plays, four classmates humiliated, then stole the homework of, the smartest girl in their class, so that she ended up with a low mark and pretended to cry. In a third play, three girls enacted the roles of the three pigs, directed by the mother pig. In a reversal of the usual plot line, the four pigs ostracized the wolf forever. In still another play, four girls being interviewed on television physically and verbally attacked their female interviewer. In a fifth play, a "mother" was killed in a car accident. Her daughter and the hospital personnel then spent their time figuring out what to do. In the sixth play, a social worker tried to take a baby away from an alcoholic family. The family threw her out.

Only one girls' group did not portray social exclusion. These girls divided themselves up into a pair and a triad and put on separate, simultaneous plays about exercising in different rooms in a gym.

The girls' and boys' plays differed in other ways too. First, as expected, the girls more frequently formed a coalition whose members synchronously directed behavior toward one lone girl. Second, the girls varied more in the amount of time each girl got on stage. The girl who was excluded got a lot less air time than the others. In contrast, the boys were more egalitarian, giving each one a fairly similar amount of time to perform.

What stood out is that in the girls' minds, the target of their exclusionary alliance seemed to deserve it. She was trying to act superior. She was the French newcomer, the smartest girl in the class, the powerful she-wolf, the glamorous television hostess, the higher status mother, and the social worker trying to break up a family. These girls believed that they were right to eliminate this superior-acting competitor. They proudly put on their plays in front of the camera; they didn't think they were behaving unethically.

To demonstrate experimentally how women too use social exclusion, my colleagues and I created a computerized game, without any particular theme. We asked individual participants to play the game against two fictional opponents [91]. If they did well enough, they won money. Each participant could choose to play either alone, with one opponent as an ally, or with both opponents as allies. The probability of winning was identical regardless of their choices.

In contrast to what most people predicted, women did not choose to play with both opponents as their allies. In fact, almost no one chose to do this. Rather, most everyone wanted to play alone and try to win the maximum amount of money possible.

But then we added a wrinkle. We mentioned that if a participant played alone, then the two opponents would be able to get together to exclude them. Even though this did not affect the participant's chances of winning, women immediately switched strategies. Instead of playing alone, they chose to ally with one player and exclude the other one [92]. Men were completely unaffected by the idea that their opponents might ally against them. After all, it had no bearing on whether they won more money.

What is the evidence, though, that in real life, women really do socially exclude another woman? Because most people won't admit to this, the next best way to find out is to ask women whether they ever have been excluded.

Sure enough, when we asked young adults to describe any occasions in the past year when they had been socially excluded by same-sex friends, women listed more occasions than men [64].

Social exclusion provides a safe, clean method for eliminating an unrelated female who can reduce physical or social resources or status available to a woman and her children. Social exclusion takes planning, however. Allies are needed. The target must be isolated. In an emergency, this may not work. A woman may not have any allies, or she needs to act quickly.

Strategy 3: A Direct Hit

She may need to proceed to strategy 3. It is a very last resort because it is dangerous. Physically assaulting or verbal insulting another person invites retaliation. A woman generally cannot afford to take the risk.

In chapter 5, I reviewed the reasons not to resort to this strategy, along with the exceptions. Because a direct hit on another woman invites retaliation, generally it decreases the chances that a woman and her children will survive and thrive. These rules are meant to increase, not decrease, survival. Strategy 3 therefore must be reserved for emergencies.

Nonetheless, life gets the better of every woman sometimes. Bad luck strikes. Repeated stress wears a woman down. No matter how privileged her life, every woman almost certainly explodes in rage or strikes out once in a while when her needs are not met.

A woman living a privileged life, however, almost always explodes at a family member who won't retaliate or end their relationship. The two most obvious targets are her small children who need her to survive and are too small to retaliate [93, 94], or possibly her husband, but only in a society that has laws preventing him from retaliating [3]. Female relatives also are possible targets; they won't abandon her. A very high-status woman with many allies also may chance a run-in with a lower-status, unrelated woman, but she must be very dominant to minimize the chances of retaliation.

Many studies suggest, however, that a privileged woman who resorts to strategy 3 afterward feels ashamed and regretful [36]. She surely has lost control of herself [36, 95]. No woman, if she can possibly help it, should risk retaliation under such benevolent circumstances.

For women with few resources, things are different. Their own and their children's survival are not assured. No one is thriving. They use strategy 3 more often. Although across diverse cultures women avoid direct physical and verbal aggression as much as possible and inflict much less injury than men do [71, 96], sometimes it is their only recourse. As assault can literally save her own or her child's life. It can secure a boyfriend or increase her status. It might help her own children succeed in life.

This is true right now for girls and women in impoverished neighborhoods in the United States [97]. If they don't fight, someone will steal their few material goods, seduce their romantic partners, or diminish their status. Across the world, by stealing food or cooking pots from another woman [96], beating up a potential mate's other girlfriend [98], preventing a co-wife from scratching her face or poisoning her child [99], a woman unequivocally improves her own and her children's chances of survival. The risk of retaliation is outweighed by the immediate benefit.

Nonetheless, unrelated women will steer clear of any woman who uses strategy 3. Such women are considered out of control and dangerous. They are beyond mean; they are a menace to society. They can hurt a woman and her children badly. When possible, all attempts must be made to exclude them permanently from the community. Alternatively, when an aggressive woman cannot be excluded, another aggressive woman might join forces with her to exclude a third party. This reduces the competition and may decrease the need to resort to strategy 3 in the future.

Chapter 5 described the rarity of women's use of this strategy. Because from early in life across diverse cultures women are much less likely than men to use direct physical or verbal aggression, there is likely an innate bias against the use of this strategy [100, 101]. Even in infancy [102], and at every age across diverse cultures [101], human females are less aggressive than males. It runs counter to the survival and well-being of women and their children, in most circumstances, to engage in such behavior [103].

Nonetheless, strategy 3 is clearly a part of all women's repertoire. I illustrated this in an experiment I described in chapter 2 in which my student and I asked children to play a game in which they collected beads and piled them on a stick [56]. Whoever reached the finish mark on their stick by collecting enough beads won a prize. On each turn, a child rolled a die and could take the number of beads shown on the die either from a pile of beads provided by the experimenter or from another child's stick. If the child chose to take another child's beads, this decreased the chances that the other child would win.

Children played two versions of the game. In the direct competition version, only the first child who reached the finish mark won the prize. In the nondirect competition version, every child who reached the finish mark before the time was up won the prize.

In the direct competition, girls took each other's beads. They did this as much as or more than the boys did. They wanted to win. Even at age 5, girls strategically took the beads of the other girl who was most likely to beat them [104]. Unlike the boys, though, when they stole another girl's beads, they looked down rather than making eye contact. They also looked worried.

In the noncompetitive version, however, girls almost never took another girl's beads. It didn't help them to win, so why resort to strategy 3? Why risk retaliation? The girls played just as hard to win, but harming another girl's chances was a waste of time. Only the boys competed in this version—just for fun.

The Reason Why: The Fragility of Women's Relationships with Unrelated Women

Women admit to fighting and even competing with immediate family members. Probably almost every mother who has ever lived has screamed in her home and commanded, insulted, made fun of, and otherwise acted superior to her family members at times. Girls and women compete directly, usually verbally, against their relatives over resources and important relationships [105]. Not only that, more than 75% of women from all income levels in the United States report hitting their children [22, 93]. In the poorest parts of American society, mothers and other female relatives actually will help daughters and nieces physically fight unrelated women [97]. While they rarely inflict serious physical harm, women from all walks of life nevertheless resort to strategy 3 quite freely within their families.

So why don't women do this with unrelated women? Genetic relationships are forever. A woman knows who her family is, and will always be. Family members share genes. Family creates permanent ties.

It is rare for a woman to find herself socially excluded by her family, unless, of course, she is a reproductive failure. Then she may be excluded and even murdered [27]. Her survival is no longer viewed as useful in terms of caring for the family's genes. If she has children or contributes to the well-being of other relatives, however, then a woman has permanent lifelong bonds.

Even when family members are present, unrelated women may be too. Even in traditional hunter-gatherer societies, a woman often interacts with other women who are unrelated to her or her husband [106]. In other societies, women marry into their husbands' families and live far from relatives [107]. In modern societies, family members often live far from one another. A woman must try to survive and thrive among mostly unrelated individuals who share genes with her children but not with her. In the most extreme case, unrelated co-wives may have to share the same husband [99].

With unrelated females and females who have no relation to a woman's children, a woman shares no genetic interests. Moreover, unrelated females are more likely to come and go. Circumstances change; they look out for their own genetic interests.

While a woman needs to form relationships with other women in her community so she can get along smoothly, she must always keep an eye on the bottom line, or the cost-benefit ratio. Building a new relationship with an unrelated woman is costly. It takes time and energy. The benefits must be absolutely clear, and the costs must be low. Her own and her children's survival and well-being must always come first.

Competition is inevitable. Food, property, friends, babysitters, status, and romantic partners often come in limited supply, even for the richest members of the world. If all homes were in equally safe neighborhoods and equally large, if food were always abundant and nutritious, if all men were equally reliable and rich, if all schools were equally good, females would not need to compete. Men could play their card games, race their horses, and engage in their frivolous competitions over just about anything, while women could sit back and relax. In reality, this is rarely the case. A woman who doesn't get the best of any of these important resources will struggle, and so will her children.

In the distant past, a woman who managed to shove another woman out of the way so that she could erect her own hut farther from the periphery of the encampment would have been safer from predators and closer to other successful individuals. She and her children would have been more likely to survive. In the same way, a modern woman who can outbid another woman for a home in the best neighborhood in town gives her children a safer and more enriched environment. At any time, a woman who managed to have babies with a husband who contributed to her own and her children's well-being would be more likely to pass on her genes successfully than her competitors who had babies with an unreliable man.

If a woman wants to invest her time, energy, and perhaps even resources in an unrelated female, she must make sure that this female does not inflict too high a cost. An unrelated female better provide the peace. serenity, and communion that women are famous for [10–13]. She must not compete. She will be monitored continually. Should the costs of this relationship ever exceed the benefits, a woman will end the relationship fast.

This happens frequently. In hundreds of interviews with girls and women about their friendships, my students and I have often heard the same story, which goes like this: A girl, I will refer to her by her initials, ME, has a Best Friend. They talk all the time and do everything together. One day, the Best Friend does something horrible. Whatever it is, it makes ME feel inferior to her Best Friend. A Third Girl appears on the scene. She makes ME feel much better; she provides a warm sanctuary. She agrees wholeheartedly with ME that the Best Friend did something inexcusable. The Third Girl then tells ME about her own similar experience with a fourth girl who used to be her own Best Friend but then made her feel inferior. The Third Girl makes ME feel so much better, and so equal. This Third Girl really would make a much better Best Friend than her former Best Friend. Good-bye old Best Friend; hello new Best Friend. Relief sets in. All is settled, until of course the new Best Friend does something horrible. . . .

We didn't hear these kinds of stories from boys. Their stories were simpler. For example, if I interviewed W, he told me he was friends with X, Y, and Z, and sometimes A, B, or C join them too. When I interview Y, he tells the same story. So does Z. The discussions are over quickly. I already know what each one is going to say before they say it.

To find out whether girls are more careful than boys in their relationships with unrelated same-sex friends, my student and I interviewed 6- to 11-year-old children from a wealthy private school in Canada. We asked each student in 17 classes whether any same-sex friendships in their class had ended [108]. At every age, girls listed more friendships that had ended than boys did. Not only that, but several boys spontaneously provided graphic details of the breakup of a girl's friendship. Not one girl mentioned the end of a boy's friendship.

We found exactly the same thing with older children and adolescents. In this case, my student Athena Christakos interviewed 120 children aged 10 through 16 from lower-middle-class public schools about their own closest same-sex friendships. At every age, girls reported that more of their friendships had ended than boys did [109].

In both studies, both girls and boys reported caring about their closest friends equally and spending equal amounts of time with them. Girls' friends, however, were newer because they had broken up with their last best friend. Even so, twice as many girls as boys reported that their current best friend had already done something to make them feel bad. In Leningrad, Chita, and Chelyabinsk in the former Soviet Union, researchers reported the same findings: Girls' friendships did not last as long as boys' friendships [110].

To try to find out why girls' friendships end, Christakos asked each boy and girl about the kinds of things that could cause the end of their friendships [109]. Everyone agreed that if a friend purposefully tried to hurt them, this would be likely to end the friendship. Only the girls, however, listed other causes. According to the girls, a friend could try to appear superior, spread negative rumors, hurt them by accident, date a boy that they had discussed, and other transgressions. The boys didn't care about these things.

For a girl, being made to feel inferior is a critical reason for ending a friendship. Even just imagining a friend breaking the rule of equality upsets a girl more than a boy. In one study, researchers asked more than 250 9- to 11-year-old American children from many ethnic backgrounds how they would feel if a same-sex friend told someone else about a bad grade they got on a school exam, didn't express sympathy toward them, wouldn't share their lunch when they had forgotten their own and were really hungry, and didn't do their part of a joint project, leading to their receiving a bad grade [111]. In all cases, girls judged their friend more negatively than boys did. Critically, girls were more likely than boys to believe that their friend was trying to put them down.

Likewise, 96 11- to 15-year-olds from Colorado were asked to imagine that their actual same-sex friend or classmate called them a name, said they were stupid, and other mean things [112]. As before, girls were much more upset and were more likely than boys to blame the peer for what happened. Boys often felt it was partly their own fault. Researchers in Finland also reported that when girls and boys had conflicts with their friends, the girls reported remaining more upset than boys [113].

My colleagues and I found that young women respond the same way [114]. We asked students to imagine that they were unable to hand in an important paper to a professor, so they asked a close same-sex friend of theirs, who always was very reliable, to deliver the paper to the professor by 5 o'clock. The friend agreed but, for whatever reason, did not hand in the paper. Before the incident, women and men rated the friend as equally reliable. After their paper was not delivered, women rated the friend as much less reliable than the men did. A similar study asked young men and young women to imagine that their closest friend had done something bad, such as spreading rumors or teasing them about their attractiveness. Women reported they would be more likely to end the friendship than men [115].

Why is it that most people, including social scientists and evolutionary biologists, think that girls and women are more sociable than men? I would argue this is because when women get along, they provide such a wonderful respite from competition. And when they compete, they do so in private, outside the prying eyes of the public, other women and researchers alike.

In my research lab we wanted to know, however whether women really view friendships as more costly than men do. One way to find out is to study an important same-sex relationship: the roommate. In societies with higher education where young adults live at the educational institution, they often live with one other same-sex student. Roommates spend a lot of time together, just as they would with their family members if they lived at home. Roommates, however, do not share any genes.

My colleagues and I wanted to know specifically whether women are more likely than men to end relationships with their roommates [114]. Consequently, we asked those in charge of assigning roommates at three colleges to keep track of all the roommate changes during one year. At all three places, more women than men had left their roommate and moved to another room. Compared with men, for women either the costs of maintaining a relationship with their roommate were higher or the benefits were lower, or perhaps both. In the event of a conflict with a roommate, women preferred to pack up all their belongings and start over, usually with a new roommate [114].

What exactly is the reason? To find out, several of us tracked down students who lived with one roommate with whom they were having a conflict. Then we found other students who were not in the midst of a roommate conflict [114]. We asked each student anonymously to answer questions about their roommate.

The results were clear. Whether they were having a conflict with their roommate, or not, women reported they were much less happy than men with their roommate. Strikingly, when there was no roommate conflict, 100% of the men said they were happy with their roommates, while fewer than 50% of the women did. Obviously, unrelated women take a toll.

We then asked those in charge of roommate assignments to name all the things they could think of that led to roommate breakups. Their lists included the roommate's smelling bad; making a mess; breaking rules; not caring about his or her appearance; being hyperactive or a sloth; being untrustworthy; having weird study habits; being emotionally insensitive, overly friendly, too religious, or too independent; refusing to ever leave the room; talking excessively; and exercising too much, to name a few. Next we categorized these aversive characteristics into those related to hygiene, values, interests, and social style.

We found that in every category, women rated their roommate as worse than men did. Amazingly, these young women even thought that their roommates were smellier, messier, and louder than the men did. This is hard to believe, as usually men care less than women about their hygiene and personal habits. Clearly, women found their roommates more costly, and less beneficial, than men did.

This corresponds to the study described in chapter 5. When asked to keep diaries of when they or someone else apologized, women reported more apologies than men. Women also were more likely than men to believe apologies were necessary. Why? Because women saw many more offenses committed every day than men did. More than anything else, this shows that women find that interactions with unrelated individuals inflict higher costs and lower benefits than men do [116].

In many traditional human cultures, a woman spends her days close to at least some female relatives. There are at least a few people around who share her own or her children's genes. These other people want those genes to survive into the next generation [117]. They have an interest in ensuring that she and her children survive and thrive. This doesn't mean that a woman need not compete over resources and valuable relationships and status. Families can be brutally competitive, and often overtly so.

But when a woman competes with family members, she knows that they share some interests with her. This should limit how much they will harm her. She also knows they are unlikely to leave her. They will be invested at least somewhat in helping her and her children stay alive and thrive. Until they die, these family members will always be there. If the goal of all of them is to ensure that their genes survive into the next generation, then they need her to survive and thrive, so she can care for their genes that reside in her children. If a woman can spend time raising her children near her own mother, she greatly increases her own and her children's survival and health [118].

If she must live with her husband's family, however, she must keep up her guard. They may choose to replace her. They will not be as invested in keeping her alive and well. They will be invested only in her children who share their genes.

That is not to ignore that some families sell their daughters to a man, a brothel owner, or as household help [27]. Girls' families can decide not to invest in them for many reasons. These girls often won't pass on their genes. They will die early. If they do pass on their genes, and they have no contact with their own relatives, the woman and their children will be less likely to survive and thrive [118, 119]. In societies where women's status is much lower than men's, this is much more likely to happen [120].

Still, if this happened too often, human beings would have disappeared from the earth. They are not disappearing; quite the contrary. As they have done since prehistoric times, families must ensure that their daughters survive and help their daughters to raise families.

References

1. Jacklin, C. N., and E. E. Maccoby, Social behavior at thirty-three months in same-sex and mixed-sex dyads. *Child Development*, 1978. 49(3): pp. 557–569.
2. Barclay, P. (2013). Strategies for cooperation in biological markets, especially for humans. *Evolution and Human Behavior*, 34, pp. 165–174.
3. Archer, J., Cross-cultural differences in physical aggression between partners: A social-role analysis. *Personality and Social Psychology Review*, 2006. 10(2): pp. 133–153.
4. Lee, R. B. *The Dobe Ju/'hoansi* 4th ed. Stamford, CT: Cengage Learning.
5. Daly, M., and M. Wilson, *Homicide*. 1988, Hawthorne, NY: Aldine de Gruyter.
6. Schieman, S., and T. McMullen, Relational demography in the workplace and health: An analysis of gender and the subordinate-superordinate role-set. *Journal of Health and Social Behavior*, 49, 2008. pp. 286–300.
7. Maltz, D. N., and R. A. Borker, *A cultural approach to male-female miscommunication*. In J. A. Gumperz (Editor) Language and social identity. New York: Cambridge University Press, 1982. pp. 195–216
8. Mehta, C. M., and J. N. Strough, Sex segregation in friendships and normative contexts across the life span. *Developmental Review*, 2009. 29(3): pp. 201–220.
9. Marlowe, F., *The Hadza: Hunter-gatherers of Tanzania: Origins of human behavior and culture*. 2010, Berkeley: University of California Press.
10. Bakan, D., *The duality of human existence: An essay on psychology and religion*. 1966, Oxford: Rand McNally.

11. Taylor, S. E., et al., Biobehavioral responses to stress in females: Tend-and-befriend, not fight-or-flight. *Psychological Review*, 2000. 107(3): pp. 411–429.

12. Gilligan, C., *In a different voice: Psychological theory and women's development.* 1982, Cambridge, MA: Harvard University Press.

13. Tannen, D., *You just don't understand: Women and men in conversation.* 2001, New York: Harper Paperbacks.

14. Bowlby, J., *Attachment and loss: Volume 1: Attachment.* 1969, London: Hogarth Press and the Institute of Psycho-Analysis.

15. Hrdy, S. B., *The woman that never evolved.* 1999, Cambridge, MA: Harvard University Press.

16. Clutton-Brock, T., Sexual selection in males and females. *Science*, 2007. 318(5858): pp. 1882–1885.

17. Clutton-Brock, T., Sexual selection in females. *Animal Behaviour*, 2009. 77(1): pp. 3–11.

18. Sapolsky, R. M., The influence of social hierarchy on primate health. *Science*, 2005. 308(5722): pp. 648–652.

19. Sapolsky, R. M., L. C. Krey, and B. S. McEwen, The neuroendocrinology of stress and aging: The glucocorticoid cascade hypothesis. *Endocrinology Review*, 1986. 7(3): pp. 284–301.

20. Sterck, E. H. M., D. P. Watts, and C. P. van Schaik, The evolution of female social relationships in nonhuman primates. *Behavioral Ecology and Sociobiology*, 1997. 41(5): pp. 291–309.

21. Schino, G., Grooming, competition and social rank among female primates: A meta-analysis. *Animal Behaviour*, 2001. 62(2): pp. 265–271.

22. Smith, H. J., *Parenting for primates.* 2005, Cambridge, MA: Harvard University Press.

23. Sapolsky, R. M., Social status and health in humans and other animals. *Annual Review of Anthropology*, 2004. 33: pp. 393–418.

24. Parker, J. D., K. C. Schoendorf, and J. L. Kiely, Associations between measures of socioeconomic status and low birth weight, small for gestational age, and premature delivery in the United States. *Annals of Epidemiology*, 1994. 4(4): pp. 271–278.

25. Bradley, R. H., and R. F. Corwyn, Socioeconomic status and child development. *Annual Review of Psychology*, 2002. 53(1): pp. 371–399.

26. Evans, G. W., The environment of childhood poverty. *American Psychologist*, 2004. 59(2): pp. 77–92.

27. Kristof, N., and S. Wudunn, *Half the sky: How to change the world.* 2010, London: Virago.

28. Evans, G. W., and M. A. Schamberg, Childhood poverty, chronic stress, and adult working memory. *Proceedings of the National Academy of Sciences of the United States of America*, 2009. 106(16): pp. 6545–6549.

29. Farah, M. J., et al., Childhood poverty: Specific associations with neurocognitive development. *Brain Research*, 2006. 1110(1): pp. 166–174.

30. Smith, E. A., Why do good hunters have higher reproductive success? *Human Nature*, 2004. 15(4): pp. 343–364.

31. Marlowe, F. W., Mate preferences among Hadza hunter-gatherers. *Human Nature*, 2004. 15(4): pp. 365–376.

32. Wood, B. M., Prestige or provisioning? A test of foraging goals among the Hadza. *Current Anthropology*, 2006. 47(2): pp. 383–387.

33. Buss, D. M., *The evolution of desire: Strategies of human mating.* 1994, New York: Basic Books.

34. Buss, D. M., Sex differences in human mate preferences: Evolutionary hypotheses tested in 37 cultures. *Behavioral and Brain Sciences*, 1989. 12(1): pp. 1–49.

35. Muller, M. N., M. E. Thompson, and R. W. Wrangham, Male chimpanzees prefer mating with old females. *Current Biology*, 2006. 16(22): pp. 2234–2238.

36. Campbell, A., and S. Muncer, Intent to harm or injure? Gender and the expression of anger. *Aggressive Behavior*, 2008. 34(3): pp. 282–293.

37. Benenson, J. F., Gender differences in social networks. *Journal of Early Adolescence*, 1990. 10(4): pp. 472–495.

38. Ahlgren, A., and D. W. Johnson, Sex differences in cooperative and competitive attitudes from the 2nd through the 12th grades. *Developmental Psychology*, 1979. 15(1): pp. 45–49.

39. Bem, S. L., The measurement of psychological androgyny. *Journal of Consulting and Clinical Psychology*, 1974. 42(2): pp. 155–162.

40. Benenson, J. F., Females' desire for status cannot be measured using male definitions. *Behavioral and Brain Sciences*, 1999. 22(02): pp. 216–217.

41. Von Hippel, W., and R. Trivers, The evolution and psychology of self-deception. *Behavioral and Brain Sciences*, 2011. 34(1): pp. 1–56.

42. Eichenbaum, L., and S. Orbach, *Between women: Love, envy, and competition in women's friendships.* 1988, New York: Viking.

43. Apter, T., and R. Josselson, *Best friends: The pleasures and perils of girls' and women's friendships.* 1999, New York: Three Rivers Press.

44. Tracy, L., *The secret between us: Competition among women.* 1991, New York: Little, Brown.

45. Chesler, P., *Woman's inhumanity to woman.* 2009, Chicago: Chicago Review Press.

46. Frieze, I. H., B. E. Whitley Jr, B. H. Hanusa, M. C. McHughAssessing the theoretical models for sex differences in causal attributions for success and failure. *Sex Roles*, 1982. 8(4): pp. 333–343.

47. Maltz, D. N., R. A. Borker, and J. A. Gumperz, A cultural approach to male-female mis-communication, in *Language and social identity*, L. Monaghan, J. E. Goodman, and J. M. Robinson, Editors. 1982, Marblehead, MA: Wiley. pp. 195–216.

48. Eckert, P., and S. McConnell-Ginet, *Language and gender.* 2003, New York: Cambridge University Press.

49. Brown, P., and S. C. Levinson, *Politeness: Some universals in language usage.* Vol. 4. 1987, New York: Cambridge University Press.

50. Leaper, C., H. R. Tenenbaum, and T. G. Shaffer, Communication patterns of African American girls and boys from low-income, urban backgrounds. *Child Development*, 1999. 70(6): pp. 1489–1503.

51. Leaper, C., and M. M. Ayres, A meta-analytic review of gender variations in adults' language use: Talkativeness, affiliative speech, and assertive speech. *Personality and Social Psychology Review*, 2007. 11(4): pp. 328–363.

52. Sheldon, A., Pickle fights: Gendered talk in preschool disputes. *Discourse processes*, 1990. 13: pp. 531.

53. Maccoby, E. E., Gender and relationships: A developmental account. *American psychologist*, 1990. 45(4): p. 513.

54. Goodwin, M. H., *He-said-she-said: Talk as social organization among black children.* 1990, Bloomington: Indiana University Press.

55. Benenson, J. F., and J. Schinazi, Sex differences in reactions to outperforming same-sex friends. *British Journal of Developmental Psychology*, 2004. 22(3): pp. 317–333.

56. Roy, R., and J. F. Benenson, Sex and contextual effects on children's use of interference competition. *Developmental Psychology*, 2002. 38(2): pp. 306–312.

57. Lever, J., Sex differences in the games children play. *Social Problems*, 1976. 23(4): pp. 478–487.

58. Mead, M., *Coming of age in Samoa.* 1928, New York: William Morrow.

59. Eagly, A. H., and B. T. Johnson, Gender and leadership style: A meta-analysis. *Psychological Bulletin*, 1990. 108(2): pp. 233–256.

60. Eagly, A. H., and S. J. Karau, Role congruity theory of prejudice toward female leaders. *Psychological Review*, 2002. 109(3): pp. 573–598.

61. Eagly, A. H., M. G. Makhijani, and B. G. Klonsky, Gender and the evaluation of leaders: A meta-analysis. *Psychological Bulletin*, 1992. 111(1): pp. 3–22.

62. Heim, P., S. Murphy, and S. K. Golant, *In the company of women: Turning workplace conflict into powerful alliances.* 2001, Los Angeles: Tarcher/Putnam.

63. Schneider, B. H., Benenson, J. F., Fulop, M., Berkics, M. and Sandor, M. Cooperation and competition, in P. K. Smith and C. H. Hart (Editors) *The Wiley-Blackwell handbook of childhood social development.* 2010, New York: Wiley-Blackwell. pp. 472–490.

64. Benenson, J., H. Markovits, B. Hultgren, T. Nyugen, G. Bullock, and R. W. Wrangham, Social Exclusion: More important to human females than males. *PLoS One*, 8(2): 2013. e55851.

65. Benenson, J. F., Dominating versus eliminating the competition: Sex differences in human intrasexual aggression. *Behavioral and Brain Sciences*, 2009. 32(3–4): pp. 268–269.

66. Thompson, M. E., S. M. Kahlenberg, I. C. Gilby, and R. W. Wrangham Core area quality is associated with variance in reproductive success among

female chimpanzees at Kibale National Park. *Animal Behaviour*, 2007. 73(3): pp. 501–512.

67. Kahlenberg, S. M., M. Emery Thompson, and R. W. Wrangham, Female competition over core areas in Pan troglodytes schweinfurthii, Kibale National Park, Uganda. *International Journal of Primatology*, 2008. 29(4): pp. 931–947.

68. Deschner, T., and C. Boesch, Can the patterns of sexual swelling cycles in female Taï chimpanzees be explained by the cost-of-sexual-attraction hypothesis? *International Journal of Primatology*, 2007. 28(2): pp. 389–406.

69. Townsend, S. W., K. E. Slocombe, M. EmeryThompson, K. Zuberbühler Female-led infanticide in wild chimpanzees. *Current Biology*, 2007. 17(10): pp. R355–R356.

70. Muller, M. N., Chimpanzee violence: Femmes fatales. *Current Biology*, 2007. 17(10): pp. R365–R366.

71. Björkqvist, K., Sex differences in physical, verbal, and indirect aggression: A review of recent research. *Sex Roles*, 1994. 30(3–4): pp. 177–188.

72. Campbell, A., Staying alive: Evolution, culture, and women's intrasexual aggression. *Behavioral and Brain Sciences*, 1999. 22(2): pp. 203–252.

73. Galen, B. R., and M. K. Underwood, A developmental investigation of social aggression among children. *Developmental Psychology*, 1997. 33(4): pp. 589–600.

74. Crick, N. R., and J. K. Grotpeter, Relational aggression, gender, and social-psychological adjustment. *Child Development*, 1995. 66(3): pp. 710–722.

75. McNeilly-Choque, M. K., C. H. Hart, C. C. Robinson, L. J. Nelson, and S. F. Olsen Overt and relational aggression on the playground: Correspondence among different informants. *Journal of Research in Childhood Education*, 1996. 11(1): pp. 47–67.

76. Smith, P. K., H. Cowie, R. F. Olafsson, and A. P. D. Liefooghe Definitions of bullying: A comparison of terms used, and age and gender differences, in a fourteen-country international comparison. *Child Development*, 2002. 73(4): pp. 1119–1133.

77. Feshbach, N. D., Sex differences in children's modes of aggressive responses toward outsiders. *Merrill-Palmer Quarterly: Journal of Developmental Psychology*, 1969. 15(3): pp. 249–258.

78. Feshbach, N., and G. Sones, Sex differences in adolescent reactions toward newcomers. *Developmental Psychology*, 1971. 4(3): pp. 381–386.

79. Gottman, J. M., and G. Mettetal, Speculations about social and affective development: Friendship and acquaintanceship through adolescence, in J. M. Gottman and J. G. Parker (Editors) *Conversations of friends: Speculations on affective development*. 1986, New York: Cambridge University Press, pp. 192–237.

80. Gottman, J. M., The world of coordinated play: Same- and cross-sex friendship in young children, in *Conversations of friends: Speculations*

on affective development, J. M. Gottman and J. G. Parker, Editors. 1986, New York: Cambridge University Press. pp. 139–191.

81. Leaper, C., and H. Holliday, Gossip in same-gender and cross- gender friends' conversations. *Personal Relationships,* 1995. 2(3): pp. 237–246.

82. Simmons, R., *Odd girl out: The hidden culture of aggression in girls.* 2002, New York: Mariner Books.

83. Owens, L., R. Shute, and P. Slee, "Guess what I just heard!": Indirect aggression among teenage girls in Australia. *Aggressive Behavior,* 2000. 26(1): pp. 67–83.

84. Russell, J., The agony of a girl who just wanted to fit in, *Boston Globe,* June 20, 2010.

85. Markham, W. T., Sex, relocation, and occupational advancement, in *Women and work: An annual review,* A. H. Stormberg, L. Larwood, and B. A. Gutek, Editors. 1987, Thousand Oaks, CA: Sage. pp. 207–231.

86. Markham, W. T., P. O. Macken, C. M. Bonjean, and J. Corder, A note on sex, geographic mobility, and career advancement. *Social Forces,* 1983. 61(4): pp. 1138–1146.

87. Markham, W. T., and J. H. Pleck, Sex and willingness to move for occupational advancement: Some national sample results. *Sociological Quarterly,* 1986. 27(1): pp. 121–143.

88. Magdol, L., Is moving gendered? The effects of residential mobility on the psychological well-being of men and women. *Sex Roles,* 2002. 47(11): pp. 553–560.

89. Benenson, J. F., T. J. Antonellis, B. J. Cotton, K. E. Noddin, and K. A. Campbell Sex differences in children's formation of exclusionary alliances under scarce resource conditions. *Animal Behaviour,* 2008. 76(2): pp. 497–505.

90. Benenson, J. F., L. Hodgson, S. Heath, and P. J. Welch Human sexual differences in the use of social ostracism as a competitive tactic. *International Journal of Primatology,* 2008. 29(4): pp. 1019–1035.

91. Benenson, J. F., H. Markovits, M. Emery Thompson, and R. W. Wrangham Strength determines coalitional strategies in humans. *Proceedings of the Royal Society B: Biological Sciences,* 2009. 276(1667): pp. 2589–2595.

92. Benenson, J. F., et al., Under threat of social exclusion, females exclude more than males. *Psychological Science,* 2011. 22(4): pp. 538–544.

93. Straus, M. A., and R. J. Gelles, Societal change and change in family violence from 1975 to 1985 as revealed by two national surveys. *Journal of Marriage and the Family,* 1986. 48(3): pp. 465–479.

94. Johansson, S., Neglect, abuse, and avoidable death: Parental investment and the mortality of infants and children in the European tradition, in *Child abuse and neglect: Biosocial dimensions,* R. J. Gelles and J. B. Lancaster, Editors. 1987, Piscataway, NJ: Transaction. pp. 57–96.

95. Campbell, A., *Out of control: Men, women and aggression.* 1993, New York: Pandora.

96. Burbank, V. K., Female aggression in cross-cultural perspective. *Behavior Science Research*, 1987. 21(1–4): pp. 70–100.

97. Ness, C. D., Why girls fight: Female youth violence in the inner city. *Annals of the American Academy of Political and Social Science*, 2004. 595(1): pp. 32–48.

98. Campbell, A., *The girls in the gang.* 1992, Cambridge, MA: Blackwell.

99. Jankowiak, W., M. Sudakov, and B. C. Wilreker, Co-wife conflict and co-operation. *Ethnology*, 2005. 44(1): pp. 81–98.

100. Maccoby, E. E., and C. N. Jacklin, *The psychology of sex differences.* 1974, Stanford, CA: Stanford University Press.

101. Archer, J., Sex differences in aggression in real-world settings: A meta-analytic review. *Review of General Psychology*, 2004. 8(4): pp. 291–322.

102. Baillargeon, R. H., et al., Gender differences in physical aggression: A prospective population-based survey of children before and after 2 years of age. *Developmental Psychology*, 2007. 43(1): pp. 13–26.

103. Benenson, J. F., and M. J. Harris, Sex differences in aggression from an adaptive perspective, in *Bullying, rejection, and peer victimization: A social cognitive neuroscience perspective*, M. J. Harris, Editor. 2009, New York: Springer. pp. 171–198.

104. Weinberger, N., and K. Stein, Early competitive game playing in same- and mixed-gender peer groups. *Merrill-Palmer Quarterly: Journal of Developmental Psychology*, 2008. 54(4): pp. 499–514.

105. Millman, M., *Warm hearts and cold cash: The intimate dynamics of families and money.* 1991, New York: Free Press

106. Hill, K. R., et al., Co-residence patterns in hunter-gatherer societies show unique human social structure. *Science*, 2011. 331(6022): pp. 1286.

107. Rodseth, L., R. W. Wrangham, A. M. Harrigan, and B. B. Smuts The human community as a primate society. *Current Anthropology*, 1991. 32(3): pp. 221–254.

108. Benenson, J. F., and K. Alavi, Sex differences in children's investment in same-sex peers. *Evolution and Human Behavior*, 2004. 25(4): pp. 258–266.

109. Benenson, J. F., and A. Christakos, The greater fragility of females' versus males' closest same-sex friendships. *Child Development*, 2003. 74(4): pp. 1123–1129.

110. Kon, I. S., and V. A. Losenkov, Friendship in adolescence: Values and behavior. *Journal of Marriage and the Family*, 1978. 40(1): pp. 143–155.

111. MacEvoy, J. P., and S. R. Asher, When friends disappoint: Boys' and girls' responses to transgressions of friendship expectations. *Child Development*, 2012. 83(1): pp. 104–119.

112. Whitesell, N. R., and S. Harter, The interpersonal context of emotion: Anger with close friends and classmates. *Child Development*, 1996. 67(4): pp. 1345–1359.

113. Lagerspetz, K. M. J., K. Björkqvist, and T. Peltonen, Is indirect aggression typical of females? Gender differences in aggressiveness in 11 to 12 year old children. *Aggressive Behavior*, 1988. 14(6): pp. 403–414.

114. Benenson, J. F., et al., Males' greater tolerance of same-sex peers. *Psychological Science*, 2009. 20(2): pp. 184–190.

115. Vigil, J. M., Asymmetries in the friendship preferences and social styles of men and women. *Human Nature*, 2007. 18(2): pp. 143–161.

116. Schumann, K., and M. Ross, Why women apologize more than men. *Psychological Science*, 2010. 21(11): pp. 1649–1655.

117. Alvarez, H., Residence groups among hunter-gatherers: A view of the claims and evidence for patrilocal bands, in *Kinship and behavior in Primates*, B. Chapais and C. Berman, Editors. 2004, Oxford: Oxford University Press. pp. 400–442.

118. Gupta, M. D., Life course perspectives on women's autonomy and health outcomes. *American Anthropologist*, 1995. 97(3): pp. 481–491.

119. Smuts, B., Male aggression against women. *Human Nature*, 1992. 3(1): pp. 1–44.

120. Bloom, S. S., D. Wypij, and M. Das Gupta, Dimensions of women's autonomy and the influence on maternal health care utilization in a north Indian city. *Demography*, 2001. 38(1): pp. 67–78.

———◆———

CHAPTER SEVEN

Organizing Her Family: The Vulnerable and the Assistants

A WOMAN KNOCKS ON THE DOOR OF HER FRIEND'S HOME. No answer, so she enters. Suddenly, she hears her friend and another person screaming in fury at one another in the kitchen. The two storm out of the kitchen only to find the woman standing there, embarrassed by what she clearly overheard. The friend's face turns bright red: She never meant this woman to hear her screaming.

Of course, female relatives fight like this all the time. Why are female relatives so much more confrontational and aggressive than female friends? I would argue that it's because female relatives have more shared genetic interests and stronger bonds than female friends. The Valuable Relationships Hypothesis states that when individuals really need one another, they tolerate more. When inevitable conflicts erupt, they figure out how to resolve them [1, 3]. The benefits of the relationship outweigh the costs of fighting.

Female friends at any age do not compete and fight directly because their relationships are simply not worth it. Unlike the careful interactions of unrelated girls or women, what occurs between females with family members contains far less smiling, fewer polite words, less attention to subtle nonverbal gestures, but many direct, mutual accusations regarding personal vulnerabilities.

A mother, children, sisters, aunts, and other female relatives are the closest allies a woman will have at any stage of her life [5–8]. In many societies, husbands, brothers, uncles, and other male relatives, despite their higher status, are also close allies [9]. Families are relatively secure places for females. Within her family, a girl or woman can compete overtly over resources, attention, and status. No need to be discreet or to avoid direct verbal or even physical confrontation. No need to fear social exclusion, not unless resources are extremely scarce. Verbal and physical abuse may occur but usually will be restrained. When they are not, a girl or woman often has no place of refuge.

From early in life, a woman is likely to gain the most resources, form the closest bonds, and eventually achieve high status within her family. Competition with her sisters and brothers, cousins, and others of her generation is severe. It occurs, however, between those who share some of her goals and, more important, some of her genes. Their common genes reside in their children's bodies. Family members need to protect them [10, 11].

The most secure place for a woman is in her family. Family members share her desire to keep her genes alive and help them thrive in the next generation. If a girl has grown up, it is because someone worked very hard to keep her alive. That someone is almost always her mother. If she has become a mother herself, even if she lives with her husband's family or without any extended family, she is needed to raise her children. Within the home, everyone knows that no one will work harder to protect them than a mother. With time and good fortune, she will become the grandmother and mother-in-law. For most women, this will be the most powerful position she holds [12].

Mothers and Children

Garrison Keillor, a Minnesotan storyteller highly respected for his accurate insights into human nature, describes the following situation [13]. A mother and father stand at the designated meeting place for the bus that will carry their son for the first time to overnight camp for the summer. This is a tradition in the United States for children of parents with money to spare.

The father proudly recounts for his son his own camp adventures: days and nights paddling through sparkling waters, frolicking in the sand on the beach, winning a trophy with his proud teammates, midnight surprise raids on another bunk, the immense joy of hot food and a shower after an extended trip through the wilderness. He genuinely hopes that his son will experience the same pleasures. Meanwhile, the boy's mother waits quietly for the bus to come. She is lost in her own thoughts. Is she thinking about the joys of camp? Not exactly: "Do the brakes work? Who is the driver? Is he licensed? Sober? Might he be carrying a pistol? Are the wheels securely fashioned to the hubs?"

Do women really care more than men about the survival and well-being of their children? Ask any nurse or doctor working in an emergency room. When a couple arrives with a sick child, even the most dedicated father cannot match his wife's emotional intensity. A mother is more distressed, more frantic, and more certain that her baby will die.

Even where fathers take care of children, many are not certain how old their child is, what day their child was born, where to find their child's doctor, or the name of their child's teacher [14]. None of these fathers, however, has any memory problems when it comes to recalling the names, ages, and statistics of the players on their favorite sports team.

Many fathers take part in activities with their children across diverse cultures [15, 16]. In the United States, these include coaching their child's baseball team, accompanying their child during trick-or-treating, and picking them up from an after-school activity. Nonetheless, a careful inspection shows that fathers can be distractible when it comes to children. While a father may dutifully push his baby's carriage, his attention is easily distracted by a pretty girl walking by, deliberations with fellow fathers about last night's baseball game, or a new business deal. Not that mothers don't get distracted and bored, as well. Nonetheless, the safety of a child is almost certainly more assured when a mother is present. A mother takes primary responsibility for passing the family's genes to her children. She invests her time, energy, and resources into her own and her children's survival and well-being. Mothers do more to feed, clothe, clean, comfort, educate, and care for sick children than fathers do. In every community ever studied, mothers take primary responsibility for their children, especially infants and other particularly vulnerable children [16–18]. Where little medical care exists, a mother almost always determines whether her children will survive [19]. Fathers, grandmothers, and other relatives vary in how much help they provide. In contrast, mothers universally help their children as much as they can.

Until recently, a mother had no choice. No surrogates existed. No breast formula was available to purchase. No baby survived without a mother's gestating and lactating. Brown [17] created a "universal people" (UP), which described the characteristics found in every human society. The most universal person is a mother:

> The core of a normal UP family is composed of a mother and children. The biological mother is usually expected to be the social mother and usually is. On a more or less permanent basis there is usually a man (or men) involved too, and he (or they) serve minimally to give the children a status in the community and/or to be a consort to the mother." (Brown, 1991, pp. 136–137)

Hunter-gatherer communities show this clearly [16]. Mothers are the primary caregivers in every hunter-gatherer community. They stay close to their infants for the infants' first 2 years, 24 hours a day. They sleep with their infants. They gather food while carrying their infants. They breastfeed whenever their infants are hungry. They respond rapidly and soothingly if an infant cries [20]. They dote over a sick child. Primatologists and experts in hunter-gatherer societies believe that these features characterize the last 30 to 40 million years of humanlike mothering [16, 21]. A mother's work keeps a new life alive.

In hunter-gatherer societies, divorce and remarriage are common. Nomadic ways of life mean continual moves. A father may not live near his child. That's because children almost always stay with their mothers [22, 23].

The United Nations millennium goals listed the education of girls as a top priority. Educated girls grow up to be women who are better able to care for their children and families [24]. Boys, regardless of whether they are educated, grow up to be men, who just don't invest as much in their families. Often, men will choose to spend their money on alcohol and tobacco or leisure activities as much as on their families. As the UNICEF millennium report [25] on the importance of education to girls states:

> Some 121 million children are not in school, most of them girls. If a family can afford school fees for only one child, it will likely be a boy who attends. If someone needs to fetch water or do housework instead of going

to school, a girl will likely be chosen. If someone needs to stay home to care for younger siblings or sick or infirm household members, this will most likely be a girl: girls will also most likely be withdrawn from school early in adolescence as the age of marriage approaches.

Yet study after study shows that educating girls is the single most effective policy to raise overall economic productivity, lower infant and maternal mortality, educate the next generation, improve nutrition and promote health.

Girls work extremely hard as children and continue to do so as women. They keep young and vulnerable children alive.

Of course, the world changes. Nowadays, in modern societies fathers are supposed to do more direct child care. How do modern fathers stack up? The best way of answering this question is to compare children living with a single father to children living with a single mother. In the past, it was very rare for children to be living with a single father. Over the last 30 years, however, there has been a large increase in single-father households, at least in the United States. By 2003, 6% of all American households contained single fathers [26]. Now it is possible to compare the child care of single fathers to that of single mothers. To make this comparison fair, however, it must be pointed out that single fathers are wealthier and better educated than single mothers.

Do single fathers use their advantages to take better care of their children? Generally not. Children of single fathers receive less health care. Single fathers are less likely to arrange for regular checkups or to have a regular doctor for their children [26]. American children living with single fathers engage in riskier health behaviors and experience greater emotional distress [27, 28].

Contrast this to what happens when children are brought up by single mothers, who are generally poorer and less well educated than the fathers of their children. Despite this, children of single mothers receive high-quality, frequent health care as much as children living with both parents. Further, children of single mothers generally do better in school than children raised by single fathers. Despite clear financial disadvantages, single mothers take better care of their children than single fathers do. This pattern has been found not only in the United States but also in European countries where there are significant proportions of single-father households. For example, Norwegian adolescents living with single fathers have much higher rates of antisocial behavior problems than adolescents living with single mothers or both parents [29].

So what do fathers do? In modern societies, fathers mostly provide fun. They toss infants high in the air; they tumble and tickle little children; they play games with older ones; and they teach their adolescent sons how to play sports and introduce them to other interesting activities [15, 30, 31]. There is also a serious side to fathers, since they train their sons in ways to make a living [32]. Of course, modern life has very specific conditions that might make it more difficult for fathers to play a more active role in child care.

In some monogamous, hunter-gatherer societies, fathers spend more time than modern fathers around mothers and their children, since they all take part in gathering food and hunting small animals. Indeed, these fathers help more with child care, and play less than European or American fathers [33]. Nonetheless, hunter-gatherer fathers almost always take less care of children than mothers do. Even in hunter-gatherer societies where fathers are the most active in caring for children, they never do more than mothers [15, 16].

What is particularly revealing is the way that hunter-gatherer fathers organize their child care. As soon as the child's mother or grandmother appears, the father typically disappears [34, 35]. When fathers get food through hunting, they share it fairly equally with all members of the community. Mothers give any food they gather first and foremost to their own children [22, 36, 37]. Likewise, when there is a battle, such as frequently occurs between Yanomamo tribes, fathers protect the whole community, not just their families [38]. Finally, in almost all hunter-gatherer societies, fathers always keep one eye directed toward unmarried women, who might want an extra morsel of meat or a helping hand—and enjoy a sexual dalliance afterward [22]. Thus, although hunter-gatherer fathers do help with child care, they do so less often and more reluctantly than mothers. Further, as society gets more advanced, and more specialized, if they have a profession, then fathers do even less child care. In agricultural societies, fathers are simply not around [39]. They herd animals or maintain crops, and many do not form any close relationships with children [40]. Of course, if fathers are out of work and mothers are not, as in some modern societies, fathers may be forced into child care.

It is not only that mothers feed, burp, clothe, clean, comfort, and care for sick children more than fathers do. Mothers provide direct care more than fathers to all their genetic relatives and to their spouse too [41]. For example, if a married woman is diagnosed with a brain tumor, there is a 21% chance that the couple will divorce. If the husband has the tumor, there is only a 3% chance that they will divorce [42]. Women are more willing than men to take care of a spouse. Men might not help their families that much, but they do help strangers more than women do [43, 44]. In fact, men receive more than 90% of all awards for heroism in the United States and Canada [43].

According to reports by the United Nations and the World Bank, mothers and fathers also use money differently [45–47]. Mothers put their children's lives first; fathers often spend their money first on themselves. This means that when mothers can control the family income, children do better. This has been found around the world. In Brazil, mothers use money to buy more nutritious food and better housing for their children than fathers do. In Mexico, mothers who can control the family income spend more on their children's food and less on alcohol, cigarettes, and clothing. In Bangladesh, mothers spend more than fathers on their children's education.

Even in richer countries, this same difference holds true. In the United Kingdom, mothers spend more on children's food, child care, and education. When fathers have the chance, they spend more on alcohol, eating out, gambling, and vacations. In Canada, mothers spend more than fathers on child care, and fathers spend more on transportation. A large-scale study in the United States, which included low- and moderate-income families, found that when fathers control the allocation of money, more children end up malnourished [45]. In fact, some single mothers are reluctant to remarry because they worry about what their new husbands will do with their money.

The death of a child hurts a mother much more than a father. A mother grieves more deeply and for longer. Mothers grieve more than fathers in the simplest hunter-gatherer communities to the most modern societies. In hunter-gatherer societies, mothers fear their child will die more than fathers do. Should the child die, which is not that uncommon, mothers experience greater anxiety, fear, and depression [22, 48].

Likewise, if an infant or young child dies in the United States, mothers are far more distressed than fathers. Mothers also develop more obsessive-compulsive behaviors, depression, and anxiety [49]. The same held true in a study in Canada with parents who had lost a child of less than a year of age. Mothers felt guiltier, believed their lives were less meaningful, yearned more for their lost child, and showed higher levels of fear [50]. In Norway, too, mothers hurt more [51].

The greater distress that mothers feel is not simply due to the extra time that they put into caring for the child. Mothers are more distressed than fathers even when a newborn dies [52]. Even when mothers do not really want to have a child, they remain highly distressed by its death. Not so with fathers. Fathers are less distressed by the death of a child that they did not really want [52].

A mother almost always invests in her children. This is not the case with fathers. A father's interest in caring for his children often is determined by his interest in their mother [15, 53–55]. If a father gets along well with the mother of his children, and particularly if he marries her [56–58], then he invests a lot in his children. He may even invest in her children from a prior marriage, though he always invests more in his own biological children. In general, a father who lives with his wife and gets to know his children early invests more in them [32]. But if things are not going well between a man and the mother of his children, he will invest less in his children. At the extreme, men disappear completely [17]. Their children never see them again and never receive anything ever again. This happens in every society.

Not so for a woman. A mother often invests in her children, usually to the end of her life—regardless of how she feels about the father. A father's resources often contribute greatly to helping a mother and her children survive and thrive. However, a mother living with an unpleasant man must make some complicated calculations. If he becomes unhappy with her, he can easily take off or limit his contribution to the family. Even in the best of cases, men buy things for themselves from money that would improve the lives of their children. This can be a difficult balancing act. She must weigh the benefits this man provides against the costs, so that she can maximize her husband's investment in her and her children. Sometimes, a man might place such strong demands on her that she ends up partially neglecting or even abusing her children. She has to figure out whether leaving her husband would be better or worse for herself and her children compared with losing her husband's resources.

Throughout human history, women have taken primary responsibility for ensuring the survival of their children. The evidence suggests that mothers are innately more prepared to do so even before a baby is born. Given the prolonged time it takes a human child to grow up, however, this is a difficult job, even in the best of circumstances. A mother's responsibilities for children never end.

Therefore, mothers benefit greatly from using whatever resources are available to help. Should a skilled substitute mother be available, such as a grandmother, older sibling, or other female relative, or day care workers or babysitters if she has some money, a mother often will turn care of her child over to them [59, 60]. A reliable and attentive husband also is highly useful. The problem is that grandmothers may live far away. Older siblings get bored. Babysitters need money. Even reliable husbands get distracted.

In the end, a mother usually bears complete responsibility for ensuring that her child is in safe hands, even if she isn't doing all the direct care herself. If she isn't overseeing her children's care at all times, then her child is much less likely to thrive, or even survive and then all the time, energy, and resources that a mother put into her child, from gestation to breastfeeding, clothing cleaning, and educating, is lost. A mother's decisions must reflect all of these concerns.

The Vulnerable: Who Women Help

Enter the world of any group of unrelated young girls in any culture with enough girls the same age. What are they doing? If they are in a preschool, they are playing in the kitchen or the dollhouse, or drawing pictures of mothers and babies and fathers, sisters and brothers, or princesses and queens in pretty places. One girl cooks; another puts the baby to sleep; a third talks on the telephone with her friend; a fourth takes a younger child to the zoo. In their pretend play, they take turns playing the roles of mother, baby, brother, father, and other relatives. Teachers find girls' play relaxing because it's so much quieter than the boys' enemy chasing [61]. In her studies of children's stories in an American preschool, Nicolopoulou [62] found that more than 75% of girls' stories are about families, and almost none are about aggression or violence.

Girls' play and their stories about family life can seem unbearably boring and predictable, but only on the surface. If you listen carefully, the seeming tranquility of little girls' play hides frightening themes. One story after another is about vulnerable individuals, all of whom need assistance.

Here are some of the stories that I have recorded in little girls' play:

1. A baby becomes sick, then dies. After heroic efforts, the hospital brings the baby back to life.

2. The princess finds a prince, but he abandons her because she is ugly. Then she becomes beautiful, and he loves her again.

3. A queen loses her way in the woods. Then, a kindly bunny brings her home.

4. A dragon comes and destroys a girl's house, and everyone runs away. Luckily, they all find each other and they build a better house and live happily ever after [63].

From earliest childhood, a woman is attracted to individual vulnerability. Being vulnerable means one's personal survival is endangered. Of course, everyone is vulnerable to some extent. But, who is most vulnerable? Who faces the most potential dangers? A baby, and after that a young child. They are the ones most likely to die, as they have been for millions of years [64, 2].

Think about what this must do to genes' desire to be passed on to the next generation. The genes need to program someone to take care of this new body where they now reside. One person should be in charge, so that there will no confusion about who is responsible. If even one extra person is in charge, confusion occurs about who should help. Social psychology experiments show that in emergencies, individuals are more likely to die if more than one person is responsible [65]. That's because no one knows who should do something; no one feels responsible. A mother always feels responsible.

Human babies are more helpless than the babies of almost any other primate species. Unlike other primate species' infants, human infants can't feed themselves or even move out of the way should danger pass by. As in other species, young babies get sick more easily. As they grow older and can move, they are prone to accidents of all kinds. Because of this, human babies and young children have to be cared for and watched constantly.

There is nothing to do about this. You can't tell a baby not to get sick. You can't tell a 3-year-old not to have an accident, and have confidence that he will obey. There is no relaxing one's vigilance when one is responsible for a vulnerable individual, only continual worry.

There is immediate pleasure, however, from solving other kinds of problems. This creates a critical distinction between the problems faced by a woman versus a man. A simple illustration brings this home. Imagine a couple in their kitchen with a young child. There is a loose board on the floor. The wife points out how dangerous this is. The husband fetches his tools and hammers down the board. He then gleefully explains to his wife how he has fixed the problem and how safe the kitchen will be. She, however, is not paying attention to him because she's had to snatch the baby's hand away from the hot stove. His problem is solved. Hers is not, and it won't be for a long, long time, if ever. As children grow older, after many years, they become more self-sufficient. A woman can relax her guard. But by then she may have a new baby or a new grandchild to worry about.

Men solve narrow problems that can be easily tackled. Done! Women don't have problems like that. Women have long-term projects, primarily the constant care they must devote over long years to keep a baby alive. Because vulnerability is a state, it has no solution.

I would suggest that a woman's genes require her attentiveness, by ensuring that a woman feels a continuing undercurrent of worry. That keeps her on her toes. As much as a mother might long to relax, feel satisfied, and even lighthearted, she can't afford to. She never is carefree. She always must be careful. Pleasure does not come easily from continually making sure that a child does not succumb to a disease, fall down the stairs, get eaten by a predator, or run over by a car. A mother cannot exclaim, "It's been 4 hours with no accidents. I've done a great job!" A mother doesn't have a job that ends after 4 hours or 40 hours or 400 hours. She has a vulnerable child—for years. For many mothers who help care for grandchildren, she has lifelong projects.

What causes a mother to maintain her interest in such a long-term project? Women find the state of vulnerability more attractive than men do. Vulnerability extends beyond human babies and young children. It includes any individual who needs long-term assistance: those with sensory, social, behavioral, emotional, mental, cognitive, and other handicaps; those with diseases; those who are elderly, poor, lost, orphaned, confused, or kidnapped. It applies to humans and nonhumans, maybe even inanimate objects. These are all particularly attractive to girls and women, and not so much to boys and men.

States of vulnerability are women's specialty. The strongest example comes from the jobs, professions, and volunteer work that women choose.

These require caring for the vulnerable, including social work, nursing, and teaching. Women in these fields often outnumber men by ratios as high as 9 to 1 [66–69]. As women increasingly become professionals, jobs in medicine and education attract them more than work that does not have vulnerability as a principal component. Fields such as math, physics, or engineering, or trades such as construction or plumbing, just don't appeal as readily to women.

Men specialize in finding answers to specific problems. But what happens if a man can't find an answer? How does he cope with his resulting sense of prolonged helplessness, and even vulnerability? By turning to a woman, of course. Many studies show that when a man fails to solve a problem, he turns to a woman for emotional support [70]. Even childless American undergraduate students, men and women alike, prefer to seek emotional support from a woman [71]. As I have described in the previous two chapters, women's conversations with other women and with family members often focus on vulnerability [70, 72–77]. Likewise, a vulnerable individual captures the attentions of any woman. A caring woman provides a safe haven from life's continuing difficulties [78].

This major difference in men's problems versus women's projects seems to me to have an enormous effect on their daily lives. When a man is in a difficult situation, he tries to find a solution—then get on with his life. Because women's projects do not have solutions, this makes no sense. A woman can never get on with her life, unless her child dies. Women's lives are intertwined with vulnerable individuals who require constant care and worry. When caring for children, a woman can easily stay worried for her entire lifetime. What a biological burden! And Freud wondered, what do women want [79, 80]? A man can't figure out what a woman wants, but a woman certainly can. What a woman wants is for herself and her children to be healthy and thriving. Then, she wants a brief respite from having to worry every second. A devoted grandmother, exceptional babysitter, or caring father can help.

Tannen [81] aptly describes the different approaches of women and men. She contrasts women's needs to soothe their worn emotions with men's desire to fix a problem and be done with it. In her subtitles "I'll fix it for you" and "I'll fix it if it kills me" she provides a man's approach to the world. Describe the problem; find the solution; continue with life until the next problem appears. Women find this approach ridiculous and infuriating. You don't fix babies, isolated animals, disabled individuals, or the elderly. You provide the best extended care you can, then cope emotionally.

Here is Tannen's illustration of a wife's versus a husband's approaches to life as recorded on a radio talk show:

The couple, Barbara and William Christopher, were discussing their life with an autistic child. The host asked if there weren't times when they felt sorry for themselves and wondered, "Why me?" Both said no, but they said it in different ways. The wife deflected attention from herself: She said that the real sufferer was her child. The husband said, "Life is problem solving. This is just one more problem to solve." (Tannen, 1990, p. 52.)

As Tannen emphasizes, it is not that a woman is not grateful when a man fixes her car or her computer or her camera, but these things are not really that important to her. Her life is composed of vulnerability, and that can never be fixed.

Underneath vulnerability, of course, is fear. You cannot take care of someone who is in danger without being afraid for them. John Gottman's [82] audiotapes of young children's conversations show this.

Gottman initially thought that girls were not really interested in fear; only boys were. After all, boys specialize in scary enemies. On the surface, boys confront fears head-on: They attack the enemy with their weapons. In chapter 5, however, I reviewed many studies that show that from the first month of life and ever after, across diverse cultures, women have more fears than men. A closer inspection of girls' conversations reveals the underlying fear.

Here's one example of two girls conversing:

c: OK, turn the car on.

m: No! No! No! No! No!

c: Rrrum!

m: No! No! Nooo! [*Screams*] You can't go on fast, you stop...

c: I stopped the car but I'm not going.

m: Oh, yeah, you're not going. Oh, oh, oh, my baby! Where is he? Where is he! Help! My bunny, where's my bunny? Need my bunny [*whining*].

c: I don't know. Here, bunny, bunny.

m: Mommy, where's my bunny?

c: Here?

m: I can't find it anywhere. [*Starts to cry*] Bunny! He's lost! I can't find him. I'm looking, I can't find it...

(Gottman, 1986, pp. 162–163)

This isn't scary in the male sense. There is no enemy. Instead, there's a lost, helpless, vulnerable animal. If this really happened, the bunny would likely die. Its caregiver would be devastated. Most boys and men wouldn't care that much.

Here's another example:

D: Well, my sister's, um, I have a friend, Sharon. He's two, but he doesn't grow.

J: Yes, he does.

D: Uh uh. He's just two all the time.

J: Why doesn't he grow?

D: Because

J: [*pausing*] We grow, don't we?

D: Huh?

J: We grow.

D: Yep.

J: Why doesn't he grow?

D: 'Cause Sharon's a boy.

J: What?

D: 'Cause Sharon's a boy.

Once again, no enemy. It's even worse, because a child who cannot grow will either die or be helpless for life. How worried must this child's mother be?

Ageliki Nicolopoulou [62] reports that half of 3- and 4-year-old girls' stories tell about some kind of danger. The other half describe what she called "stable social relationships" (Nicolopoulou, 1997, p. 166). To my mind, a stable social relationship is the male equivalent of defeating the enemy. The best offense and defense against prolonged vulnerability is having someone to help.

Here is a story from the collection of nursery school and kindergarten teacher Vivian Gussin Paley [61], told by her student Mary Ann:

Once upon a time there lived two princesses who were prettier than ever and rosier than a rose. They went to the woods. They saw the wicked witch hiding and she tried to catch them, but they were too fast. Then they went to the woods again. The wicked witch tried to catch them again. Luckily she did. She put them in a cage. There were no windows and doors. They could not breathe, so they died.... But that was a cage where it was raining gold. It woke them up. The gold was magic and it made a door and then they went home. Then two princes knocked on the door. When the princesses saw them they wanted to marry them, so they got married. (Paley, 1984, p. 100)

While there is an enemy, it succeeds in killing the princesses. The seeming non sequitur, however, is money and men. Long-term assistants are required to help whenever anyone stops breathing and needs to be revived.

Paley's student Janie reflects the same juxtaposition:

Once there was a pretty girl and she planted pretty flowers in her pretty garden. And she was very pretty. Her name was Snow White. Then a witch gave her a poison apple, so she died. Then a pretty diamond necklace came on her neck and she came alive and she was still pretty. (Paley, 1984, p. 101)

Again, the enemy succeeds; being pretty enough to attract a man is the solution.

What can we see in these stories? There are two obvious themes. First, even at 3 and 4 years of age, death is clearly on girls' minds' too. Unlike for boys, however, for girls there is no easy answer to it—no enemy to be defeated, putting a quick end to the problem.

Second, the answer to life for these particular girls is money and long-term relationships. More generally, I suggest that these stories of girls, so calm in their telling, mirror a woman's early fear of how she will support herself and her children.

For the sake of comparison, here is a fairly typical boys' example:

Once upon a time there was a *wolf*. And then a *T-Rex* came. And then *Godzilla* came. And then *Pterodactyl* came. Then they had a fight, and then T-Rex killed Godzilla. And then Godzilla came back alive again. Then there was a bunch of bad guys, and then the Godzilla knocked the bad guys down and they were trying to get him. Then a little *super hero* came. Then he was flying and he landed. Then he flipped, and then Godzilla realized it was Batman, so then he blowed fire at him, and then he falled down and he was dead. Then a *Brontosaurus* came, and Godzilla jumped on him, and then he got squished. Then they had a major fight. Then they stopped the fight, and everyone looked at each other, and then they didn't do the fight anymore. The End. (Nicolopoulou, 1997, p. 167)

The enemy must be killed, as often as possible. You try to kill the enemy; the enemy tries to kill you. If you die, too bad. The key is that it's over. The enemy might attack at a future date, but there are many pleasurable things to do before that happens.

Not for women. If you're lucky, you'll find riches, be pretty, and marry a prince. But this is just the beginning of the story. The future is a long, long road.

If you're not lucky, if you aren't rich and don't marry a prince, or anyone else, it's a long, very hard road. In human history, and still in many parts of the world, it's a road filled with children who have died, and many relatives who die young. A mother herself can be perfectly healthy, but then die suddenly in childbirth. Her children then will usually die too.

In most places, caring for one vulnerable child after another, for years on end, requires health and endurance. Human mothers have children more closely spaced than in any other closely related species [83]. After a child turns 3 years, a breastfeeding mother usually is getting ready to have another one. A nonbreast feeding, modern mother may already have another one. Finding resources to feed children and a place to raise them requires endless stamina, a task far more daunting than confronting a boy's enemy who arrives from time to time.

There is a harsh truth in these stories. Women's lives require assistance with long-term projects in which women continually look after the vulnerable in their lives. A beloved baby could get sick. A successful teenager could kill himself in a car accident. Meanwhile, grandmothers die, and husbands can run off with younger, prettier neighbors. Life for women can be more like a Stephen King horror novel, in which the mundane goes awry, and life continues. There is no violent showdown between the good guys and the bad guys that ends no matter what the outcome.

For women, what happens if a child's body stops growing? What happens when someone gets lost and cannot find the way home? What happens when the baby who screams for food and constantly needs to be comforted suddenly no longer moves? What does it feel like when there is no father anymore to help the mother feed herself and her baby? What about when there is no mother either?

From a vulnerable person's perspective, this is more frightening than an enemy. Superman can combat the enemy. This works as long as there is a home. There will never be a Superwoman to complement Superman. Few want to hear the tedious details, punctuated by occasional emergencies, of the prolonged child care provided by Superwoman. Absolutely no one wants to hear about it when Superwoman's care fails to work.

This is real fear. It's so frightening that most people will not speak about it. Girls come close when they are feeling very brave. Women speak in hushed tones. No boy or man would ever touch it. What's the point of saving the world from destruction if no one is left in the world who loves you? How many men have I observed refusing to discuss the fate of a very sick child, the death of a child, the loss of a child's mother? These same men go bravely off to war displaying their loyalty to their country.

Sex differences in approaches to problems versus projects appear early in life. As one example, children were told stories about someone like them who lost a dog or was disliked in school. Then each child was asked how they thought the child would feel [84, 85]. Not surprisingly, girls reported being more afraid and sadder than boys. Furthermore, even though they were not asked, almost a third of the boys spontaneously offered a solution to the problem [85]. For example, when responding to the story about the boy who lost his dog, a girl said she would feel sad, whereas a boy said he would "follow the tracks of the dog" or "call the police." If only all lost dogs could be found!

Of course, the point of being attracted to vulnerability is to care for babies and children. Around the world, like virtually all female mammals, starting early in life, human females take a special interest in their babies. For example, in Peru, Kenya, Guatemala, and the United States, girls hold their younger infant siblings twice as often as boys do [39]. Although boys theoretically are as capable of caring for infants, girls enjoy doing so more.

In virtually every culture that has been studied young girls interact more with babies than boys do. This holds true in hunter-gatherer tribes, for example, the Hadza of Tanzania [22], the Kung San of Botswana [86], the Toba of Argentina [87], and the Dogon of Mali [23]. Well before maternal hormones begin circulating, girls appear primed to care for younger siblings. They also are more willing than boys to comply with their mother's requests. In many cultures, by the age of 5, girls often begin their roles as maternal helpers.

This has a clear biological basis. When a girl's brain is exposed to abnormally high levels of testosterone prenatally, she shows less interest in and warmth toward infants. She has less desire to grow up to become a mother.

Girls with excess testosterone before birth are even less likely to want to play with dolls or to play the role of mother or wife [88, 89].

Of course, boys and men can love babies too. In fact, many times their physiological and behavioral responses to babies are similar to those of girls and women [90]. However, love does not provide enough glue to ensure that they stick by the baby's side continuously.

Fear does more. I suggest that along with an attraction to vulnerability, what ultimately binds a woman most strongly to a vulnerable baby or child is sheer terror. Women live in fear for the lives of their vulnerable children. Men do not. Men have a lot of other ideas in their heads. The result is that most girls and mothers never break their ties to their children.

Heart rate is a sign of anxiety and fear [91, 92]. A crying baby produces a greater increase in heart rate in mothers than in fathers [93, 94]. Even women who have not given birth respond to videotapes of crying babies more than men do [95].

In a woman who has had children, the levels of the hormone oxytocin, often called the "love hormone," are linked to her feelings of affection for her baby. Tellingly, higher levels of oxytocin also make a mother more worried about her baby's safety, health, and future, and determine how often she checks up on her baby [96].

Even animal studies find that a critical part of the tie that binds a nonhuman mother to her baby is fear for the baby's survival. How do researchers know this? The mother spends her time continually checking on her infants [97]. Fear is a stronger insurance policy than love because feelings of love are complicated and depend on both partners being in the right state at the same moment. Fear is simpler. A continual underlying fear for a child's safety depends less on the immediate circumstances.

In modern, technologically advanced societies, most babies survive, but this is not true in many parts of the world, nor was it true historically until very recently. As I recounted in chapter 5, more than 40% of children still die before their 15th birthday. Women's genes must direct them to do the best they can to stop this from happening.

Falling ill in the past would have been a terrible event for anyone, but especially for children. Even today, 9 million children still die every year in Third World countries, mostly due to diarrhea, pneumonia, malaria, malnutrition, and infected cuts [98]. This is down from twice that many two decades ago [24]. In modern countries, disease, accidents, and lack of resources still kill vulnerable children disproportionately. In underdeveloped countries and in the past, the death toll is much higher.

Consequently, genes almost certainly guide a mother to fear for her own survival and that of her babies. She has to pay attention and work 24 hours a day, 7 days a week, year after year, to keep her baby alive. She does this knowing that at any moment, a disease, accident, or predator can undo all her work, sometimes in a matter of seconds. Think about that. To keep a baby alive until his or her 15th birthday requires 15 years times 365 days a year times 24 hours a day times 60 minutes a hour times 60 seconds a minute, or a total of 473,040,000 seconds of worrying per child. Of course, most mothers worry far longer than after their child turns 15, and most mothers have many children, and then grandchildren.

What a mixed blessing. No wonder that mothers everywhere wonder whether they can cope. Not surprisingly, some mothers can't cope. This leads to another, dark and hidden part of being a mother. Even love and worry are no guarantee that a mother can successfully bring up a baby. As young girls' stories show, you need physical resources and human help. A woman who is isolated and poor is off to a bad start. She has a much smaller chance of succeeding.

What does a mother do? In extreme cases, a mother may kill her newborn baby. Many mothers who live in difficult circumstances end up neglecting or abusing their own children, even in rich countries [20, 99]. Millions of mothers abort their fetuses every year. In the year 2003, 31 abortions were estimated to have taken place for every 100 live births worldwide [100].

Infanticide and child abuse elicit strong emotions, as they should. We live in a society that believes very strongly in the transformative bonds of love and motherhood. When men murder others from the same community, we accept this as a regrettable, but normal, criminal act. This is true even if the victims are children, even a man's own children. Sometimes, women kill their husbands or other adults, and this also is too bad, another unfortunate crime.

But a mother who kills or even abuses her own children is another story. This is more than a crime. This is *deranged*. It's a crime against nature. Women who kill their children are usually considered mentally or morally ill. Few things garner as much publicity and outrage.

If mother-infant bonds were as strong as everyone would like to think, then infanticide would have been rare, no matter what the circumstances. In fact, infanticide was quite common in the historical past. Anthropologist

Laila Williamson [101] notes that "infanticide has been practiced on every continent and by people on every level of cultural complexity, from hunter gatherers to high civilizations, including our own ancestors. Rather than being an exception, then, it has been the rule" (Williamson, 1978, p. 61) Simple population pressure resulted in a fairly high level of infanticide, estimated at well over 15% of all births in Neolithic communities (about 10,000–3,000 B.C.). Even today, infanticide continues to be practiced by women, mostly outside the sphere of Western influence [102].

Do mothers randomly kill or abuse their children? Are there characteristics of a mother that determine whether she will abuse or kill her child? If abusive or infanticidal mothers were morally defective or clinically insane, we should be able to find and help them. It turns out that with very few exceptions, mothers who kill their infants are not insane. Abuse and killing of children are not random, and are not due to unusual characteristics of a mother. Rather, they are predicted by a mother's lack of resources and social support. Being a single mother is the best predictor of infanticide, abuse, or neglect universally [20, 103, 104].

A study of almost 400 recent cases of parents killing their own children in Canada supports the conclusion that the vast majority of mothers who kill their children are not morally defective or temporarily insane. Virtually all mothers who killed young infants did so because of lack of financial resources or social support. A few mothers killed an older child, but these women did suffer from severe mental illness. The only other situation in which a mother killed an older child occurred when the child suffered from so severe an illness or handicap that the mother no longer felt able to care for the child. These mothers often took their own lives as well [105].

Men also killed their own children. But when fathers did this, they mostly did so because they were furious: furious mostly at their wives, whom they accused of infidelity. Often men would kill their wives along with their children. Whereas mothers kill out of an inability to care for their children, fathers kill for revenge [106].

Sarah Hrdy [59] is an expert on the different ways in which nonhuman and human mothers have killed their infants and children. Her analysis shows clearly that mothers do not kill their children as a result of some random aberration or loss of sanity. Human mothers most often kill a child when the chances are high that their sacrifice and hard work will not succeed in keeping that child alive.

When a baby's chances of survival are lower, the chances of infanticide are higher. There are many reasons a baby may not survive. Being born unhealthy or deformed, living in an environment lacking in food, and living in a place with major climate changes or wars are obvious reasons.

Other reasons are more complex. In many past and current societies, sons contribute more to a family's fortunes, since daughters marry into other families. In these societies, female infants are much more likely to be killed. In societies in which daughters remain with their families and sons leave home, male infants are more likely to be killed. In societies where children are not valued for many reasons, mothers may kill children regularly. A mother may kill a baby because she already has too many other children of the same sex or because the child's prospects for marrying are low, or because not enough children of the other sex are being born. Mothers are far more likely to kill a baby when it arrives too soon after another child, jeopardizing the older child's survival. The mother's health and energy level at the time of birth also affect her desire to invest in a new child. An ill or difficult child may create too much stress, or an easy child may be too easily ignored, leading a mother to abuse or neglect it.

Finally, and most critically, the assistance available to the mother greatly influences her willingness to invest in a baby. A mother with a biological father willing to invest, or female kin willing to assist, or older daughters available to act as child minders, or money with which to pay unrelated female babysitters, or wet nurses willing to breastfeed her baby is far more likely to invest in her child.

Infanticide is a decision. It is a decision by a mother who knows she will have to invest a lot of time, energy, and resources for years and years into a baby and who does not feel that she will succeed.

It is difficult to accept this. After all, we live in a generally rich society where even poor people have some access to resources and assistance. But consider the following situation: A mother is poor; her husband left her, just after she became pregnant. She already has two children who need her constant care, and they are already suffering because they don't have enough food. If she tries to give adequate care to a new baby in these circumstances, she may end up with three dead children. If she kills her newborn, her existing children have a better chance of surviving. Throughout most of human history, women have had to make these unpleasant calculations. If circumstances are really difficult, a mother simply cannot manage to care for a newborn baby, the most vulnerable and needy of all, and ignore the risk to those children in whom she already has invested so much.

Abuse and neglect are less extreme than killing. The dynamics, however, are similar. Mothers usually abuse and neglect their children when they cannot properly care for them [107]. Even today, millions of mothers abuse or neglect to feed or find medical care for their female infants and young children [24, 107]. In cultures where children are not valued and resources and attention are scarce, childhood neglect is much more common [59, 108]. A mother's level of stress influences her threshold for abusing her infant [109]. If mothers' lives are made easier, abuse decreases. Regular visits from a kind stranger are enough to reduce child abuse and neglect [110].

This brings us to another face of human mothering: a mother's reactions to her children. Children are completely dependent on their mother for survival, even if all she does is make the arrangements for others to care for them. Children therefore learn to observe attentively and with great concern the behaviors of their mothers [111]. Signs of affection and fearfulness for a child's safety signal to the child that survival is likely. Even under the best circumstances, however, not many mothers can provide continued responsiveness to all their children all the time. How do mothers react to their children?

As I described in chapter 5, girls and women display a whole constellation of nice behaviors when they are with each other. They smile, speak polite words, pay close attention to nonverbal gestures, acknowledge one another's ideas. They don't brag. They never issue commands. They almost never hit one another.

Do these same women react in the same way to their children? Not in the least. A mother displays very different behaviors toward her child than toward other unrelated females. There is no smiling or politeness with her child. Quite the opposite.

A mother has to make sure that her child survives. Smiling and being polite are more than useless: They prevent her from doing her job. Instead, mothers issue orders, criticize their children, yell at them, and administer physical punishment. Mothers both praise and criticize children more than fathers do [112, 113]. In fact, it looks suspicious to most people when a mother smiles too often at her child [114]. What is she trying to hide? Anyone privy to the interactions in a home know that it is filled with emotions and conflicts between genetically related individuals. Families, with mothers at the head, do not resemble the polite society of unrelated girls or women. Too much is at stake.

Young children know best of all how mothers react. When a girl takes on the role of mother during play, for those few minutes, she stops being polite and deferential [115]. She becomes directive, assertive, commanding, and domineering. In fact, when girls play at mother, they sound just like boys. Girls' play shows dominance and energy when they have children to mind, students to teach, or helpless individuals to take care of. In these contexts, exerting their authority is acceptable. These girls know that when you have to take care of someone who is vulnerable and unable to take care of him- or herself, female public social conventions go out the window.

In modern societies, some mothers live under quite easy conditions. Their environment generally is safe from diseases, predators, and criminals. They have enough resources that they have time to spend just interacting with their children. They have time to spend gazing into their children's eyes and sharing their nonverbal expressions. They mirror their infants' moods and appear to be enmeshed in a tight bond. Psychiatrists have identified this as an ideal model for mother-child relations [116, 117].

I think this is most likely nonsense. Most mothers in human history have never had the time or the circumstances to indulge in such relatively useless behaviors. They were too busy keeping themselves and their children alive. In fact, observations in nontechnological societies show that mothers in more usual circumstances do not overly engage in mutual eye contact or reading nonverbal emotional signals or long conversations with their children [39]. In fact, in many societies, particularly hunter-gatherer and agricultural ones, mothers don't even look much at their infants. They sling them under their breasts, attach them to their backs or chests, carry them on their heads, or put them in a carriage and wheel them along, often with the baby's eyes covered [54]. In a difficult world, understanding the nuances of a baby's emotional responses is useless.

It's not that undivided attention would not make a baby happier, or even more secure. It almost certainly would [118]. Perhaps the world is becoming less violent and more caring [119], because mothers do have more time to focus just on their babies' and young children's needs. This conveys to children that the world is safe, that the child will most likely live and thrive. How happy this must make a young child. But such attention likely improves happiness, and perhaps caring for others, but does not keep a baby alive. Insecurely attached children live too.

Close bodily contact during the day and night combined with a mother's fast response to her infant's crying are sufficient to respond to a potential threat. A baby is quite capable of emitting an unpleasant scream right from birth, and anyone within earshot grasps that the baby is distressed. While the nuances of babies' expressions might be of fascination to relaxed parents in the Western world, such subtleties seem unlikely to influence a baby's survival.

Even in the most modern societies, most mothers do not have the resources and leisure to provide children with consistent care and attention. Mothers vary greatly in how much they can invest in a particular child, at a particular moment in time [120]. Children rapidly learn whether and how much their mother can be relied upon when they are in distress. Unless a mother has sufficient personal, physical, and social resources to be a consistent presence, her child must learn to treat her with great wariness [118].

Unsurprisingly, infants with problems such as low birth weight or prematurity, as well as infants born to mothers with fewer resources from poorer environments, are much less likely to turn to their mothers when distressed [118]. When difficulties in the environment or in the mother or child exist, then most infants do not reliably trust their mothers in times of external danger or internal distress. Nonetheless, even an unreliable mother is better than no mother as the child's best bet for survival.

What a mother provides is an unbroken tie to her child [78]. No other individual forms such a close and unbreakable bond. Once a mother decides to keep her child alive, though she may behave abusively and neglectfully at times, she remains the primary caregiver. It is the tie that binds more tightly than any other. At the best of times, this is a remarkably heavy burden. How do mothers cope?

The Assistants: Who Helps Women?

In the United States, Halloween costumes are mirrors into children's souls. Boys dress up as superheroes or enemies. What costumes do girls choose? Do they dress up as caretakers of the vulnerable, such as mothers, teachers, nurses, doctors, veterinarians, or social workers? Do they dress up as vulnerable creatures, such as babies, students, sick patients, or disabled individuals? Nope.

What do girls wear on Halloween? The Halloween Express website provides a good selection. There you'll find angels, Batgirl, Barbie, cats, clowns, devils (Bride of Satan, Devil Princess, Naughty or Nice?), Disney and other popular television characters such as Cinderella, Little Mermaid, Minnie Mouse, Dorothy or Gilda from *The Wizard of Oz*, Little Red Riding Hood, Sleeping Beauty, southern belle, Princess Tiana, Tinkerbell, gothic vampires, Wonder Woman, divas (ballerina, go-go girl, disco dolly, Hannah Montana, Disco Diva, MegaStar, Queen Child,), fairies, and princesses. It doesn't take long to get the point. All of these girls' costumes are pretty. Some are downright sexy. These costumes are designed to attract men.

Why don't girls dress up as caregivers to the vulnerable, or as the vulnerable themselves, just like boys become superheroes and enemies? Why practice attracting men? I suggest that it's because bringing up children is so hard that, early in life, girls begin searching for assistants. Assistance can make the difference between life and death for a mother and her children. Assistance makes the difference between a hardscrabble and an easy life. Only for females from families overflowing with resources does assistance from a mate not matter so strongly. So, while boys take on the enemy directly, girls attempt to obtain reinforcements before committing to a lifetime of child care.

Anthropologists coined the term "cooperative breeders" to describe female animals who cannot rear their offspring without assistants. Although it is unclear whether a human mother could succeed in raising her children without any help from others, having assistance clearly increases the odds enormously that she and her children will survive and thrive.

For humans more than any other species, taking care of a baby requires a huge investment of time, energy, and resources. This is so difficult that throughout human history, human females are the only females of any species who frequently killed their own newborns when conditions were too difficult. It is likely that the presence of an assistant is the most important factor in whether a woman decides to kill her newborn.

The best sources of help are her own genetic relatives and those of the father of her children. While the father of her children and his family don't share any of her own genes, they share her children's genes. Both families want these genes to live.

Whenever a woman had a say in choosing a husband, it would have been critical to choose well. A healthy, strong, reliable food provider would make an ideal mate. In hunter-gatherer communities today, that is who women choose [121]. Not only that, but they choose again, and again sometimes, due to lots of divorce and remarriage. They must constantly assess the qualities of potential mates and make a good choice. In some societies, women may have less freedom to choose a mate. When they can acquire critical information that can influence their parents' or brothers' choices for them, however, it surely makes sense for them to pass it along.

Like most things in the world, good men are a scarce resource. In modern Western societies, women who marry rich men live longer [122] and produce children who are more successful socially, academically, and professionally [123]. Little wonder, then, that even young girls quickly grasp the importance of being able to attract a worthy man.

Why is a man so important? Honestly, why couldn't a new mother just get help from other, unrelated women? After all, who is better placed to help a mother with children than another mother who understands completely the problems and pitfalls?

I always suggest that my female students, who attend a college that is predominantly female, simply dispense with monogamy. Rather, they should either live together with their children or join in a polygynous (several co-wives, one husband) marriage in some other country. Living in a harem makes sense. There are many advantages. First, all the co-wives can share an excellent man; none of them has to settle for second best. None has to fear never marrying at all.

Second, despite the often touted joys of marriage, wife abuse and even killing of wives by husbands is widespread around the world. This happens more often when a woman is isolated from her family and the man controls the resources [5, 124, 125]. Even in the United States, where women are more equal to men, every year several million women are abused by their husbands [126]. Co-wives could join forces. They could overpower their husband. They would all be safer and have more control.

Third, if many women lived together, the sexual division of labor whereby women universally get the lower-status positions could be overthrown. The women themselves would simply divvy up their tasks. Some women could work outside the home, whether gathering fruit and vegetables or running a corporation, whereas others could remain at home, attentively guarding everyone's children. While the breadwinners brought home extra resources, the babysitters would carefully ensure that everyone's child was safe and well taken care of. Surely, this makes sense.

Well, it makes more sense to men. Whenever I talk about the advantages of polygyny to my students, the young men enthusiastically concur. These wide-eyed, sexually charged young males imagine themselves as the husband. What they fail to realize is that, in any polygynous society, most of the men can't marry at all. If one man monopolizes several women, then by definition, a lot of men are out of a wife.

But what of the original idea? Doesn't it make sense for a mother to look for help from other women in a similar situation? It doesn't seem to for my female students. Every time that I bring it up, they invariably find the idea of polygyny appalling. They want one husband all to themselves. Why? Well, they are convinced that other mothers are not as reliable as they might appear. In fact, instead of seeing other mothers as a potential source of help, they see them as competition. Are they right?

Researchers have studied polygynous households in more than 50 different cultures. They have indeed found that, instead of helping each other, co-wives compete fiercely. They fight to put the interests of their own children first, and they fight over sexual and emotional access to their husband [127]. As I described in chapter 5, open fighting occurs most frequently and most viciously between fertile unrelated co-wives. Not only are they not sympathetic and helpful, but co-wives engage in some of the most intense violence that occurs between women.

This competition takes a toll on the children as well. We know this from a classic study in the Dogon's villages in Mali. Beverly Strassman [128] compared children of first wives in polygynous marriages to children of only wives in monogamous marriages over an 8-year period. A higher percentage of children in polygynous households died.

So, my female students' intuitions appear to be correct. Relying on other mothers for help is risky. You just can't get around the competition. A woman and her children do better when she is in a strong monogamous relationship with a man, despite the dangers posed by a man. In fact, this can explain women's strong desire to have exclusive one-on-one relationships, even with other women [129, 130]. Surprisingly, even in homosexual relationships, across diverse countries, lesbians break up more frequently than gay men [131]. A woman doesn't want another unrelated woman's help in raising her children. A woman wants a husband devoted entirely to herself and her children.

Of course, help can come from other sources. Other than a husband, who else can a mother turn to for help? Who won't compete with her? The answer is not other, unrelated mothers. Anyone who shares genes with her children, however, is potentially useful. That means her own family, and eventually the family of her husband. They do offer help, on occasion. Of course, members of her own family, such as her sisters, usually have their own children. They will not have much time, energy, or resources to spare [23]. A woman's mother also may have several sets of grandchildren, so she can be of only limited benefit [23]. A husband's family is never really sure he is the father of her children, even if she says so. Thus, they can help, but they might be a bit suspicious and more inclined to help their daughters' rather than their daughter-in-laws' children. A husband, particularly one without any other children, therefore is the ideal candidate. Irrespective of where the assistance comes from, however, a woman benefits greatly from finding someone to help her care for her children.

Indeed, I argue that from early in life, women's genes direct them to ask for help. Even before they turn 2 years old, girls ask both mothers and fathers for help more than boys do [132]. The same greater help-seeking behavior in young girls has been described by anthropologists in many diverse cultures [133].

This continues as children grow older. In one study, girls and boys aged 3 to 5 were given a puzzle to put together, with only a male adult nearby [134]. The girls made more than three times as many statements as the boys to the adult indicating that they might need help, such as "I don't know where this one goes" or "I can't do this one." This was not necessarily because these girls were having difficulty. Girls made these statements regardless of how fast they solved the puzzle. In contrast, boys made these statements only when they couldn't put the puzzle together. This suggests that young girls think they need help more than boys, even when they don't. My students and I couldn't believe this at first. Why should girls who are good at puzzles make statements suggesting that they need help? We decided to expand the original puzzle study. We asked 3- and 6-year-old children attending lower- and middle-income schools to do four simple tasks: draw an animal, build a house of blocks, assemble a puzzle, and match sounds on an electronic memory game. A male and a female experimenter took turns being present. To make sure that the role of the experimenters was clear to both girls and boys, they offered to help each child before each task. All children took all the tasks seriously and got right down to work. On every task, girls asked for help more quickly than boys did, regardless of whether the experimenter was a male or a female [135].

The same thing has been found with adolescent girls. More than a thousand adolescent students from Australia were asked to think about a real problem they had recently faced and whether they had asked for help. Girls' problems concerned health, family, and relationships. More important, girls asked for help more often than boys when faced with a real-life problem [136]. The same thing has been found for girls in the United States, Germany, Israel, Finland, and Japan [137, 138].

Of course, what these studies mostly show is that girls ask for help from available authority figures. In fact, hundreds of American studies have looked at use of medical care, psychiatric care, and other institutionalized care. These have all found that women seek help more from professionals and clergy members than men do [139–141]. Even if nothing is physically wrong with them, women visit the doctor more [142]. The same holds for psychotherapy. Psychotherapy in its most popular form consists of forming a relationship with a stranger who provides an emotional, healing bond in exchange for money. Women visit therapists much more often than men for a whole host of conditions, including depression, anxiety, drug abuse, alcoholism, and stress [143–146].

Females' greater help-seeking behavior from an authority figure applies to even the most extreme type of emotional distress. One reviewer [141] of the cross-cultural research put it like this:

> "Women seek help—men die." This conclusion was drawn from a study of suicide prevention in Switzerland (Angst and Ernst, 1990): 75% of those who sought professional help in an institution for suicide prevention were female, and 75% of those who committed suicide in the same year were male. (Möller-Leimkühler, 2002, p. 3)

Why do girls and women look for help so often? One interpretation is that they just remain more dependent. For example, anthropologists Alice Schlegel and Herbert Barry [147] studied adolescent behavior in more than 150 different societies. They observed that during adolescence girls remain closer than boys to their families, particularly their mothers. They suggested initially that girls were simply less self-reliant than boys.

This conclusion is too simple. Schlegel and Barry also found that when girls shared a close bond with their mothers, they actually accomplished more tasks on their own. Human females need the support of another, but not necessarily to accomplish an actual task. Girls and women may actually be more independent than boys and men. Girls and women need to know someone else is around—to help look after their children, protect them from marauding males, or keep the predators away. Then, girls and women can go about their business.

Having parents, especially mothers, who were available and willing to invest in her and her children would have been a major advantage to a woman. This support would have allowed a mother to worry less about her children's survival and freed her to do other important tasks. The absence of such support would prevent a mother from doing much more than minimally ensuring her children's survival, unless she could find a man to provide support. Viewing a woman's behavior in terms of self-reliance or autonomy misses the point. For much of human history, women have found it almost impossible to keep their children alive without assistance. Finding help is not dependency, but necessity. Necessity is not the mother of invention in this case; mothers do not have time for inventions unless they first have assistants.

I suggest that from early in life, women thrive within a close relationship with their parents or, as a substitute, with a modern authority figure—one who has extra time, energy and resources to aid her. This allows a woman to depend on parents, or whoever the authority figure is, for help raising children. This in turn frees her from worry and permits her to be more independent. When an authority figure is unavailable, then she may turn to the younger generation, those with extra time and energy, if not resources, for help.

Consistent with this, Schlegel and Barry [147] noted that, in most societies, girls and women live entwined within relationships with the older and younger generations. Just as girls help mothers with younger siblings and food preparation, girls get help from mothers with the same tasks. From early in childhood, women's care for vulnerable family members and need for assistance from older family members and authority figures defines being female. According to Schlegel and Barry:

> Across societies in the sample, girls have more contact and greater intimacy with mothers than boys do with parents of either sex. Brought along with their mothers into the company of women, girls participate in multigenerational groups. Boys, even when they work alongside their fathers, have less contact and intimacy with them and other men than girls do with women. Leisure hours—and sometimes working hours as well—are spent in the company of age-mates.

This sex difference cuts across a wide range of societies. As it occurs in sexually egalitarian as well as male-dominant societies and among informally organized foragers as well as in traditional states, it is unlikely to be strictly "cultural," that is, a pattern that each culture or each cultural tradition invents for itself or borrows from its neighbors. We suggest that the difference is a feature of our species.... we link gender differences to the fundamental contrast between girls and boys in their relation to adults versus peers... it should not be overlooked in any comparison between the sexes.... Through their relations with their mothers and other adult women, girls continue within the hierarchy...more than do boys. (Schlegel & Barry, 1991, pp. 182–184)

While men's domestic roles vary from society to society, women depend on the assistance of those who share a stake in their genetic material.

Women live embedded in hierarchical relationships, first with older kin and soon after with younger kin, because this was important to the survival of their children. A review of 45 traditional societies with no access to modern medicine or contraception shows this to be the case [148]. As the authors state:

In every single study that examined the impact of multiple family members on child survival (apart from the mother), at least one relative has a significant impact on child survival. This widespread importance of kin apart from the mother supports the hypothesis that women are cooperative breeders, sharing child-rearing with other family members. However, which relatives help is less consistent than the fact of help itself. (Sear & Mace, 2008, p. 5)

In fact, many studies have shown the huge benefits of having a mother's mother, and other female relatives, living close by. The help of maternal relatives increases the chances that a child will live. Researchers examined the records of births and deaths in Canada and Finland in the 1700s and 1800s, looking for the presence of a nearby grandmother [149]. When a mother's mother lived within 20 kilometers, she had an enormous impact on the survival of her grandchildren. A close maternal grandmother kept two extra grandchildren alive for each extra decade that she lived beyond age 50. Grandmothers had little effect, however, on the survival of children less than 2 years of age, since at this age babies are primarily a mother's responsibility [16]. But when a child is between 2 and 15 years of age, a healthy grandmother can provide extra food, help with chores, protect the child from danger, and allow the mother time to rest and to produce and care for a new baby. The presence of a grandmother allows mothers to begin reproducing almost 2.5 years earlier, thereby increasing the number of grandchildren she leaves. In India, a mother who has her own mother nearby stays healthier and keeps more of her own children alive [7]. Of course, a grandmother without time, energy, and resources would be of little help [23].

In fact, supportive families may even be more important than the choice of a father, at least sometimes. In hunter-gatherer societies, a father does not help much with increasing his child's chances of surviving [23, 148]. In these societies, fathers provide animal food and honey for the entire community [83, 150]. While a man likely provides more meat to his own family [121], he is busy. He spends a lot of time with other men. He works on his hunting gear. He must be ready to protect the community from enemies. A man's primary contribution, then, may not add to the benefits of his child in particular, but rather to the community's welfare more generally. In a hunter-gatherer society like the Hadza of Tanzania, where the majority of mothers divorce and remarry, often leaving their child's father behind in a former camp, a woman's relatives would be far more important than a temporary husband. In modern societies, this may be true as well [151]. With extended families living far away, however, a husband becomes much more important to a woman and her children's well-being [123].

Historically, women have relied on help from extended family to raise their children. This appears basic to the way women think. After one highly successful American woman after another sought treatment from her in her clinical practice, the psychiatrist Jean Baker Miller [152] concluded that for emotional health, a woman requires a lifelong relationship. According to Miller:

> Women stay with, build on, and develop in a context of connections with others. Indeed, women's sense of self becomes very much organized around being able to make and then to maintain affiliations and relationships. Eventually, for many women the threat of disruption of connections is perceived not as just a loss of a relationship but as something closer to a total loss of self. (Miller, 1976, p. 83)

What Miller misses, however, is that the relationship need be not only long-term but also hierarchical. As Schlegel and Barry point out, women need hierarchical relationships, so that the helper has energy and resources and is not too busy to help. Only then can a relationship mirror the essential comfort provided when a woman has the strong support of her family, especially her mother. Without this, even the most successful women turn to a therapist—someone who (hopefully) knows more about life and has the time and energy to spend helping.

Thus, I suggest that whereas girls and women form polite, smiling relationships with female peers of the same age, these age-mates will not be able to assist them with keeping their genes alive. These relationships cannot ever be that important because they do not help a woman pass her genes to the next generation. In equal relationships, neither female has the time, energy, or resources to help the other one. Depending on the stage of life, a girl or woman must instead invest in helping her mother to raise younger siblings, finding a mate for herself, raising her own children, or helping to raise her grandchildren. Female peers can at best sympathize with one another about the difficulties each has in other relationships, with people like family members or boyfriends, or spouses, who do actually assist them in raising children. This is true for young, unmarried women [153] and married women with children [154] alike.

These family relationships are the ones on which girls and women depend to allow them to function. These hierarchical relationships are with someone who has the time, energy, and resources to help a woman care for her children, then allow her to get her other work done. In hierarchical relationships with family members, a girl and woman can express her honest feelings and overtly compete for attention and resources. These are the critical relationships a woman needs for herself and her children to survive and thrive.

While most people, researchers and nonresearchers alike, believe human males are the hierarchical sex, this ignores the people on whom each sex depends to solve their unique problems. Boys and men need others to help them fight the enemy. These others are most often peers. It is females, with their intergenerational ties to children and the older generation, those with more time, energy, resources, or to males with their higher status, who are more hierarchical.

Men view familial and spousal relationships from an entirely different perspective [155]. Few men ever take primary responsibility for keeping their genes alive and helping them thrive. Thus, they don't need that much assistance. The time they need assistance is when the enemy strikes. Then, they need their able-bodied male peers, not the hierarchical relationships within families.

In contrast, men are less egalitarian toward women. Thus, men form a close bond with a wife or friend, or lots of wives and lots of friends. A man is happy to be dominant to all of them and to help them all out when he has some free time. A man can more easily switch familial relationships, temporarily or permanently, because genetic investment is not his main concern. His (former) wife is taking care of his genes.

Take the case of divorce. Divorced men remarry far more quickly than divorced women. I would argue that this is because men don't have to worry as much as women do about who they are marrying. A woman needs to be sure that a man will help, and not hurt, her and her children. Across diverse cultures, a man who lives in the house with another man's children is 60 times more likely than the biological father to kill those children [103, 156]. Generally a man is more interested in whether a woman can have and take care of his children [157]. Unsurprisingly, men are more likely to get divorced when they have been married longer, whereas the opposite is true for women [158]. This is true in hunter-gatherer communities too [22]. A man married for a long time has a spouse who cannot produce any more children. This is the extent of his genetic problem. An older woman now has children and grandchildren to care for. She really could use the help of her spouse.

This makes men much more flexible than women about their former spousal relationships. They are far happier than women to retain their ties to the spouse they divorced—and to form ties with their replacement: their former wife's new spouse [159]. Men do not get stuck holding the baby, or their baby grandchildren. Women do. A woman is not happy being abandoned for another woman who now receives her former husband's extra time, energy, and resources. She needs these still. But her former husband is happy to see her. She's still doing all the work—and more now that he's gone.

The comfort of being taken care of by someone in a position of authority also at least partly explains why women are often attracted to older men and men of higher status [157, 160]. Across the world, men dominate women in terms of owning more resources, holding more territory, and profiting from higher status [5]. Thus, when a girl or woman has no female relatives to help her, a man can take on the role of the older female generation, as long as he will support her [157]. A man has not only more resources, territory, and status but also more energy and free time. A woman needs all of these to keep herself and her children alive and well. A woman thrives most in a relationship with her mother, older female relatives, or a husband. I suggest that any higher-status person with time, energy, and resources to invest in her and her children, however, should do. In modern societies, a therapist or a doctor can serve as temporary substitutes but not a long-term solution.

From early in life, across diverse cultures, women find authority figures more attractive than men do. Again, this indicates a biological basis. Put a toddler with his or her mother in a room with lots of attractive toys. A girl will take longer to leave her mother, stay closer to her mother, and become more distressed if separated from her mother [161]. Preschool girls also are more likely than boys to stay closer to their teachers [162], especially if lots of other children are around [163]. In middle childhood and adolescence, the same holds true. At one study at a summer camp, girls spent more time near their counselors or activities structured by adults than boys did [164]. Many studies have repeatedly found that, by 7 years of age, girls try to stay close to their mothers, while boys increasingly begin to avoid them [166, 166].

Likewise, by 3 years of age, if not earlier, girls comply more than boys with commands and requests from authority figures [61]. The same occurs with teachers as children grow into adolescents: Girls are much more likely than boys to comply with the demands of authority figures, even when those authority figures are male [167]. In adolescence, fewer battles for dominance occur between mothers and daughters than between mothers and sons. This has been observed in simple agricultural societies [39] and in American households [168, 169]. In the United States, the most common fights are between mothers and boys. These can result in vicious circles in which each tries to control the other, and the mothers often lose [170]. Boys do comply with fathers more, but fathers are simply less present [171]. Girls nevertheless comply with fathers much more than boys ever do.

Throughout most of human history, girls and women have retained ties to older generations [172], with clear hierarchical structures. Within the family, authority and help are usually strongly associated. Who can a mother rely on most but her own mother or aunt or older sister? Anyone else has competing goals that could present a threat to her or her children. So a girl, or a young mother, must respect the authority of her own mother, since this is the best assurance of getting help with her own children.

Eventually, her own mother will die, however, and then a mother herself becomes the authority figure. She already has accumulated experience caring for and being the authority figure to her own dependent children. In some societies, she wields considerable power as a mother-in-law or matriarch of the family [12]. In others, her power is less formal but welcomed by her daughters. A girl then undergoes a psychological transformation from reliance upon her mother as authority figure to becoming the authority figure for her daughters, and perhaps even her grandchildren. Boys and men live embedded in a world of relative equals, mostly unrelated to one another, who combat the enemy and join in activities together, competing over small variations in status. Girls and women, in contrast, focus on older and younger female relatives, and others who have time, energy, and resources to help them raise their children.

What happens, then, when girls and women interact with unrelated equals, their peers? As I emphasized in chapters 5 and 6, they must be very careful. But they likely try hard to find someone who can be a family substitute.

Dangerous Liaisons

Tamara, age 20, writes of her memories of her best friend [173]:

> For two years, seventh and eighth grade, it was as if we were the same person. We understood each other perfectly. We thought the same thing at the same time, finished each other's sentences, felt the same way always. We were so in sync with one another that I started to get confused about who was who. I would look at her handwriting and think it was mine. I would look at her, and though we looked nothing alike, I would almost think it was me. I lost myself in her, so that after a while I couldn't figure out anymore where she stopped and I began. Together, we were invincible—it was me and her against the world. The only thing that either of us feared was losing the other. She wrote me a letter once, the only one I still have, where she confessed to me that the thing that most frightened her was when she realized that we were different. I felt the same way. Yet we naively believed that those differences didn't matter. We were one and nothing could change that.
>
> But we were wrong, because no matter how hard we tried to deny it, we were different people. Ninth grade turned out to be the most traumatic

year of my life.... Throughout that year, we tried to get back the absolute oneness we'd had. Every night, we talked on the phone for hours, trying to work things out.... Toward the end of the year, I destroyed everything I had that was connected to her. I cut off my hair, stopped eating normally, destroyed my journals, letters, cassettes. I couldn't deal with the loss because when she changed she took everything with her. We had been like the same person; I had given my whole self to her. Then she became the enemy. (Apter & Josselson, 1998, pp. 83–85)

Writing in her 60s, the late Nora Ephron passed on important information to women that she picked up over the course of her life. In her chapter entitled "What I Wish I'd Known," she provides a list of important advice, including the following suggestion [174]:

"Whenever someone says the words 'Our friendship is more important than this,' watch out, because it almost never is" (Ephron, 2006, p. 125).

The friendship pattern described by Tamara is quite common. The advice dispensed by Nora Ephron likely reflects repeated disappointments.

Why do girls growing up in Western society invest so much time, energy, and thought in their female friends? Dozens of studies have described the intense, one-on-one [129, 175, 176], exclusive [130, 177], intimate [70, 73], loyal [173, 178] relationships that women beginning in early childhood form with unrelated female peers.

They have focused on a girl's great desire to have her closest friend attend only to her, to share everything with her, for life. They don't want anyone else being friends with their friend. They don't want their friends ever to leave. Studies show this desire exists from early childhood well into adulthood [129, 130]. Boys and men do not form exclusive friendships. They are not jealous if their friends are friends with one another. They don't think about how long their friendships are going to last.

What purpose do these wishes serve for women? I suggest they are a girl's or woman's best attempt to make her female friend into a family member. In families, having the undivided attention of one's spouse or female family member allows a woman greater freedom to pursue her own goals. Should her husband, mother, or cousin agree to invest in her children, a woman can gather food or run a corporation far more easily. Being forced to share her husband's investment with a co-wife, or anyone else, or tolerating her mother's investment in her sisters, brothers, or cousins is a great loss. It is a loss of the assistant's investment of time, energy, and resources in a woman and her children. Not only that, but women's genetic relationships are for life. If possible, women want their husbands to be there for life, too. I suggest, therefore, that girls and women apply the same standard to a best friend.

The problem is that best friends aren't family. They share no common genes that bind them for life, no ultimate investment in the same people. A female's demands for exclusivity are not in any other girl's or woman's best interest.

The result is that these intense, exclusive, intimate, seemingly family-like relationships are destined to fail, causing much heartbreak [179]. As researchers who have studied hundreds of adolescents concluded more than 50 years ago, female friends are simply not as important to one another as they think they are [167]. Whereas girls and women can be responsive and sympathetic listeners, their real interests lie with those who can help them, with those who have time and energy and resources to give to them. As I described in chapter 2, when a conflict arises between same-sex friends, my students and I showed that young women were more likely than young men to state that they would stay angrier longer and be much slower to reconcile. Their physiological responses also indicated that, compared with men, when confronting a same-sex peer, they were more afraid and less willing to try to repair the relationship [180].

If a woman, because of her wealth, or husband, or family members, can find assistance rearing children, then she may be able to earn her own money and acquire her own status. She then might be in a position to help younger, unrelated women. Will she? Will younger women be able to rely on older and more senior women, rather than husbands or family members to help them?

So far, the answer is no. In business and science, high-status women invest less than high-status men in lower-status same-sex individuals [181, 182, 4]. Recently, my colleagues and I asked young women and men how much money they would share with a less powerful same-sex ally with whom they had worked on a joint project. Women gave much less than men did [183]. They also collaborated less than men did with lower-status same-sex partners. Women invested in equals however as much as men did. Equals are more likely to reciprocate. Only when women are paid to help the vulnerable, the weak, or those of low status should they agree. The resources or money they earn can go toward increasing their own and their children's chances of surviving and flourishing. But someone has to care for their children if they are to earn this extra money. No wonder, then, that women hate having female bosses [184, 6].

Why are men more helpful to those of lower status? It might be because men benefit from larger groups. Should the enemy appear, whether in war or in a competing enterprise, the larger the group, the better. Even lower-status men can help. For a woman, if she spends her time, energy, and resources investing in a lower-status member of her group, she has less time, energy, and resources for her family. Until women can be assured that their children are well cared for, they have to put their children, and those who will care for their children, first.

When it comes to friendships between girls or women, each learns that the other may smile, be polite, and interested in one another's potential assistants and vulnerabilities. Neither, however, is going to give her time, energy, and money or other resources to the other's family members. Each asks too much. Each needs more than the other can give. When they are mothers, each needs someone who has extra time, energy, and resources to invest in her children. Neither has any of these to give away. Impoverished mothers report that the people who often cause them the most stress are other unrelated mothers, just like themselves [185, 186]. Further, they are often competing over the very same resources or potential mate.

At all ages, female friends must still be watched closely. Smiling, soft-spoken, polite girls and women use mutual eye contact, accurate decoding of nonverbal emotions, and persistent exchange of demographic information and vulnerability assessments to evaluate one another's intentions. Any sign of competition, and the relationship must end. Too much is at stake. In adolescence and adulthood, an extra female can rapidly ruin a woman's marriage, or at least reduce a husband's investment in his original family.

Husbands must be watched carefully too. Like female friends, they are not family members. They do not share genetic ties to a woman. Unlike female friends, they share a common tie with a woman to their joint children. Nonetheless, a husband can leave, knowing a woman will almost certainly care for their children [155]. He can find a younger and more energetic female. This happens in the simplest hunter-gatherer societies [22] and all around the world [160]. In hunter-gatherer societies, divorce is predicted best by a man's chances of forming another bond with a woman who will produce children [187].

Even close relatives must be closely watched. A girl or woman who feels that her sister is getting more of their mother's share of attention or resources should rightly be furious. Her own children will suffer. Nonetheless, her fury may be restrained if her nieces and nephews have more needs at the moment. When a mother does not favor one sibling over the other [188] and helps each [189], this reduces hostility and competition between siblings.

The danger to a woman's and her children's survival and well-being increases specifically, however, when female friends mix with husbands. A married man who has produced children with one woman usually keeps an eye out for additional mating opportunities [190]. A married woman must continually be on the lookout for signs of her spouse's infidelity. Around the world, therefore, married women are less welcoming to a single woman than to a single man [159]. Married men, in contrast, are just as happy to invite over single men as single women. They likely know that their wives have less time, energy, and resources than they do to invest in a new sexual partner. Their wives are too busy caring for their children.

Not that mothers never find new sexual partners. But a mother must think carefully about this. There are many obstacles: violently jealous husbands; societally sanctioned murder; killing by nonbiological fathers of her children; and potential neglect of her children's needs while she invests in a new man [124, 160, 191]. In contrast, women almost never kill their philandering husbands. They would risk retaliation if they failed. The benefits of a new sexual partner, or even husband, therefore must be weighed carefully against the potential costs. Accordingly, even in modern society, a divorced woman takes much longer than a divorced man to remarry [159]. She must spend a lot of time thinking first.

Fathers needn't bother with these complex calculations. They know the mother of their children will almost always be there for the children. Of course, around the world, stealing another man's wife or girlfriend is probably the number one cause of murder within a community [192], even in hunter-gatherer societies [22]. But a man doesn't worry as much about this, as long as his wife can care for his children.

There is one final reason that a single man is less of a threat to a marriage. When the enemy strikes, men profit from forming relationships with unrelated men. Thus, a man's desire to seduce his friend's wife must be balanced against the value his friend provides in terms of potential cooperation in solving joint problems. Men who are friends appear to be less attracted to a woman if they know that it is their friend's girlfriend or wife [193]. A man who is attracted to a woman experiences a rise in testosterone—but only if the woman is not his friend's sexual partner. Men gain a lot from other men, especially when they are relative equals. They stand to lose out if they threaten their male bonds. If he doesn't kill him in a rage, a man might even be willing to form a relationship with his wife's new husband. This happens much more frequently than a woman forming a relationship with her husband's new wife [159].

Once again, a man's greater flexibility and apparent kindness reflect the fact that his former and future wives will ultimately take primary responsibility for ensuring the survival and well-being of his children. If another man wants to help a husband's former wife, why should the biological father object? In contrast, not too many women help care for a new husband's children by another woman. It is rare for a woman's children to live with their father and his new wife. Further, they need to focus on their own children. A mother generally remains with her children, no matter what happens.

Female friends therefore are not merely not good sources of assistance; they are competitors. If a woman thinks her female friend poses a potential danger to her marriage, she must gather a posse and attempt to exclude this friend as quickly as possible. A direct hit may be necessary in an emergency.

Conclusion to Part II: The Unique Problems of Girls and Women

Women's lives have always been constrained by a lifetime devoted to caring for vulnerable children. They must protect themselves, first and foremost, then their children. Their basic fear helps reduce the chances of a harmful accident, an illness, or a social conflict. They must exhibit caution at all times. Life is more serious for women, who always bear more responsibility for ensuring that their genes survive into the next generation. Letting down her guard could damage a woman's ability to have children, even before they are born.

In this respect, every woman is on her own. The best assistance comes from those with a mutual stake in protecting a woman's children's genes. Those assistants must have the time, energy, and resources, however, to help her raise her children. Thus, a woman's most important relationships are based on genetic ties and remain stable throughout her life. If she is lucky, she will form a close bond with her mother, and to the father of her children. Being in a strong, lasting relationship of this kind can provide her with enough additional help to reduce the level of worry that comes with the long-term care required for vulnerable children.

A woman's relationships with friends reflect this biological dynamic. Women are relatively vulnerable. A female friend is a luxury, someone who understands and shares the difficulties of life.

Unrelated females, however, cannot cooperate to raise their mutual children. Each one simply benefits too much from getting help from someone not burdened with raising children. Thus, friendship between women is characterized by a series of strategies calculated to ensure that a friend remains tightly bound, with no signs of competition. Girls' and women's friendships are intense and exclusive and strictly egalitarian, so no one gets ahead. They are based on constant sharing of demographic information and personal vulnerabilities, and repeated verification of each other's feelings, both verbally and nonverbally. But underneath these behaviors are competition and fear. What passes for intimacy is actually insurance. When the signs turn negative, girls' and women's friendships change, often into their opposite. Heartbreak and fury replace what each genuinely wished would turn into a lifelong bond. Competition for mates ultimately reduces any benefits that a close female friend might provide.

Modern life has made family members less available to women. But modern women can turn to alternate authority figures in order to recreate the internal feelings of a supportive family structure. Thus, when things are going badly, or even when they are not, a woman will consult a doctor, a teacher, or a therapist. This is not out of some real sense of personal danger; in fact, women live longer and are healthier than men. Women, however, remain the primary caregivers for their children and must suffer the constant stress and worry that this entails. Being able to have a relationship with an older or higher-status person who is free from the responsibilities of child care can mirror what might be available within a family. Even if this is commercial at its heart, such a relationship can provide the extra support required to maintain a woman's equilibrium.

What a woman wants is the assurance that she and her children, and those assistants who can ease her load, are healthy and thriving. More than anything, a woman truly wants herself and her children "to live happily ever after."

References

1. de Waal, F. B. M., The integration of dominance and social bonding in primates. *Quarterly Review of Biology*, 1986. 61(4): pp. 459–479.
2. Volk, A. A. and J. A. Atkinson, Infant and child death in the human environment of evolutionary adaptation. *Evolution and Human Behavior*, 2013. 34(3): pp. 182–192.
3. Waal, F. B. M., and A. Roosmalen, Reconciliation and consolation among chimpanzees. *Behavioral Ecology and Sociobiology*, 1979. 5(1): pp. 55–66.
4. Moss-Racusin, C. A., J. F. Dovidio, V. L. Brescoll, M. J. Graham, and J. Handelsman, Science faculty's subtle gender biases favor male students. *Proceedings of the National Academy of Sciences*, 2012. 109 (41): pp. 16474–16479.
5. Smuts, B., The evolutionary origins of patriarchy. *Human Nature*, 1995. 6(1): pp. 1–32.
6. Schieman, S., and T. McMullen, Relational demography in the workplace and health: An analysis of gender and the subordinate-superordinate role-set. *Journal of Health and Social Behavior*, 49, 2008. pp. 286–300.
7. Gupta, M. D., Life course perspectives on women's autonomy and health outcomes. *American Anthropologist*, 1995. 97(3): pp. 481–491.
8. Smuts, B., Male aggression against women. *Human Nature*, 1992. 3(1): pp. 1–44.
9. Chapais, B., *Primeval kinship: How pair-bonding gave birth to human society*. 2008, Cambridge, MA: Harvard University Press.
10. Hamilton, W. D., The genetical evolution of social behaviour. II. *Journal of Theoretical Biology*, 1964. 7(1): pp. 17–52.
11. Nowak, M. A., C. E. Tarnita, and E. O. Wilson, The evolution of eusociality. *Nature*, 2010. 466(7310): pp. 1057–1062.
12. Rosaldo, M. Z., L. Lamphere, and J. Bamberger, *Woman, culture, and society*. 1974, Stanford, CA: Stanford University Press.
13. Keillor, G., A parent's prayer, *New York Times* June 30, 2010.
14. Lareau, A., My wife can tell me who I know: Methodological and conceptual problems in studying fathers. *Qualitative Sociology*, 2000. 23(4): pp. 407–433.
15. Hewlett, B. S., *Father-child relations: Cultural and biosocial contexts*. 1992, New Brunswick, NJ: Aldine Transaction.
16. Konner, M., Hunter-gatherer infancy and childhood: The!Kung and others, in *Hunter-gatherer childhoods*, B. S. Hewlett and M. E. Lamb, Editors. 2005, New Brunswick, NJ: Aldine Transaction. pp. 19–64.
17. Brown, D. E., *Human universals*. 1991, Philadelphia: Temple University Press.
18. Ember, C. R., A cross-cultural perspective on sex-differences, in *Handbook of cross-cultural development*, R. H. Munroe, R. L. Munroe, and B. B. Whiting, Editors. 1984, New York: Garland. pp. 531–580.

19. Campbell, A., Staying alive: Evolution, culture, and women's intrasexual aggression. *Behavioral and Brain Sciences*, 1999. 22(2): pp. 203–252.

20. Smith, H. J., *Parenting for primates.* 2005, Cambridge, MA: Harvard University Press.

21. Martin, R. D., The evolution of human reproduction: A primatological perspective. *American Journal of Physical Anthropology*, 2007. 134(S45): pp. 59–84.

22. Marlowe, F., *The Hadza: Hunter-gatherers of Tanzania: Origins of human behavior and culture.* 2010, Berkeley: University of California Press.

23. Strassman, B. I., Cooperation and competition in a cliff-dwelling people. *Proceedings of the National Academy of Sciences*, 2011. 108(S2): pp. 10894–10901.

24. Kristof, N., and S. Wudunn, *Half the sky: How to change the world.* 2010, London: Virago.

25. UNICEF. *Millennium Development Goals #3. Promote gender equality and empower women.* 2000; available from http://www.unicef.org/mdg/gender.html.

26. Leininger, L. J., and K. M. Ziol Guest, Reexamining the effects of family structure on children's access to care: The single father family. *Health Services Research*, 2008. 43(1 Pt. 1): pp. 117–133.

27. Demuth, S., and S. L. Brown, Family structure, family processes, and adolescent delinquency: The significance of parental absence versus parental gender. *Journal of Research in Crime and Delinquency*, 2004. 41(1): pp. 58–81.

28. Cavanagh, S. E., Family structure history and adolescent adjustment. *Journal of Family Issues*, 2008. 29(7): pp. 944–980.

29. Breivik, K., and D. Olweus, Children of divorce in a Scandinavian welfare state: Are they less affected than US children? *Scandinavian Journal of Psychology*, 2006. 47(1): pp. 61–74.

30. Lamb, M. E., J. H. Pleck, E. L. Charnov, and J. A. Levine A biosocial perspective on paternal behavior and involvement, in *Parenting across the life span: Biosocial dimensions*, J. B. Lancaster, J. Altmann L. R. Sherrod, and A. Rossi Editors. 1987, New York: Aldine Transaction. pp. 111–142.

31. Parke, R. D., *Fatherhood.* 1996, Cambridge, MA: Harvard University Press.

32. Youniss, J., and J. Smollar, *Adolescent relations with mothers, fathers, and friends.* 1985, Chicago: University of Chicago Press.

33. Katz, M. M., and M. J. Konner, The role of the father: An anthropological perspective, in *The role of the father in child development*, M. E. Lamb, Editor. 1981, New York: Wiley. pp. 155–185.

34. Flinn, M., Paternal care in a Caribbean village, in *Father-child relations: Cultural and biosocial contexts*, B. S. Hewlett, Editor. 1992, New York: Walter de Gruyter. pp. 57–84.

35. Marlowe, F. W., Who tends Hadza children, in *Hunter-gatherer childhoods: Evolutionary, developmental, and cultural perspectives*, B. S. Hewlett

and M. E. Lamb, Editors. 2005, New Brunswick, NJ: Aldine Transaction. pp. 177–190.

36. Hawkes, K., J. F. O'Connell, N. G. Blurton Jones, Hunting and nuclear families. *Current Anthropology*, 2001. 42(5): pp. 681–709.

37. Hawkes, K., J. F. O'Connell, and N. G. Blurton Jones, Hadza women's time allocation, offspring provisioning, and the evolution of long postmenopausal life spans. *Current Anthropology*, 1997. 38(4): pp. 551–577.

38. Chagnon, N. A., Yanomamo social organization and warfare, in *War: The anthropology of armed conflict and aggression*, M. Fried, R. Harris, and R. Murphy, Editors. 1968, Garden City, NY: History Press. pp. 109–159.

39. Whiting, B. B. and C. P. Edwards *Children of different worlds: The formation of social behavior*. 1988, Cambridge, MA: Harvard University Press.

40. Bronstein, P., Parenting, in *Encyclopedia of women and gender*, J. Worrell, Editor. 2001, Boston: Academic Press. pp. 795–808.

41. Eagly, A. H., The his and hers of prosocial behavior: An examination of the social psychology of gender. *American Psychologist*, 2009. 64(8): pp. 644–658.

42. Glantz, M. J., et al., Gender disparity in the rate of partner abandonment in patients with serious medical illness. *Cancer*, 2009. 115(22): pp. 5237–5242.

43. Eagly, A. H., and M. Crowley, Gender and helping behavior: A meta-analytic review of the social psychological literature. *Psychological Bulletin*, 1986. 100(3): pp. 283–308.

44. Johnson, R. C., et al., Cross-cultural assessment of altruism and its correlates. *Personality and Individual Differences*, 1989. 10(8): pp. 855–868.

45. Kenney, C. T., Father doesn't know best? Parents' control of money and children's food insecurity. *Journal of Marriage and Family*, 2008. 70(3): pp. 654–669.

46. Herz, B. K., and G. B. Sperling, *What works in girls' education: Evidence and policies from the developing world*. 2004, New York: Council on Foreign Relations Press.

47. King, E., and A. D. Mason, *Engendering development: Through gender equality in rights, resources, and voice*. 2001, Washington, DC: World Bank.

48. Shostak, M., *Nisa: The life and words of a!Kung woman*. 1981, Cambridge, MA: Harvard University Press.

49. Moriarty, H. J., R. Carroll, and M. Cotroneo, Differences in bereavement reactions within couples following death of a child. *Research in Nursing and Health*, 1996. 19(6): pp. 461–469.

50. Lang, A., L. N. Gottlieb, and R. Amsel, Predictors of husbands' and wives' grief reactions following infant death: The role of marital intimacy. *Death Studies*, 1996. 20(1): pp. 33–57.

51. Dyregrov, A., Parental reactions to the loss of an infant child: A review. *Scandinavian Journal of Psychology*, 1990. 31(4): pp. 266–280.

52. Benfield, D. G., S. A. Leib, and J. H. Vollman, Grief response of parents to neonatal death and parent participation in deciding care. *Pediatrics*, 1978. 62(2): pp. 171–177.

53. Belsky, J., L. Youngblade, M. Rovine, and B Volling, Patterns of marital change and parent-child interaction. *Journal of Marriage and the Family*, 1991. 53(2): pp. 487–498.

54. Hewlett, B. S., and M. E. Lamb, *Hunter-gatherer childhoods: Evolutionary, developmental, and cultural perspectives.* 2005, New Brunswick, NJ: Aldine Transaction.

55. Anderson, K. G., H. Kaplan, and J. Lancaster, Paternal care by genetic fathers and stepfathers I: Reports from Albuquerque men. *Evolution and Human Behavior*, 1999. 20(6): pp. 405–431.

56. Manning, W. D., and K. A. Lamb, Adolescent well-being in cohabiting, married, and single-parent families. *Journal of Marriage and Family*, 2003. 65(4): pp. 876–893.

57. Hofferth, S. L., Residential father family type and child well-being: Investment versus selection. *Demography*, 2006. 43(1): pp. 53–77.

58. Hofferth, S. L., and K. G. Anderson, Are all dads equal? Biology versus marriage as a basis for paternal investment. *Journal of Marriage and Family*, 2003. 65(1): pp. 213–232.

59. Hrdy, S. B., *Mother nature: A history of mothers, infants, and natural selection.* New York: Pantheon, 1999.

60. Kramer, K. L., Children's help and the pace of reproduction: Cooperative breeding in humans. *Evolutionary Anthropology: Issues, News, and Reviews*, 2005. 14(6): pp. 224–237.

61. Paley, V. G., *Boys and girls: Superheroes in the doll corner.* 1984, Chicago: University of Chicago Press.

62. Nicolopoulou, A., Worldmaking and identity formation in children's narrative play-acting, in *Sociogenetic perspectives on internalization*, B. D. Cox and C. Lightfoot, Editors. 1997, Mahwah, NJ: Erlbaum. pp. 157–187.

63. Benenson, J. F., and R. Del Bianco, Sex differences in children. *Canadian Journal of Research in Early Childhood Education*, 1997. 6(2): pp. 107–125.

64. Casanova, J. L., and L. Abel, Inborn errors of immunity to infection. *Journal of Experimental Medicine*, 2005. 202(2): pp. 197–201.

65. Darley, J. M., and B. Latane, Bystander intervention in emergencies: Diffusion of responsibility. *Journal of Personality and Social Psychology*, 1968. 8 (4): pp. 377–383.

66. Diekman, A. B., E. R. Brown, A. M. Johnston, and E. K. Clark Seeking congruity between goals and roles. *Psychological Science*, 2010. 21(8): pp. 1051–1057.

67. Tomaskovic-Devey, D., et al., Documenting desegregation: EEO-1 estimates of US gender and ethnic segregation 1966–2000. *American Sociological Review*, 2006. 71(4): pp. 565–588.

68. Berenbaum, S. A., and S. Resnick, The seeds of career choices: Prenatal sex hormone effects on psychological sex differences, in *Why aren't more women in science*, S. J. Ceci and W. M. Williams, Editors. 2007, Washington, DC: American Psychological Association. pp. 147–157.

69. Padavic, I., and B. F. Reskin, *Women and men at work.* 2002, Thousand Oaks, CA: Pine Forge Press.

70. Winstead, B., and J. Griffin, Friendship styles, in *Encyclopedia of women and gender*, J. Worell, Editor. 2001, Boston: Academic Press. pp. 481–492.

71. Burleson, B. R., and A. W. Kunkel, Revisiting the different cultures thesis: An assessment of sex differences and similarities in supportive communication, in K. Dindia and D. J. Canary (Editors) *Sex differences and similarities in communication.* 2006, Mahwah, NJ: Erlbaum. pp. 137–159.

72. Blieszner, R., and R. G. Adams, *Adult friendship.* 1992, Thousand Oaks, CA: Sage.

73. Buhrmester, D., and K. Prager, Patterns and functions of self-disclosure during childhood and adolescence, in *Disclosure processes in children and adolescents*, K. Rotenberg, Editor. 1995, Cambridge: Cambridge University Press. pp. 10–56.

74. Coates, J., *Women talk: Conversation between women friends.* 1996, Oxford: Wiley-Blackwell.

75. Cross, C. P., L. T. Copping, and A. Campbell, Sex differences in impulsivity: A meta-analysis. *Psychological Bulletin*, 2011. 137(1): pp. 97–130.

76. O'Connor, P., *Friendships between women: A critical review.* 1992, New York: Guilford.

77. Wright, P. H., Toward an expanded orientation to the study of sex differences in friendship, in *Sex differences and similarities in communication: Critical essays and empirical investigations of sex and gender in interaction*, D. J. Canary and K. Dindia, Editors. 1998, Mahwah, NJ: Erlbaum. pp. 41–63.

78. Bowlby, J., *Attachment and loss: Volume 1: Attachment.* 1969, London: Hogarth Press and the Institute of Psycho-Analysis.

79. Freud, S. Female sexuality, in *The standard edition of the complete psychological works of Sigmund Freud*, Vol. 21 J. Strachey, Editor. London: Hogarth Press. 1931, New York: Norton. pp. 221–243.

80. Freud, S., *Femininity. The standard edition of the complete psychological works of Sigmund Freud*, J. Strachey, Editor. London: Hogarth Press. Vol. 22 1933. pp. 112–135.

81. Tannen, D., *You just don't understand: Women and men in conversation.* 1990 New York: Ballantine.

82. Gottman, J. M., The world of coordinated play: Same- and cross-sex friendship in young children, in *Conversations of friends: Speculations on affective development*, J. M. Gottman and J. G. Parker, Editors. 1986, New York: Cambridge University Press. pp. 139–191.

83. Kaplan, H., K. Hill, J. Lancaster, and A. M. Hurtado A theory of human life history evolution: Diet, intelligence, and longevity. *Evolutionary Anthropology*, 2000. 9(4): pp. 156–185.

84. Feshbach, N. D., and K. Roe, Empathy in six- and seven-year-olds. *Child Development*, 1968. 39(1): pp. 133–145.

85. Hoffman, M. L., and L. E. Levine, Early sex differences in empathy. *Developmental Psychology*, 1976. 12(6): pp. 557–558.
86. Konner, M., Relations among infants and toddlers in comparative perspective. In M. Lewis and L. A. Rosenblum (Editors) *Friendship and peer relations*, 1975. New York: Wiley, pp. 99129.
87. Bove, R. B., C. R. Valeggia, and P. T. Ellison, Girl helpers and time allocation of nursing women among the Toba of Argentina. *Human Nature*, 2002. 13(4): pp. 457–472.
88. Collaer, M. L., and M. Hines, Human behavioral sex differences: A role for gonadal hormones during early development? *Psychological Bulletin*, 1995. 118(1): pp. 55–107.
89. Mathews, G. A., B. A. Fine, G. S. Conway, C. G. D. Brook and M. Hines Personality and congenital adrenal hyperplasia: Possible effects of prenatal androgen exposure. *Hormones and Behavior*, 2009. 55(2): pp. 285–291.
90. Berman, P. W., Are women more responsive than men to the young? A review of developmental and situational variables. *Psychological Bulletin*, 1980. 88(3): pp. 668–695.
91. Ekman, P., R. W. Levenson, and W. V. Friesen, Autonomic nervous system activity distinguishes among emotions. *Science*, 1983. 221(4616): pp. 1208–1210.
92. Fernández, C., et al., Physiological responses induced by emotion-eliciting films. *Applied Psychophysiology and Biofeedback*, 2012. 37 (2): pp. 1–7.
93. Frodi, A. M., and M. E. Lamb, Sex differences in responsiveness to infants: A developmental study of psychophysiological and behavioral responses. *Child Development*, 1978. 49(4): pp. 1182–1188.
94. Frodi, A. M., et al., Fathers' and mothers' responses to the faces and cries of normal and premature infants. *Developmental Psychology*, 1978. 14(5): pp. 490–498.
95. Furedy, J. J., et al., Sex differences in small-magnitude heart-rate responses to sexual and infant-related stimuli: A psychophysiological approach. *Physiology and behavior*, 1989. 46(5): pp. 903–905.
96. Feldman, R., A. Weller, O. Zagoory-Sharon and A. Levine, Evidence for a neuroendocrinological foundation of human affiliation. *Psychological Science*, 2007. 18(11): pp. 965–970.
97. Hinde, R. A., Relations between levels of complexity in the behavioral sciences. *Journal of Nervous and Mental Disease*, 1989. 177(11): pp. 655–667.
98. Landers, J., Trends in population growth, in *The Cambridge encyclopedia of human evolution*, S. Jones, R. Martin, and D. Pilbeam, Editors. 1992, Cambridge: Cambridge University Press.
99. Straus, M. A., and J. H. Stewart, Corporal punishment by American parents: National data on prevalence, chronicity, severity, and duration, in relation to child and family characteristics. *Clinical Child and Family Psychology Review*, 1999. 2(2): pp. 55–70.

100. Sedgh, G., S. Henshaw, S. Singh, E. Åhman, and I. H. Shah Induced abortion: Estimated rates and trends worldwide. *Lancet*, 2007. 370(9595): pp. 1338–1345.

101. Williamson, L., Infanticide: an anthropological analysis, in *Infanticide and the value of life*, M. Kohl, Editor. 1978, Buffalo, NY: Prometheus Books. pp. 61–75.

102. Eisenberg, L., The biosocial context of parenting in human families, in *Mammalian parenting: Biochemical, neurobiological, and behavioral determinants*, N. Krasnegor and R. Bridges, Editors. 1990, New York: Basic Books pp. 9–24.

103. Daly, M., and M. Wilson, The Darwinian psychology of discriminative parental solicitude, in *Nebraska Symposium on Motivation: Comparative perspectives in modern psychology*, D. W. Leger, Editor. 1987, Lincoln: University of Nebraska Press. pp. 91–144.

104. LeVine, S., and R. LeVine, Child abuse and neglect in sub-Saharan Africa, in *Child abuse and neglect: Cross-cultural perspectives*, J. E. Korbin, Editor. 1981, Berkeley: University of California Press. pp. 35–55.

105. Harris, G. T., N. Z. Hilton, M. E. Rice, and A. W. Eke, Children killed by genetic parents versus stepparents. *Evolution and Human Behavior*, 2007. 28(2): pp. 85–95.

106. Daly, M., and M. Wilson, *Homicide*. 1988, Hawthorne, NY: Aldine de Gruyter.

107. Korbin, J. E., Child abuse and neglect: The cultural context, in *The battered child*, R. E. Helfer and R. S. Kempe, Editors. 1987, New York: Guilford. pp. 23–41.

108. Johansson, S., Neglect, abuse, and avoidable death: Parental investment and the mortality of infants and children in the European tradition, in *Child abuse and neglect: Biosocial dimensions*, R. J. Gelles and J. B. Lancaster, Editors. 1987, Piscataway, NJ: Transaction Press. pp. 57–96.

109. Martorell, G. A., and D. B. Bugental, Maternal variations in stress reactivity: Implications for harsh parenting practices with very young children. *Journal of Family Psychology*, 2006. 20(4): pp. 641–647.

110. Bugental, D. B., and A. Schwartz, A cognitive approach to child mistreatment prevention among medically at-risk infants. *Developmental Psychology*, 2009. 45(1): pp. 284–288.

111. Hrdy, S. B., *Mothers and others: The evolutionary origins of mutual understanding*. 2009, Cambridge, MA: Belknap Press.

112. Leaper, C., K. J. Anderson, and P. Sanders, Moderators of gender effects on parents' talk to their children: A meta-analysis. *Developmental Psychology*, 1998. 34(1): pp. 3–27.

113. Leaper, C., and M. M. Ayres, A meta-analytic review of gender variations in adults' language use: Talkativeness, affiliative speech, and assertive speech. *Personality and Social Psychology Review*, 2007. 11(4): pp. 328–363.

114. Bugental, D. E., L. R. Love, and R. M. Gianetto, Perfidious feminine faces. *Journal of Personality and Social Psychology*, 1971. 17(3): pp. 314–318.

115. Goodwin, M. H., *He-said-she-said: Talk as social organization among black children*. 1990, Bloomington: Indiana University Press.

116. Beebe, B., and F. M. Lachmann, *Infant research and adult treatment: Co-constructing interactions*. 2005, New York: Analytic Press.

117. Stern, D. N., *The interpersonal world of the infant*. 1985, New York: Basic Books.

118. Ainsworth, M. D. S., M. C. Blehar, E. Waters, and S. Wall *Patterns of attachment: A psychological study of the strange situation*. 1978, Hillsdale, NJ: Erlbaum.

119. Pinker, S., *The better angels of our nature: Why violence has declined*. 2011, New York: Viking.

120. Van IJzendoorn, M. H., et al., The similarity of siblings' attachments to their mother. *Child Development*, 2000. 71(4): pp. 1086–1098.

121. Wood, B. M., Prestige or provisioning? A test of foraging goals among the Hadza. *Current Anthropology*, 2006. 47(2): pp. 383–387.

122. Montez, J. K., M. D. Hayward, D. C. Brown and R. A. Hummer, Why is the educational gradient of mortality steeper for men? *Journals of Gerontology Series B: Psychological Sciences and Social Sciences*, 2009. 64(5): pp. 625–634.

123. Sigle-Rushton, W., and S. McLanahan, Father absence and child well-being: A critical review, in *The future of the family*, D. P. Moynihan, T. M. Smeeding, and L. Rainwater, Editors. 2004, New York: Russell Sage Foundation: pp. 116–155.

124. Archer, J., Cross-cultural differences in physical aggression between partners: A social-role analysis. *Personality and Social Psychology Review*, 2006. 10(2): pp. 133–153.

125. Yanca, C., and B. S. Low, Female allies and female power: A cross-cultural analysis. *Evolution and Human Behavior*, 2004. 25(1): pp. 9–23.

126. Straus, M. A., and R. J. Gelles, Societal change and change in family violence from 1975 to 1985 as revealed by two national surveys. *Journal of Marriage and the Family*, 1986. 48(3): pp. 465–479.

127. Jankowiak, W., M. Sudakov, and B. C. Wilreker, Co-wife conflict and co-operation. *Ethnology*, 2005. 44(1): pp. 81–98.

128. Strassman, B. I., Polygyny, family structure, and child mortality: A prospective study among the Dogon of Mali, in *Adaptation and human behavior: An anthropological perspective*, L. Cronk, N. A. Chagnon, and W. Irons, Editors. 2000, Hawthorne, NY: Aldine de Gruyter. pp. 45–63.

129. Markovits, H., J. Benenson, and E. Dolenszky, Evidence that children and adolescents have internal models of peer interactions that are gender differentiated. *Child Development*, 2001. 72(3): pp. 879–886.

130. Parker, J. G., C. M. Low, A. R. Walker, and B. K. Gamm, Friendship jealousy in young adolescents: Individual differences and links to sex,

self-esteem, aggression, and social adjustment. *Developmental Psychology*, 2005. 41(1): pp. 235–250.

131.   Kurdek, L. A., What do we know about gay and lesbian couples? *Current Directions in Psychological Science*, 2005. 14(5): pp. 251–254.

132.   Fagot, B. I., The influence of sex of child on parental reactions to toddler children. *Child Development*, 1978. 49(2): pp. 459–465.

133.   Whiting, J. W. M., and B. B. Whiting, Aloofness and intimacy of husbands and wives. *Ethos*, 1975. 3(2): pp. 183–207.

134.   Thompson, R. B., Gender differences in preschoolers' help-eliciting communication. *Journal of Genetic Psychology*, 1999. 160(3): pp. 357–368.

135.   Benenson, J. F., and M. Koulnazarian, Sex differences in help-seeking appear in early childhood. *British Journal of Developmental Psychology*, 2008. 26(2): pp. 163–169.

136.   Boldero, J., and B. Fallon, Adolescent help-seeking: What do they get help for and from whom? *Journal of Adolescence*, 1995. 18(2): pp. 193–209.

137.   Seiffge-Krenke, I., and S. Shulman, Coping style in adolescence. *Journal of Cross-Cultural Psychology*, 1990. 21(3): pp. 351–377.

138.   Crystal, D. S., M. Kakinuma, M. DeBell, and T. Miyashito Who helps you? Self and other sources of support among youth in Japan and the USA. *International Journal of Behavioral Development*, 2008. 32(6): pp. 496–508.

139.   Belle, D., Gender differences in children's social networks and supports, in *Children's social networks and social supports*, D. Belle, Editor. 1989, Oxford: Wiley. pp. 173–188.

140.   Galdas, P. M., F. Cheater, and P. Marshall, Men and health help-seeking behaviour: Literature review. *Journal of Advanced Nursing*, 2005. 49(6): pp. 616–623.

141.   Möller-Leimkühler, A. M., Barriers to help-seeking by men: A review of sociocultural and clinical literature with particular reference to depression. *Journal of Affective Disorders*, 2002. 71(1–3): pp. 1–9.

142.   Tabenkin, H., M. A. Goodwin, S. J. Zyzanksi, K. C. Stange, and J. H. Medalie Gender differences in time spent during direct observation of doctor-patient encounters. *Journal of Women's Health*, 2004. 13(3): pp. 341–349.

143.   Addis, M. E., and J. R. Mahalik, Men, masculinity, and the contexts of help seeking. *American psychologist*, 2003. 58(1): pp. 5–14.

144.   Levinson, D., and A. Ifrah, The robustness of the gender effect on help seeking for mental health needs in three subcultures in Israel. *Social Psychiatry and Psychiatric Epidemiology*, 2010. 45(3): pp. 337–344.

145.   McKay, J. R., M. J. Rutherford, J. S. Cacciola, R. Kabasakalian-McKay A. I. Alterman, Gender differences in the relapse experiences of cocaine patients. *Journal of Nervous and Mental Disease*, 1996. 184(10): pp. 616–622.

146.   Weissman, M. M., and G. L. Klerman, Sex differences and the epidemiology of depression. *Archives of General Psychiatry*, 1977. 34(1): pp. 98–111.

147. Schlegel, A., and H. Barry III, *Adolescence: An anthropological inquiry.* 1991, New York: Free Press.

148. Sear, R., and R. Mace, Who keeps children alive? A review of the effects of kin on child survival. *Evolution and Human Behavior*, 2008. 29(1): pp. 1–18.

149. Lahdenpera, M., V. Lummaa, S. Helle, and M. Tremblay Fitness benefits of prolonged post-reproductive lifespan in women. *Nature*, 2004. 428(6979): pp. 178–181.

150. Hawkes, K., The evolutionary basis of sex variations in the use of natural resources: Human examples. *Population and Environment*, 1996. 18(2): pp. 161–173.

151. McLanahan, S., and G. D. Sandefur, *Growing up with a single parent: What hurts, what helps.* 1994, Cambridge, MA: Harvard University Press.

152. Miller, J. B., *Toward a new psychology of women.* 1970, Boston: Beacon Press.

153. Levin, J., and A. Arluke, An exploratory analysis of sex differences in gossip. *Sex Roles*, 1985. 12(3): pp. 281–286.

154. Aries, E. J., and F. L. Johnson, Close friendship in adulthood: Conversational content between same-sex friends. *Sex Roles*, 1983. 9(12): pp. 1183–1196.

155. Dawkins, R., *The selfish gene.* 1976, New York: Oxford University Press.

156. Daly, M., and M. Wilson, *The truth about Cinderella: A Darwinian view of parental love.* 1998, New Haven, CT: Yale University Press.

157. Buss, D. M., Sex differences in human mate preferences: Evolutionary hypotheses tested in 37 cultures. *Behavioral and Brain Sciences*, 1989. 12(1): pp. 1–49.

158. Buckle, L., and G. G. Gallup, Marriage as a reproductive contract: Patterns of marriage, divorce, and remarriage. *Ethology and Sociobiology*, 1996. 17(6): pp. 363–377.

159. Hetherington, E. M., and J. Kelly, *For better or for worse: Divorce reconsidered.* 2003, New York: Norton.

160. Buss, D. M., *The evolution of desire: Strategies of human mating.* 1994, New York: Basic books.

161. Goldberg, S., and M. Lewis, Play behavior in the year-old infant: Early sex differences. *Child Development*, 1969. 40(1): pp. 21–31.

162. Serbin, L. A., J. M. Connor, and C. C. Citron, Sex-differentiated free play behavior: Effects of teacher modeling, location, and gender. *Developmental Psychology*, 1981. 17(5): pp. 640–646.

163. Fabes, R. A., C. L. Martin, and L. D. Hanish, Young children's play qualities in same, other, and mixed sex peer groups. *Child Development*, 2003. 74(3): pp. 921–932.

164. Huston, A. C., C. J. Carpenter, J. B. Atwater, and L. M. Johnson Gender, adult structuring of activities, and social behavior in middle childhood. *Child Development*, 1986. 57(5): pp. 1200–1209.

165. Del Giudice, M., Sex, attachment, and the development of reproductive strategies. *Behavioral and Brain Sciences*, 2009. 32(01): pp. 1–21.

166. Del Giudice, M., and J. Belsky, Sex differences in attachment emerge in middle childhood: An evolutionary hypothesis. *Child Development Perspectives*, 2010. 4(2): pp. 97–105.

167. Douvan, E. A. M., and J. Adelson, *The adolescent experience*. 1966, New York: Wiley.

168. Kuczynski, L., and G. Kochanska, Development of children's noncompliance strategies from toddlerhood to age 5. *Developmental psychology*, 1990. 26(3): pp. 398.

169. Murray, K. T., and G. Kochanska, Effortful control: Factor structure and relation to externalizing and internalizing behaviors. *Journal of Abnormal Child Psychology*, 2002. 30(5): pp. 503–514.

170. Conger, R. D., G. R. Patterson, and X. Ge, It takes two to replicate: A mediational model for the impact of parents' stress on adolescent adjustment. *Child Development*, 1995. 66(1): pp. 80–97.

171. Kochanska, G., D. R. Forman, N. Aksan, and S. B. Dunbar Pathways to conscience: Early mother-child mutually responsive orientation and children's moral emotion, conduct, and cognition. *Journal of Child Psychology and Psychiatry*, 2005. 46(1): pp. 19–34.

172. Alvarez, H., Residence groups among hunter-gatherers: A view of the claims and evidence for patrilocal bands, in *Kinship and behavior in Primates*, B. Chapais and C. Berman, Editors. 2004, Oxford: Oxford University Press. pp. 400–442.

173. Apter, T., and R. Josselson, *Best friends: The pleasures and perils of girls' and women's friendships*. 1998, New York: Three Rivers Press.

174. Ephron, N., *I feel bad about my neck: And other thoughts on being a woman*. 2006, New York: Vintage.

175. Benenson, J. F., Greater preference among females than males for dyadic interaction in early childhood. *Child Development*, 1993. 64(2): pp. 544–555.

176. Markovits, H., J. Benenson, and S. White, Gender and priming differences in speed of processing of information relating to social structure. *Journal of Experimental Social Psychology*, 2006. 42(5): pp. 662–667.

177. Eder, D., and M. T. Hallinan, Sex differences in children's friendships. *American Sociological Review*, 1978. 43(2): pp. 237–250.

178. Whitesell, N. R., and S. Harter, The interpersonal context of emotion: Anger with close friends and classmates. *Child Development*, 1996. 67(4): pp. 1345–1359.

179. Benenson, J. F., and A. Christakos, The greater fragility of females' versus males' closest same-sex friendships. *Child Development*, 2003. 74(4): pp. 1123–1129.

180. Benenson, J., et al. Social Exclusion: More important to human females than males. *PLoS One*, 2013, 8(2): e55851.

181. Rosser, S. V., *Breaking into the lab: Engineering progress for women in science*. 2012, New York: New York University Press.

182. Kanter, R. M., *Men and women of the corporation*. 1977, New York: Basic Books.

183. Benenson, J., H. Markovits, & R. W. Wrangham Rank influences human sex differences in dyadic cooperation. *Current Biology*, 2014.

184. Eagly, A. H., M. G. Makhijani, and B. G. Klonsky, Gender and the evaluation of leaders: A meta-analysis. *Psychological Bulletin*, 1992. 111(1): pp. 3–22.

185. Belle, D., The impact of poverty on social networks and supports. *Marriage and Family Review*, 1983. 5(4): pp. 89–103

186. Belle, D., The stress of caring: Women as providers of social support, in *Handbook of stress: Theoretical and clinical aspects*, L. Goldberger and S. Breznitz, Editors. 1982, New York: Free Press. pp. 496–505.

187. Blurton Jones, N., Marlowe, F. W., Hawkes, K., and O'Connell, J. F. Paternal investment and hunter-gatherer divorce rates. In L. Cronk, N. Chagnon, and W. Irons (Editors). *Adaptation and human behavior: An anthropological perspective* 2000: pp. 69–90.

188. Stocker, C., J. Dunn, and R. Plomin, Sibling relationships: Links with child temperament, maternal behavior, and family structure. *Child Development*, 1989. 60 (3): pp. 715–727.

189. Stocker, C. M., and S. M. McHale, The nature and family correlates of preadolescents' perceptions of their sibling relationships. *Journal of Social and Personal Relationships*, 1992. 9(2): pp. 179–195.

190. Trivers, R., *Parental investment and sexual selection*. 1972, Chicago: Aldine.

191. Daly, M., and M. I. Wilson, Some differential attributes of lethal assaults on small children by stepfathers versus genetic fathers. *Ethology and Sociobiology*, 1994. 15(4): pp. 207–217.

192. Daly, M., and M. Wilson, An evolutionary psychological perspective on homicide, in *Homicide: A sourcebook of social research*, M. D. Smith and M. A. Zahn, Editors. 1999, Thousand Oaks, CA: Sage. pp. 58–71.

193. Flinn, M. V., and D. Ponzi, Hormonal mechanisms for regulation of aggression in human coalitions. *Human Nature*, 2012. 23(1): pp. 68–88.

INDEX